Canon Rebel T1i / 500D:
From
Snapshots to
Great Shots

Jeff Revell

Peachpit Press

Canon Rebel T1i / 500D: From Snapshots to Great Shots
Jeff Revell

Peachpit Press
1249 Eighth Street
Berkeley, CA 94710
510/524-2178
510/524-2221 (fax)

Find us on the Web at www.peachpit.com
To report errors, please send a note to errata@peachpit.com
Peachpit Press is a division of Pearson Education

Copyright © 2010 by Peachpit Press
All photography © Jeff Revell except where noted

Editor: Ted Waitt
Production Editor: Lisa Brazieal
Interior Design: Riezebos Holzbaur Design Group
Compositor: WolfsonDesign
Indexer: James Minkin
Cover Design: Aren Howell
Cover Image: Jeff Revell
Back Cover Author Photo: Scott Kelby

Notice of Rights

All rights reserved. No part of this book may be reproduced or transmitted in any form by any means, electronic, mechanical, photocopying, recording, or otherwise, without the prior written permission of the publisher. For information on getting permission reprints and excerpts, contact permissions@ peachpit.com.

Notice of Liability

The information in this book is distributed on an "As Is" basis without warranty. While every precaution has been taken in the preparation of the book, neither the author nor Peachpit shall have any liability to any person or entity with respect to any loss or damage caused or alleged to be caused directly or indirectly by the instructions contained in this book or by the computer software and hardware products described in it.

Trademarks

All Canon products are trademarks or registered trademarks of Canon Inc.

Many of the designations used by manufacturers and sellers to distinguish their products are claimed as trademarks. Where those designations appear in this book, and Peachpit was aware of a trademark claim, the designations appear as requested by the owner of the trademark. All other product names and services identified throughout this book are used in editorial fashion only and for the benefit of such companies with no intention of infringement of the trademark. No such use, or the use of any trade name, is intended to convey endorsement or other affiliation with this book.

ISBN-13   978-0-321-64725-2
ISBN-10   0-321-64725-4

9 8 7 6 5 4 3 2 1

Printed and bound in the United States of America

DEDICATION

For my best buddies—my sons, Alex & Matt

I love you guys.

ACKNOWLEDGMENTS

Lately, deciding which cameras to write about has been pretty simple. Canon has been releasing such groundbreaking DSLRs that the choosing has pretty much been done for me. When Canon released the new Rebel T1i/500D, I placed a phone call to my favorite Canon Tech Rep, Scott Andrews. I told Scott that the T1i was next on my list and asked if he had one I could use for research purposes. Sure enough, he stopped on his way down to a shuttle launch in Florida and set me up with everything I needed to write this book. Thanks again, Scott and Canon, for all your support in writing this book.

There are many other people who help to get this book off the ground. Some of them aren't even aware that they were making a contribution, but that doesn't mean that their assistance/guidance didn't help to get this book from my head to the bookshelf.

Don and **Ed**, thanks for letting me tag along on the model shoot in Seattle where I got the chance to photograph some great models.

Rose Marie and **Laura Ann**, thanks for being such great models and helping me get some great images for this book.

Ted Waitt, not only are you a great editor but I think you could also have a lucrative career in cat herding. His eye for detail and ability to ask the right questions have kept me on the right track throughout this series.

The entire **Peachpit crew**, because working with such professionals really inspires and brings out the best in me.

Veronica and **Daphne**, for being the cutest nieces ever and letting your uncle take so many great pictures of you.

Debbie Chewning, for always listening to my rants and helping to keep me grounded. I couldn't ask more from a friend.

Scott Kelby, for being my friend, my mentor, and just the goofy guy that makes me laugh, usually when I need it most.

My brothers, **Chris** and **Russ,** and sister, **LeeAnne**, I wish I could see you more often because I really miss having you guys around. Sorry, this doesn't mean I'm moving to Texas.

All the great folks who have accompanied me on photowalks, for sharing your experiences, desires, and enthusiasm for photography.

Mike Meyer, for always keeping an eye on me. Not to mention the pie.

Finally, my wife, **Suzanne**, and sons, **Matt** and **Alex**; you are my joy and inspiration and make each day worth living.

Contents

Introduction

Walk into any bookseller, go to the photography section, and you will see countless books on the subject of photography. Look a little further and you will locate the camera-specific books. It is this divide between the camera-specific and instructional photography books that inspired me to write this book. What I was seeing in the store was a lot of books that were just sort of missing the mark—especially when it came to using a specific brand and model of camera along with actual photographic instruction. So with that, I set about to write this book on the Canon T1i, not as a rehash of the owner's manual but as a resource to teach photography with the wonderful technology present in the T1i. I have put together a short Q&A to help you get a better understanding of just what it is that you can expect from this book.

Q: IS EVERY CAMERA FEATURE GOING TO BE COVERED?

A: Nope, just the ones I felt you need to know about in order to start taking great photos. Believe it or not, you already own a great resource that covers every feature of your camera: the owner's manual. Writing a book that just repeats this information would have been a waste of my time and your money. What I did want to write about was how to harness certain camera features to the benefit of your photography. As you read through the book, you will also see callouts that point you to specific pages in your owner's manual that are related to the topic being discussed. For example, in Chapter 6 I discuss the use of the AE-L button but there is more information available on this feature in the manual. I cover the function that applies to our specific needs but also give you the page numbers in the manual to explore this function even further.

Q: SO IF I ALREADY OWN THE MANUAL, WHY DO I NEED THIS BOOK?

A: The manual does a pretty good job of telling you how to use a feature or turn it on in the menus, but it doesn't necessarily tell you *why* and *when* you should use it. If you really want to improve your photography, you need to know the whys and whens to put all of those great camera features to use at the right time. To that extent, the manual just isn't going to cut it. It is, however, a great resource on the camera's features, and it is for that reason that I treat it like a companion to this book. You already own it, so why not get something of value from it?

Q: WHAT CAN I EXPECT TO LEARN FROM THIS BOOK?

A: Hopefully, you will learn how to take great photographs. My goal, and the reason the book is laid out the way it is, is to guide you through the basics of photography as they relate to different situations and scenarios. By using the features of your T1i and this book, you will learn about aperture, shutter speed, ISO, lens selection, depth of field, and many other photographic concepts. You will also find plenty of large full-page photos that include captions, shooting data, and callouts so you can see how all of the photography fundamentals come together to make great images. All the while, you will be learning how your camera works and how to apply its functions and features to your photography.

Q: WHAT ARE THE ASSIGNMENTS ALL ABOUT?

A: At the end of most of the chapters, you will find shooting assignments, where I give you some suggestions as to how you can apply the lessons of the chapter to help reinforce everything you just learned. Let's face it—using the camera is much more fun than reading about it, so the assignments are a way of taking a little break after each chapter and having some fun.

Q: SHOULD I READ THE BOOK STRAIGHT THROUGH OR CAN I SKIP AROUND FROM CHAPTER TO CHAPTER?

A: Here's the easy answer: yes and no. No, because the first four chapters give you the basic information that you need to know about your camera. These are the building blocks for using the camera. After that, yes, you can move around the book as you see fit because those chapters are written to stand on their own as guides to specific types of photography or shooting situations. So you can bounce from portraits to shooting landscapes and then maybe to a little action photography. It's all about your needs and how you want to address them. Or, you can read it straight through. The choice is up to you.

Q: I DON'T SEE ANY CHAPTERS DEVOTED TO VIDEO.

A: I know that one of the reasons you probably bought the T1i was its ability to capture video. I have covered some basic video setup information in Chapter 2 but I really wanted the focus of this book to center around the photographic capabilities and possibilities. Don't worry, though; read the next Q&A and I think you will be happy.

Q: IS THERE ANYTHING ELSE I SHOULD KNOW BEFORE GETTING STARTED?

A: In order to keep the book short and focused, I had to be pretty selective about what I put in each chapter. The problem is that there is a little more information that might come in handy after you've gone through all the chapters. So as an added value for you, I have written two bonus chapters called "Pimp My Ride" and "T1i Video: Beyond the Basics." The first chapter is full of information on photo accessories that will assist you in making better photographs. In it, you will find my recommendation for things like filters, tripods, and much more. The second chapter will lead you through some video tips and techniques to make your T1i movies even better. To access the bonus chapters, just log in or join peachpit.com (it's free), then enter the book's ISBN. After you register the book, a link to the bonus chapters will be listed on your Account page under Registered Products.

Q: IS THAT IT?

A: One last thought before you dive into the first chapter. My goal in writing this book has been to give you a resource that you can turn to for creating great photographs with your Canon T1i. Take some time to learn the basics and then put them to use. Photography, like most things, takes time to master and requires practice. I have been a photographer for 25 years and I'm still learning. Always remember, it's not the camera but the person using it who makes beautiful photographs. Have fun, make mistakes, and then learn from them. In no time, I'm sure you will transition from a person who takes snapshots to a photographer who makes great shots.

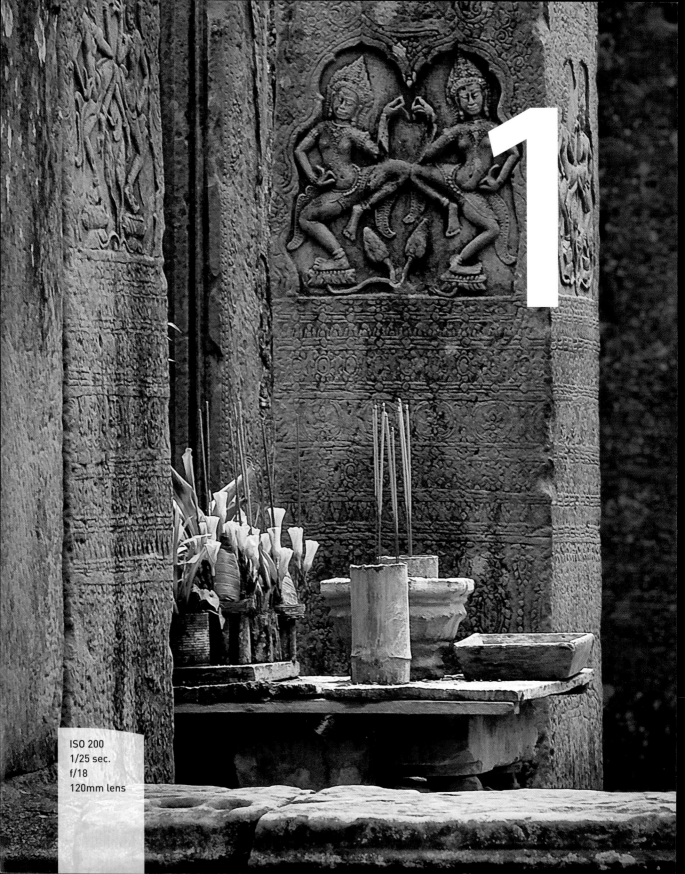

1

ISO 200
1/25 sec.
f/18
120mm lens

The T1i Top Ten List

TEN TIPS TO MAKE YOUR SHOOTING MORE PRODUCTIVE RIGHT OUT OF THE BOX

Whenever I get a new camera, I am always anxious to jump right in and start cranking off exposures. What I really should be doing is sitting down with my instruction manual to learn how to use all of the camera features, but what fun is that? After all, we all know that instruction manuals are for propping up that short leg on the family room table, right?

Of course, this behavior always leads me to frustration in the end—there are always issues that would have been easily addressed had I known about them before I started shooting. Maybe if I had a Top Ten list of things to know, I could be more productive without having to spend countless hours with the manual. So this is where we begin.

The following list will get you up and running without suffering many of the "gotchas" that come from not being at least somewhat familiar with your new camera. So let's take a look at the top ten things you should know before you start taking pictures with your Canon T1i.

PORING OVER THE CAMERA

CAMERA FRONT

Remote Sensor

Shutter Release

Red-Eye Reduction Lamp/
Self-Timer Lamp

EF Lens
Alignment

EF-S Lens
Alignment

Microphone

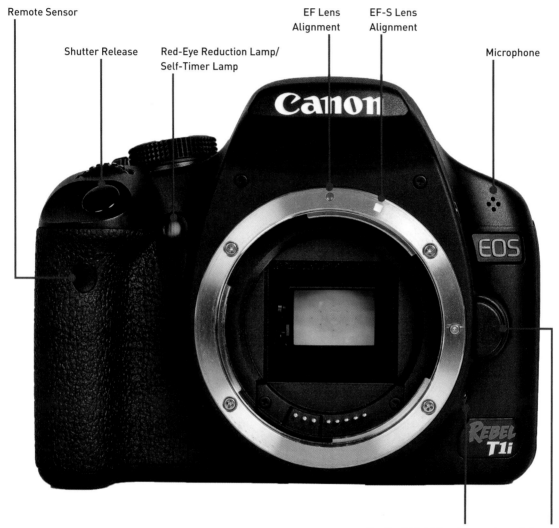

Depth-of-Field Preview

Lens Release

CAMERA BACK

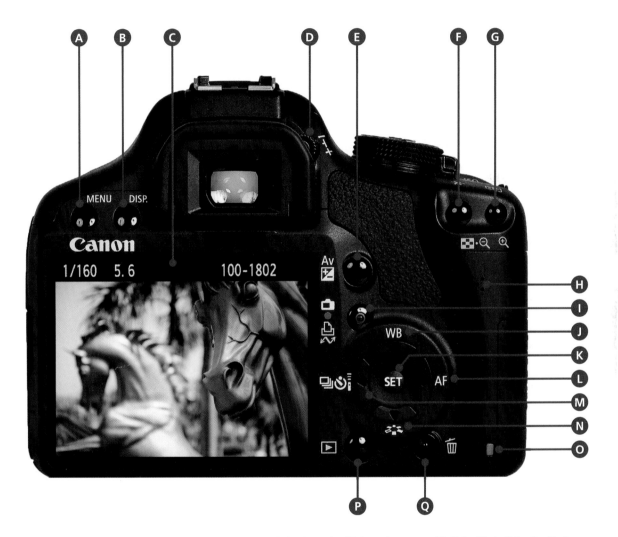

A Menu
B Display
C Rear LCD
D Dioptric Adjustment
E Aperture/Exposure Compensation
F ✱ AE/AF Lock/Focus/Reduce Image

G Focus Point Selection/Enlarge Image
H Speaker
I Live View/Movie Shooting
J White Balance/Up Cross Key
K Set
L Autofocus Selection/Right Cross Key

M Drive Mode Selection/Left
   Cross Key
N Picture Style/Down Cross Key
O Card Busy
P Image Review
Q Trash

CAMERA TOP

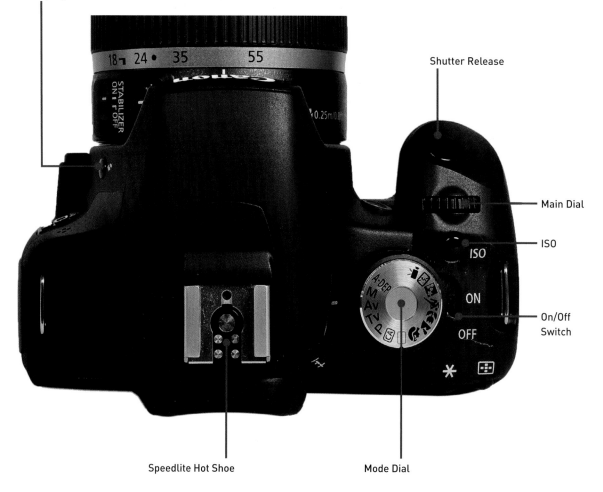

Pop-Up Flash

Shutter Release

Main Dial

ISO

On/Off Switch

Speedlite Hot Shoe

Mode Dial

1. CHARGE YOUR BATTERY

I know that this will be one of the hardest things for you to do because you really want to start shooting, but a little patience will pay off later.

When you first open your camera and slide the battery into the battery slot, you will be pleased to find that there is probably juice in the battery and you can start shooting right away. What you should really be doing is getting out the battery charger and giving that power-cell a full charge. Not only will this give you more time to shoot, it will start the battery off on the right foot. No matter what claims the manufacturers make about battery life and charging memory, I always find I get better life and performance when I charge my batteries fully and then use them right down to the point where they have nothing left to give. To check your battery level, insert it into the camera, turn on the camera, and look for the battery indicator on the rear LCD. You can also press the shutter release button to wake up the camera. This will activate the rear LCD display and allow you to see the battery level indicator located in the bottom-right portion of the display panel (**Figure 1.1**).

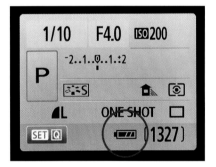

FIGURE 1.1
The LCD shows how much charge is left on your battery.

KEEPING A BACKUP BATTERY

If I were to suggest just one accessory that you should buy for your camera, it would probably be a second battery. Nothing stinks more than being out in the field and having your camera die. Keeping a fully charged battery in your bag will always give you the confidence that you can keep on shooting without fail. Not only is this a great strategy to extend your shooting time, it also helps to lengthen the life of your batteries by alternating between them. No matter what the manufacturers say, batteries do have a life and using them half as much will only lengthen their usefulness.

2. TURN OFF THE RELEASE SHUTTER WITHOUT CARD SETTING

Nothing will ruin your day faster than shooting for a couple of hours only to find that you didn't have a memory card in your camera and thus haven't saved any of the pictures that you've taken. This was always a concern with film shooters, and it hasn't gone away with digital SLRs. You see, camera manufacturers want to give prospective buyers a way to test out the camera without having to keep a memory card in it, so they came up with a setting called Release Shutter without Card. When your camera is set up in this mode, it will act and shoot just as it would when you have a memory card inserted. It will even display your shot on the rear LCD display. Unfortunately, this is where most photographers get fooled into thinking they are saving their images. If they were to look at the LCD, they would see that Canon was nice enough to overlay a message on the display that clearly says No Card. This is nice, but if you are shooting without looking at the display, you could be easily fooled.

Unfortunately, there is no visual clue within the viewfinder to alert you to this No Card status. So here is the simple solution.

TURNING OFF THE RELEASE SHUTTER WITHOUT CARD SETTING

1. Turn the camera on.
2. Press the Menu button on the back of the camera to bring up the menu list.
3. Use the Main dial to select the far-left menu tab.
4. Now scroll down to the Release shutter without card option using the Cross keys and press the Set button (**A**).
5. Use the Cross keys to select the Disable option, and then press the Set button once again (**B**).
6. Press the Menu button again to return to shooting mode.

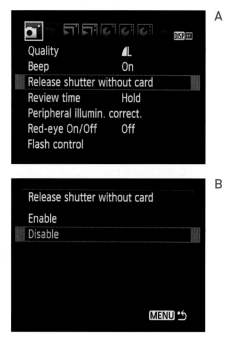

Now when you try to take a photo without a memory card inserted in the camera, you will see a message in the bottom left of your viewfinder that flashes the word Card. This is your clue that you need to insert your memory card before the camera will fire. The rear display will also display a large No Card message if you activate the shutter button.

We will have an in-depth discussion on memory cards and proper formatting in Chapter 2.

3. SET YOUR JPEG IMAGE QUALITY

Your new T1i has a number of image quality settings to choose from, and depending on your needs, you can adjust them accordingly. Most people shoot with the JPEG option because it allows them to capture a large number of photos on their memory cards. The problem is that unless you understand what JPEG is, you might be degrading the quality of your images without realizing it.

The JPEG format has been around since about 1994 and stands for Joint Photographic Experts Group. JPEG was developed by this group as a method of shrinking the size of digital images down to a smaller size for the purpose of reducing large file sizes while retaining the original image information. (Technically, JPEG isn't even a file format—it's a mathematical equation for reducing image file sizes—but to keep things simple, we'll just refer to it as a file format.) The problem with JPEG is that, in order to reduce a file size, it has to throw away some of the information. This is referred to as "lossy compression." This is important to understand because, while you can fit more images on your memory card by choosing a lower-quality JPEG setting, you will also be reducing the quality of your image. This effect becomes more apparent as you enlarge your pictures.

The JPEG file format also has one other characteristic: to apply the compression to the image before final storage on your memory card, the camera has to apply all of the image processing first. Image processing involves such factors as sharpening, color adjustment, contrast adjustment, noise reduction, and so on. Many photographers now prefer to use the RAW file format to get greater control over the image processing. We will take a closer look at this in Chapter 2, but for now let's just make sure that we are using the best-quality JPEG possible.

The T1i has six quality settings for the JPEG format. There are two settings each for the Large, Medium, and Small settings. The two settings represent more or less image compression based on your choice. The Large, Medium, and Small settings determine the actual physical size of your image in pixels. Let's work with the highest-quality setting possible. After all, our goal is to make big, beautiful photographs, so why start the process with a lower-quality image?

SETTING THE IMAGE QUALITY

1. Press the Menu button on the back of the camera to bring up the menu list.

2. Use the Main dial to select the far-left menu tab.

3. At the top of this menu tab locate the Quality option (**A**).

4. Press the Set button to bring up the options screen.

5. Use the left/right Cross keys to select the first L (this will render a 15-megapixel image with a dimension of 4752 pixels by 3168 pixels) (**B**).

6. Press the Set button to lock in this change.

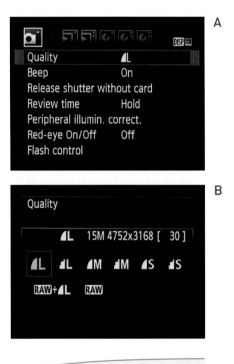

A

B

As you will see when scrolling through the quality settings, the higher the quality, the fewer pictures you will be able to fit on your card. If you have a 2 GB memory card, the quality setting we have selected will allow you to shoot about 460 photographs before you fill up your card. Always try to choose quality over quantity. Your pictures will be the better for it.

Manual Callout

For a complete chart that shows the image quality settings with the number of possible shots for each setting, turn to page 70 in your user manual.

4. TURN OFF THE AUTO ISO SETTING

The ISO setting in your camera allows you to choose the level of sensitivity of the camera sensor to light. The ability to change this sensitivity is one of the biggest advantages to using a digital camera. In the days of film cameras, you had to choose the ISO by film type. This meant that if you wanted to shoot in lower light, you had to replace the film in the camera with one that had a higher ISO. So not only did you have to carry different types of film, but you also had to remove one roll from the camera to replace it with another, even if you hadn't used up the current roll. Now all we have to do is go to our menu and select the appropriate ISO.

Having this flexibility is a powerful option but, just as with the Quality setting, the ISO setting has a direct bearing on the quality of the final image. The higher the ISO, the more digital noise the image will contain. Since our goal is to produce high-quality photographs, it is important that we get control over all of the camera controls and bend them to our will. When you turn your camera on for the first time, the ISO will be set to Auto. This means that the camera is determining how much light is available and will choose what it believes is the correct ISO setting. Since you want to use the lowest ISO possible, you will need to turn this setting off and manually select the appropriate ISO.

Which ISO you choose depends on your level of available or ambient light. For sunny days or very bright scenes, use a low ISO such as 100 or 200. As the level of light is reduced, raise the ISO level. Cloudy days or indoor scenes might require you to use ISO 400. Low-light scenes, such as when you are shooting at night, will mean you need to bump up that ISO to 1600. The thing to remember is to shoot with the lowest setting possible for maximum quality.

SETTING THE ISO

1. Activate the camera by lightly pressing the shutter release button.

2. Press the ISO button on the top of the camera.

3. Use the Main dial to select an ISO between 100 and 6400.

4. Lightly press the shutter release button or press the ISO button again to lock in your change.

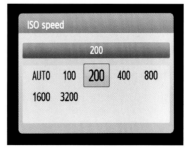

NOISE

Noise is the enemy of digital photography, but it has nothing to do with the loudness of your camera operation. It is a term that refers to the electronic artifacts that appear as speckles in your image. They generally appear in darker shadow areas and are a result of the camera trying to amplify the signal to produce visible information. The more the image needs to be amplified—e.g., raising the sensitivity through higher ISOs—the greater the amount of noise there will be.

SET YOUR ISO ON THE FLY

You can also change the ISO without taking your eye from the viewfinder by following the same steps as above. When you press the ISO button, you will see all of the camera settings in the viewfinder disappear, leaving just the ISO information viewable. Once you press the Set button, your new ISO setting will be displayed along with the regular shooting data. This will get easier to do as you become more familiar with the camera buttons.

5. SET YOUR FOCUS POINT AND MODE

The Canon focusing system is legendary for its speed and accuracy. The Artificial Intelligence (AI) focus modes will give you a ton of flexibility in your shooting. There is, however, one small problem that is inherent with any focusing system. No matter how intelligent it is, the camera is looking at all of the subjects in the scene and determining which is closest to the camera. It then uses this information to determine where the proper focus point should be. It has no way of knowing what your main emphasis is, so it is using a "best guess" system. To eliminate this factor, you should set the camera to single-point focusing so that you can ensure that you are focusing on the most important feature in the scene.

The camera has nine separate focus points to choose from. They are arranged in a diamond pattern with eight points around the outside of the diamond and one in the center. To start things off, you should select the focus point in the middle. Once you have become more familiar with the focus system, you can experiment with the other points, as well as the automatic point selection.

You should also change the focus mode to One Shot so that you can focus on your subject and then recompose your shot while holding that point of focus.

SETTING THE FOCUS POINT AND FOCUS MODE

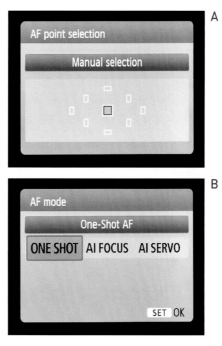

1. To choose a single point of focus, wake the camera (if necessary) by lightly pressing the shutter release button.

2. Press the focus point selection button located in the upper-right area of your camera back.

3. Now use the Cross keys or the Main dial to move the focus point to the center spot, as seen on the rear LCD display (you can also do this in the viewfinder by moving the red dot to the desired position) (**A**).

4. Lightly press the shutter release button once more to set your new focus point.

5. To set the focus mode, press the AF button, which doubles as the right Cross key.

6. Using the Cross keys or Main dial, select the One Shot mode, then press the Set button (**B**).

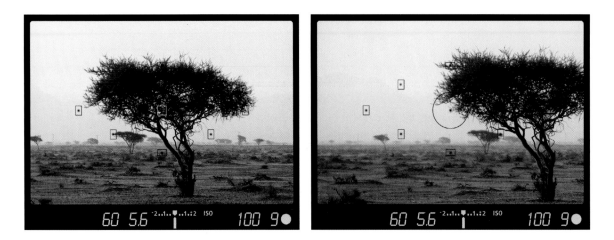

FIGURE 1.2
Using the center single focus point in One Shot mode allows you to focus on your subject in the center, then recompose your photograph for a better composition.

The camera is now ready for single focusing. You will hear a chirp when the camera has locked in and focused on the subject. To focus on your subject and then recompose your shot, just place the focus point in the viewfinder on your subject, depress the shutter release button halfway until the camera chirps and, without letting up on the shutter button, recompose your shot and then press the shutter button all the way down to make your exposure (**Figure 1.2**).

6. SET THE CORRECT WHITE BALANCE

White balance correction is the process of rendering accurate colors in your final image. Most people don't even notice that light has different color characteristics because the human eye automatically adjusts to different color temperatures, so quickly, in fact, that everything looks correct in a matter of milliseconds.

When color film ruled the world, photographers would select which film to use depending on what their light source was going to be. The most common film was balanced for daylight, but you could also buy film that was color balanced for tungsten light sources. Most other lighting situations had to be handled by using color filters over the lens. This process was necessary for the photographer's final image to show the correct color balance of a scene.

Your camera has the ability to perform this same process automatically, but you can also choose to override it and set it manually. Guess which method we are going to use? You are catching on fast! Once again, your photography should be all about maintaining control over everything that influences your final image.

Luckily, you don't need to have a deep understanding of color temperatures to control your camera's white balance. The choices are given to you in terms that are easy to relate to and that will make things pretty simple. Your white balance choices are:

- **Auto:** The default setting for your camera. It is also the setting used by all of the Basic modes (see Chapter 3).

- **Daylight:** Most often used for general daylight/sun-lit shooting.

- **Shade:** Used when working in shaded areas that are still using sunlight as the dominant light source.

- **Cloudy:** The choice for overcast or very cloudy days. This and the Shade setting will eliminate the blue color cast from your images.

- **Tungsten:** Used for any occasion where you are using regular household-type bulbs for your light source. Tungsten is a very warm light source and will result in a yellow/orange cast if you don't correct for it.

- **Fluorescent:** Used to get rid of the green-blue cast that can result from using regular fluorescent lights as your dominant light source. Some fluorescent lights are actually balanced for daylight, which would allow you to use the Daylight white balance setting.

- **Flash:** Used whenever you're using the built-in flash or using a flash on the hot shoe. You should select this white balance to adjust for the slightly cooler light that comes from using a flash. (The hot shoe is the small bracket located on the top of your camera, which rests just above the eyepiece. This bracket is used for attaching a more powerful flash to the camera [see Chapter 8 and the bonus chapter].)

- **Custom:** Indicates that you are using a customized white balance that is adjusted for a particular light source. If you know what the color temperature of your light source is, you can manually create a white balance setting that is specifically for that light source.

Your camera has two different "zones" of shooting modes to choose from. These are located on the Mode dial, and they're called the Basic and Creative zones. All of the Basic modes, which are identifiable by small icons, are automatic in nature and do not allow for much, if any, customization. The Creative modes, defined by the letter symbols, allow for much more control by the photographer (**Figure 1.3**).

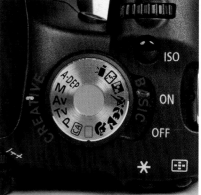

FIGURE 1.3
The camera's shooting modes are divided into the Basic zone and the Creative zone.

SETTING THE WHITE BALANCE

1. After turning on or waking the camera, select one of the shooting modes in the Creative zone such as P (you can't select the white balance when using any of the Basic modes).

2. Press the WB button on the back of the camera to bring up the white balance menu. It is the top button on the Cross keys.

3. Use the left/right Cross keys to select the proper white balance for your shooting situation.

4. Press the Set button to lock in your selection.

5. Check the camera display to ensure that the proper white balance is selected.

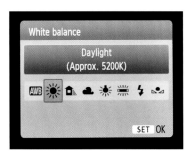

WHITE BALANCE AND THE TEMPERATURE OF COLOR

When you select different white balances in your camera, you will notice that underneath several of the choices is a number, e.g., 5200K, 7000K, or 3200K. These numbers refer to the Kelvin temperature of the colors in the visible spectrum. The visible spectrum is the range of light that the human eye can see (think of a rainbow or the color bands that come out of a spectrum). The visible spectrum of light has been placed into a scale called the Kelvin temperature scale, which identifies the thermodynamic temperature of a given color of light. Put simply, reds and yellows are "warm" and greens and blues are "cool." Even more confusing can be the actual temperature ratings. Warm temperatures are typically lower on the Kelvin scale, ranging from 3000 degrees to 5000 degrees, while cool temperatures run from 5500 degrees to around 10000 degrees. Take a look at this list for an example of Kelvin temperature properties.

KELVIN TEMPERATURE PROPERTIES

Flames	1700K–1900K	Daylight	5000K
Incandescent bulb	2800K–3300K	Camera flash	5500K
White fluorescent	4000K	Overcast sky	6000K
Moonlight	4000K	Open shade	7000K

The most important thing to remember here is how the color temperature of light will affect the look of your images. If something is "warm," it will look reddish-yellow, and if something is "cool," it will have a bluish cast.

7. ADJUST THE VIEWFINDER DIOPTER

If you wear glasses, or are just like me and your eyes are getting older, you might have trouble looking through the viewfinder. Actually, you will be able to see through the viewfinder but what you see might not look like it is in crisp focus. This may not be a huge problem when you are using autofocus, but if you are trying to manually focus your lens you will find that your images look a bit soft. To remedy this, you should use the dioptric adjustment knob, located to the right of the viewfinder, to adjust things for your particular vision. There is no "correct" setting for this adjustment so you will have to dial it in yourself. It's really easy if you know this little trick.

ADJUSTING THE DIOPTER

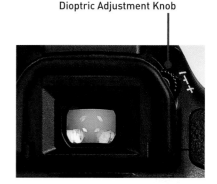

Dioptric Adjustment Knob

1. Remove your lens and point your camera at a light-colored wall or surface.

2. Place your index finger on the dioptric adjustment knob and look through the viewfinder (if you normally wear glasses you should have them on).

3. Rotate the wheel until the focus points in the viewfinder look sharp.

4. That's it. Just replace your lens and start shooting with a clearer view.

8. KNOW HOW TO OVERRIDE AUTO FOCUS

As good as the Canon autofocus system is, there are times when it just isn't doing the job for you. Many times this has to do with how you would like to compose a scene and where the actual point of focus should be. This can be especially true when you are using the camera on a tripod, where you can't pre-focus and then recompose before shooting (as discussed earlier). To take care of this problem, you will need to manually focus the lens. I am only going to cover the kit lens that came with my Canon T1i (the EF-S 18–55mm IS), so if you have purchased a different lens be sure to check the accompanying instruction manual for the lens.

On the 18–55mm kit lens, you simply need to slide the switch located at the base of the lens (located on the lens barrel near the body of the camera) from the AF setting to the MF setting (**Figure 1.4**). You can now turn the focus ring at the end of the lens to set your focus. You will also see an MF displayed on the shooting display of your LCD screen, which indicates that you are in manual focus mode. Now that you're in manual focus mode, the camera will not give you an audible chirp when you have correctly focused unless you are focusing on an area that is covered by one of the focus points in the viewfinder.

We'll cover manual focus in more detail in future chapters.

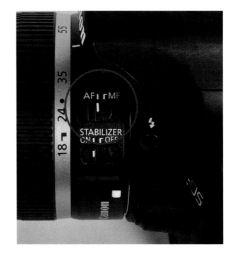

FIGURE 1.4
Slide the focus switch on the lens to the MF position to manually focus.

9. REVIEW YOUR SHOTS

One of the greatest features of a digital camera is its ability to give us instant feedback. By reviewing your images on the camera's LCD screen, you can instantly tell if you got your shot. This visual feedback allows you to make adjustments on the fly and make certain that all of your adjustments are correct before moving on.

When you first press the shutter release button, your camera quickly processes your shot and then displays the image on the LCD display. The default setting for that display is only two seconds. Personally, I don't find this to be nearly enough time to take in all the visual feedback that I might want. Instead of using this "quick glance" method, change your display time to the Hold setting. This will keep the image up on the display until you decide that you are ready to move on to your next shot. (Note that this option will drain your batteries a little faster than the default setting.)

CHANGING YOUR REVIEW TIME SETTING

1. Press the Menu button and the use the Main dial to select the leftmost menu item.

2. Using the Cross keys, scroll down to Review time and press the Set button (**A**).

3. Scroll down to Hold and then press the Set button once again (**B**).

4. Press the Menu button to leave the menus and continue shooting.

Now that you have the image display set, let's check out some of the other visual information that will really help you when shooting.

There are four display modes that give you different amounts of information while reviewing your photos. The default view (**Figure 1.5**) simply displays your image along with the shutter speed, f-stop, and image number (these will appear above your image on the display).

To get more visual feedback, press the Display (Disp.) button located to the left of the viewfinder. Press it once and you will see your Quality setting, along with the image number that you are currently viewing ("3/307" would mean that you're looking at the third image of 307 total images). See **Figure 1.6**.

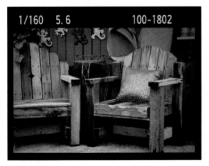

FIGURE 1.5
The default display mode on the T1i.

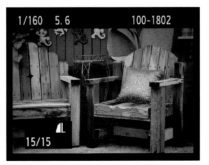

FIGURE 1.6
Pressing the Display (Disp.) button lets you scroll through the different display modes.

Pressing the button a second time results in a huge amount of information being displayed along with the image. You will now be able to see the following items in your display: shutter speed, aperture, exposure compensation, image name, image thumbnail, histogram, shooting mode, ISO, white balance setting, picture style, quality setting, size of the image in megabytes, color space, image number, date, and time (**Figure 1.7**).

FIGURE 1.7
This display mode offers you a ton of information at a glance.

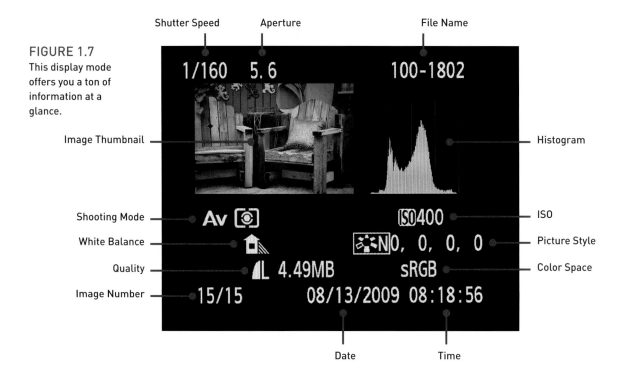

That's a huge amount of information available on a 3" screen! You probably won't want to use this display option as your default review setting, but if you are trying to figure out what settings you used or if you want to review the histogram (see "The Value of the Histogram" sidebar on pages 20–21), you now have all of this great information available.

The fourth display option allows you to view the regular image histogram, as well as a color histogram for your image. Personally, I prefer to use just the standard histogram, but you may find this feature handy when checking to see if you were able to capture all of the information in your scene (**Figure 1.8**).

Additionally, both histogram modes result in a small, thumbnail-sized version of your image. So while there is a lot of information concerning the camera settings, you get less visual feedback in terms of seeing the actual photo. You would probably be best served by selecting one of the first two viewing modes, and then using the histogram modes when you need to review your shooting data.

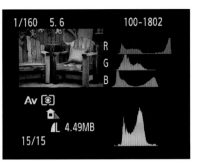

FIGURE 1.8
The fourth display option shows you a color histogram.

The different display modes are activated by pressing the Display (Disp.) button while an image is actively being displayed on your LCD screen. The display mode will remain for all future images that are displayed until you press the Display button again. Also, pressing the shutter release or Menu button will result in closing the image display. To get your image back up on the LCD screen, simply press the blue Image Review playback button on the back of the camera.

DELETING IMAGES

Deleting or erasing images is a fairly simple process that is covered on pages 159-160 of your manual. To quickly get you on your way, simply press the Image Review playback button and spin the Main dial until you find the picture that you want to delete. Then press the Trash button beneath the Cross keys, use the right Cross key to select Erase, and then press the Set button (**Figure 1.9**).

Caution: Once you have deleted an image, it is gone for good. Make sure you don't want it before you drop it in the trash.

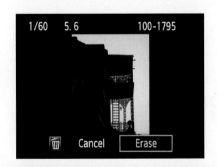

FIGURE 1.9
Deleting images on the T1i is simple.

THE VALUE OF THE HISTOGRAM

Simply put, histograms are two-dimensional representations of your images in graph form. There are two different histograms that you should be concerned with: the luminance and the color histograms. Luminance is referred to in your manual as "brightness" and is most valuable when evaluating your exposures. In **Figure 1.10**, you see what looks like a mountain range. The graph represents the entire tonal range that your camera can capture, from the whitest whites to the blackest blacks. The left side represents black, all the way to the right side, which represents white. The heights of the peaks represent the number of pixels that contain those luminance levels (a tall peak in the middle means your image contains a large amount of medium-bright pixels). Looking at this figure, it is hard to determine where all of the ranges of light and dark areas are and how much of each I have. If I look at the histogram, I can see that the largest peak of the graph is in the middle and trails off as it reaches the edges. In most cases, you would look for this type of histogram, indicating that you captured the entire range of tones, from dark to light, in your image. Knowing that is fine, but here is where the information really gets useful.

When you evaluate the histogram that has a spike or peak riding up the far left or right side of the graph, it means that you are clipping detail from your image. In essence, you are trying to record values that are either too dark or too light for your sensor to accurately record. This is usually an indication of over- or under-exposure. It also means that you need to correct your exposure so that the important details will not record as solid black or white pixels (which is what happens when clipping occurs). There are times, however, when some clipping is acceptable. If you are photographing a scene where the sun will be in the frame, you can expect to get some clipping because the sun is just too bright to hold any detail. Likewise, if you are shooting something that has true blacks in it—think coal in a mineshaft at midnight—there are most certainly going to be some true blacks with no detail in your shot. The main goal is to ensure that you aren't clipping any "important" visual

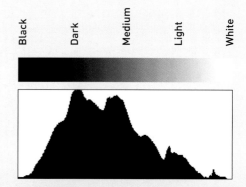

FIGURE 1.10
This is a typical histogram, where the dark to light tones run from left to right. The black-to-white gradient above the graph demonstrates where the tones lie on the graph and would not appear above your camera histogram display.

information, and that is achieved by keeping an eye on your histogram. Take a look at **Figure 1.11**. The histogram displayed on the image shows a heavy skew toward the left with almost no part of the mountain touching the right side. This is a good example of what an underexposed image histogram looks like. Now look at **Figure 1.12** and compare the histogram for the image that was correctly exposed. Notice that even though there are two distinct peaks on the graph, there is an even distribution across the entire histogram.

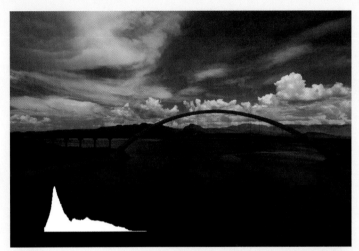

FIGURE 1.11
This image is about two stops under-exposed. Notice the histogram is skewed to the left.

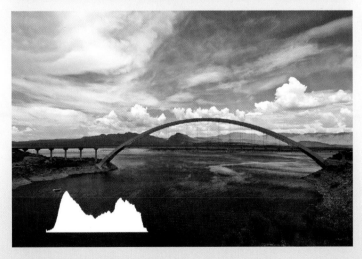

FIGURE 1.12
This histogram reflects a correctly exposed image.

10. HOLD YOUR CAMERA FOR PROPER SHOOTING

Digital SLR cameras are made to favor the right-handed individual. The basics of properly holding the camera begins with grasping the camera body with the right hand. You will quickly find that most of the important camera controls are within easy reach of your thumb and forefinger. The next step is to create a stable base for your camera to rest on. This is accomplished by placing the camera body on the up-facing palm of your left hand (**Figure 1.13**). Now you can curl your fingers around the lens barrel to quickly zoom or manually focus the lens.

Now that you know where to put your hands, let's talk about what to do with the rest of your body parts. By using the under-hand grip, your elbows will be drawn closer to your body. You should concentrate on pulling them in close to your body to stabilize your shooting position. You should also try to maintain proper upright posture. Leaning forward at the waist will begin to fatigue your back, neck, and arms. Nothing ruins a day of shooting like a sore back, so make sure you stand erect with your elbows in. Finally, place your left foot in front of your right foot, and face your subject in a slightly wide stance. By combining all of these aspects into your photography, you will give yourself the best chance of eliminating self-imposed camera shake (or hand shake) in your images, resulting in much sharper photographs.

FIGURE 1.13
The proper way to hold your camera to ensure sharp, blur-free images. (Photos: Alex Revell)

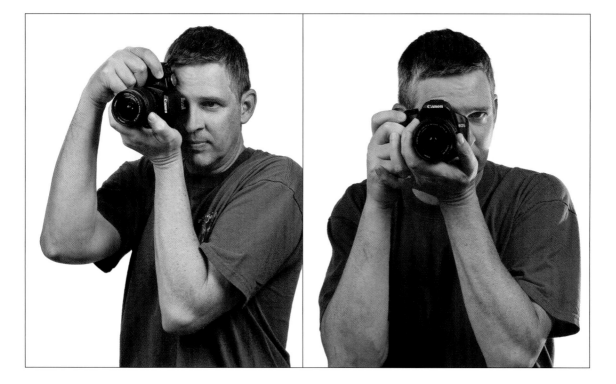

Chapter 1 Assignments

Let's begin our shooting assignments by setting up and using all of the elements of the Top Ten list. Even though I have yet to cover the Creative shooting modes, you should set your camera to the P (Program) mode. This will allow you to interact with the various settings and menus that have been covered thus far.

Basic camera setup

Charge your battery to 100% to get it started on a life of dependable service. Next, using your newfound knowledge, set up your camera to address the following: Shooting without a card, Image Quality, and Auto ISO.

Selecting the proper white balance

Take your camera outside into a daylight environment and then photograph the same scene using different white balance settings. Pay close attention to how each setting affects the overall color cast of your images. Next, move inside and repeat the exercise while shooting in a tungsten lighting environment. Finally, find a fluorescent light source and repeat once more.

Focusing with single point and One Shot

Change your camera setting so that you are focusing using the single-point focus mode. Try using all of the different focus points to see how they work in focusing your scene. Then set your focus mode to One Shot and practice focusing on a subject and then recomposing before actually taking the picture. Try doing this with subjects at varying distances.

Evaluating your pictures with the LCD display

Set up your image display properties and then review some of your previous assignment images using the different display modes. Review your shooting information for each image and take a look at the histograms to see how the content of your photo affects their shapes.

Discovering the manual focus mode

Change your focus mode from auto focus to manual focus and practice a little manual focus photography. Get familiar with where the focus ring is and how to use it to achieve sharp images.

Get a grip: proper camera holding

This final assignment is something that you should practice every time you shoot: proper grip and stance for shooting with your camera. Use the described technique and then shoot a series of images. Try comparing it with improper techniques to compare the stability of the grip and stance.

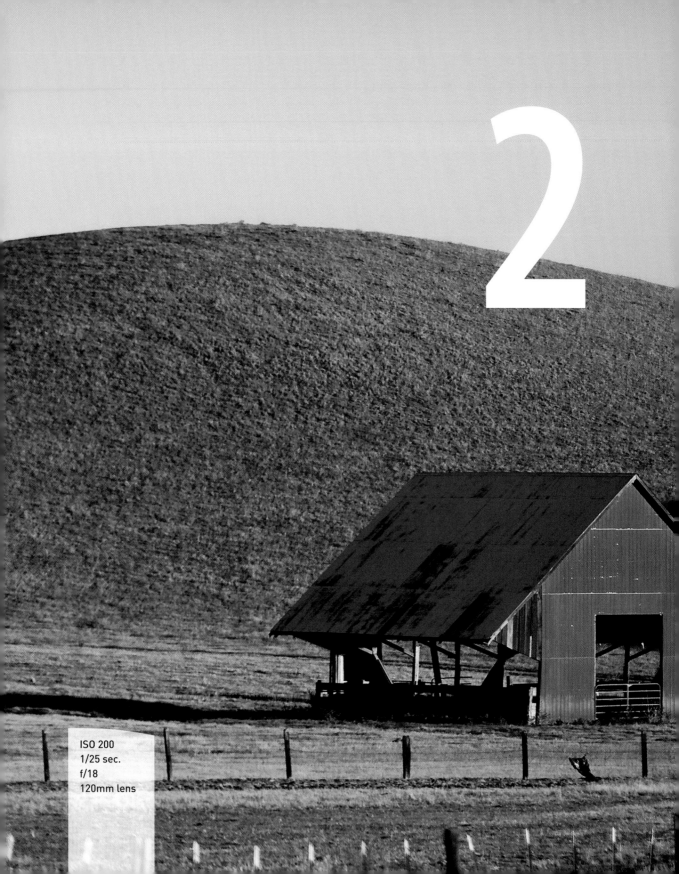

2

ISO 200
1/25 sec.
f/18
120mm lens

First Things First

A FEW THINGS TO KNOW AND DO BEFORE YOU BEGIN TAKING PICTURES

Now that we've covered the top ten tasks to get you up and shooting, we should probably take care of some other important details. You must become familiar with certain features of your camera before you can take full advantage of it. Additionally, we will take some steps to prepare the camera and memory card for use. So to get things moving, let's start off with something that you will definitely need before you can take a single picture: a memory card.

PORING OVER THE PICTURE

While strolling around Bainbridge Island with some friends, I came upon this small garden scene. It was early evening and it was slightly overcast, which was casting a soft even light down on the area, softening the shadows and adding great saturation to the plants.

The fence made a nice leading line to draw the viewer's eye into the scene.

The image was slightly underexposed to get more details in the white fence.

I used a normal lens setting to get a fairly tight composure.

I added warmth and saturation by using the landscape picture style.

ISO 400
1/250 sec.
f/5.6
48mm lens

PORING OVER THE PICTURE

The exposure was set so that detail was not lost in the shadows.

SUQUAMISH TRIBE

Suquamish Tribe

My buddy Don and I were taking a photowalk along the Seattle waterfront and came upon a small marina. Mixed in with all of the large yachts and fishing boats was this small blue boat that looked so out of place. I really loved the weathered look of the boat as it sat in a darker section of the marina. I decided to use a telephoto lens to isolate it from the other ships and make it the sole subject of my photo.

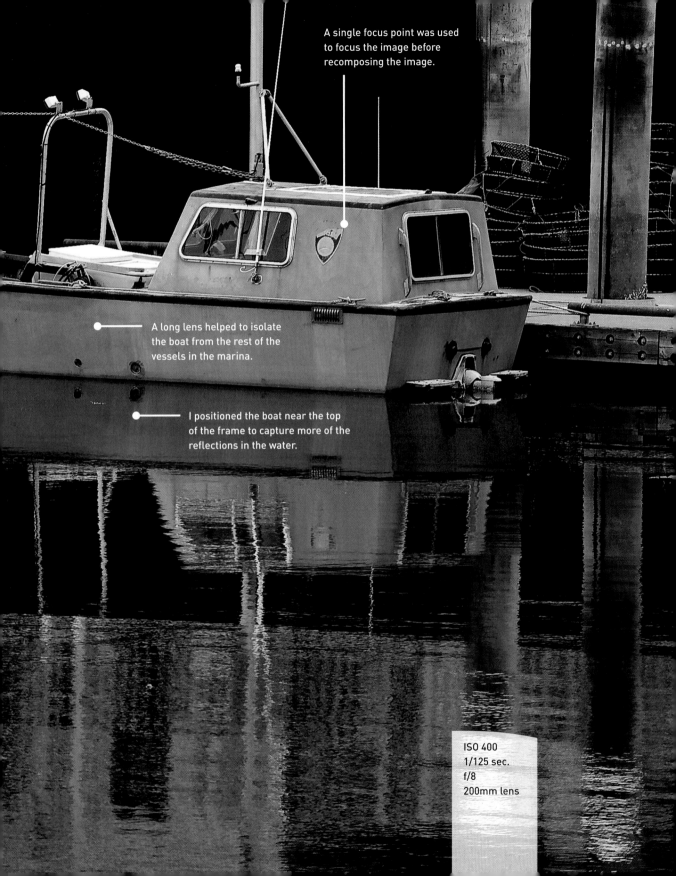

A single focus point was used to focus the image before recomposing the image.

A long lens helped to isolate the boat from the rest of the vessels in the marina.

I positioned the boat near the top of the frame to capture more of the reflections in the water.

ISO 400
1/125 sec.
f/8
200mm lens

CHOOSING THE RIGHT MEMORY CARD

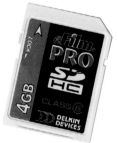

Memory cards are the digital film that stores every shot you take until you move them to a computer. The cards come in all shapes and sizes, and they are critical for capturing all of your photos. It is important not to skimp when it comes to selecting your memory cards. The T1i uses Secure Digital (SD) memory cards (**Figure 2.1**).

FIGURE 2.1
Make sure you select an SD card that has enough capacity to handle your photography needs.

If you have been using a point-and-shoot camera, chances are that you may already own a Secure Digital (SD) media card. Which brand of card you use is completely up to you, but here is some advice about choosing your memory card:

- Size matters, at least in memory cards. At 15.1 megapixels, the T1i will require a lot of storage space, especially if you shoot in the RAW or RAW+JPEG mode (more on this later in the chapter) or shoot HD video. You should definitely consider using a card with a storage capacity of at least 4 GB.

- Consider buying High Capacity (SDHC) cards. These cards are generally much faster, both when writing images to the card as well as when transferring them to your computer. If you are planning on using the Continuous mode (see Chapter 5) for capturing fast action, you can gain a boost in performance just by using an SDHC card with a Class rating of at least 4 or 6. The higher the class rating, the faster the write-speed. Having a fast card will also benefit your video capture by keeping the flow of video frames moving quickly to your card.

- Buy more than one card. If you have already purchased a memory card, consider getting another. Nothing is worse than almost filling your card and then having to either erase shots or choose a lower-quality image format so that you can keep on shooting. With the cost of memory cards what it is, keeping a spare just makes good sense.

FORMATTING YOUR MEMORY CARD

Now that you have your card, let's talk about formatting for a minute. When you purchase any new SD card, you can pop it into your camera and start shooting right away—and probably everything will work as it should. However, what you should do first is format the card in the camera. This process allows the camera to set up the card to record images from your camera. Just as a computer hard drive must be formatted, formatting your card ensures that it is properly initialized. The card may work in the camera without first being formatted, but chances of failure down the road are much higher.

As a general practice, I always format new cards or cards that have been used in different cameras. I also reformat cards after I have downloaded my images and want to start a new shooting session. Note that you should always format your card in the camera, not your computer. Using the computer could render the card useless. You should also pay attention to the manufacturer's recommendations in respect to moisture, humidity, and proper handling procedures. It sounds a little cliché, but when it comes to protecting your images, every little bit helps.

Most people make the mistake of thinking that the process of formatting the memory card is equivalent to erasing it. Not so. The truth is that when you format the card all you are doing is changing the file management information on the card. Think of it as removing the table of contents from a book and replacing it with a blank page. All of the contents are still there, but you wouldn't know it by looking at the empty table of contents. The camera will see the card as completely empty so you won't be losing any space, even if you have previously filled the card with images. Your camera will simply write the new image data over the previous data.

FORMATTING YOUR MEMORY CARD

1. Insert your memory card into the camera.

2. Press the Menu button and navigate to the first setup menu screen (the fifth from the left).

3. Press the down Cross key on the back of the camera to highlight the Format option and press Set (**A**).

4. The default selection for the Format screen is Cancel, just in case you didn't really want to format the card (**B**). Press the right Cross key to highlight OK. The screen will warn you that you will lose any data by formatting your card, so make sure that you have saved any images that you want onto your computer or elsewhere before formatting.

5. Press the Set button to finalize the formatting of the card.

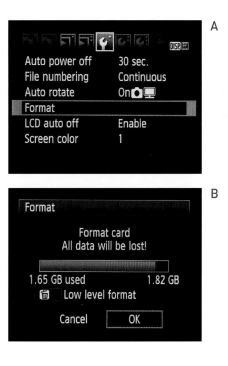

Note that when you perform the card formatting, you can select something called Low-Level Formatting, which performs a much more intensive formatting of the card. During the process, the camera will format all of the recordable sectors on the card. This process takes much longer than a normal formatting and does not need to be performed every time you format. You only need to do this if you see a slow-down in card performance. To enable the Low-Level Formatting option, simply follow the directions above but press the Trash button before starting the format process. This will put a checkmark next to the Low level format option (**Figure 2.2**).

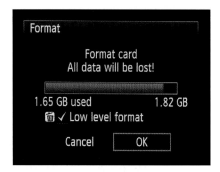

FIGURE 2.2
Press the Trash button to enable Low-Level Formatting.

UPDATING THE T1i'S FIRMWARE

I know that you want to get shooting, but having the proper firmware can impact the way the camera operates. It can fix problems as well as improve operation, so you should probably take care of it sooner rather than later. Updating your camera's firmware is something that the manual completely omits, yet it can change the entire behavior of your camera operating systems and functions. The firmware of your camera is the set of computer operating instructions that controls how your camera functions. Updating this firmware is a great way to not only fix little bugs but also gain access to new functionality. You will need to check out the information on the Canon Firmware update page (www.canon.com/eos-d/) to review how a firmware update will impact your camera, but it is always a good idea to be working with the most up-to-date firmware version available.

CHECKING THE CAMERA'S CURRENT FIRMWARE VERSION NUMBER

1. Rotate the Mode dial to select P (or any of the other modes in the Creative zone).

2. Press the Menu button to display the menu.

3. Turn the Main dial to get to the third camera setup menu, and you will see the currently installed firmware version number at the bottom of the settings. If this version is not the latest one listed on the Canon website, follow the steps in the next section to load the latest version.

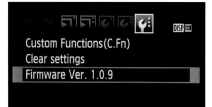

At the time this book was published, the current version of the firmware for the T1i was 1.0.9 and no update was available. Make sure you check the Canon web page often for any updates and then follow the directions below for updating your camera.

UPDATING THE FIRMWARE DIRECTLY FROM YOUR COMPUTER

1. Download the firmware update file from the Canon website (**A**). (You can find the file by going to the Download Library section of the EOS camera site and entering the information about your camera.)

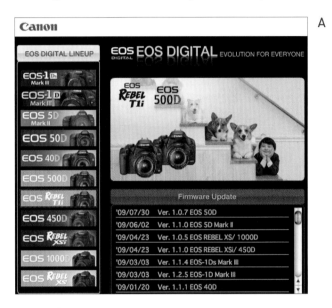

A

2. Download the Firmware Update file that matches your computer operating system (Windows or Macintosh).

3. Extract the downloaded firmware file as per your operating system (B).

4. Attach your camera to the computer via USB and turn the camera on (**C**).

B

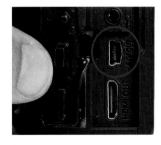

C

5. Open the EOS Utility program and select the Camera Settings/Remote Shooting option (**D**). (This program was included on the CD in your camera box. You will need to install it prior to performing this operation.)

6. When the panel opens, click the Set-Up icon and then click the Firmware button at the bottom of the panel.

7. Click OK and then locate the extracted firmware file to begin the update (**E**).

8. Click Yes on the confirmation screen to begin the update. Note that the software will not allow you to continue the update unless the camera is plugged into the AC power adapter or the battery is fully charged.

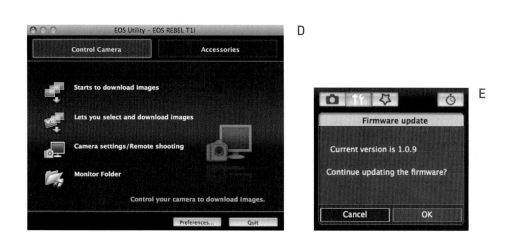

CLEANING THE SENSOR

Cleaning camera sensors used to be a nerve-racking process that required leaving the sensor exposed to scratching and even more dust. Now cleaning the sensor is pretty much an automatic function. Every time you turn the camera on and off, the sensor in the camera vibrates to remove any dust particles that might have landed on it.

There are three choices for cleaning in the camera setup menu: Auto Cleaning, Clean Now, and Clean Manually. By default, the camera is set to automatically clean the sensor every time you power on and off. You can disable this function, but it is best to leave it on.

The one cleaning function that you will need to use via this menu is the Clean Now feature. This should be done every time that you remove the lens from the camera body. That is because removing or changing a lens will leave the camera body open and susceptible to dust sneaking into the body. If you never change lenses, you shouldn't have too many dust problems. But the more often you change lenses, the more chances you are giving dust to enter the body. It's for this reason that I have the Clean Now function added to the custom My Menu list (see Chapter 10).

Every now and then, there will just be a dust spot that is impervious to the shaking of the Auto Cleaning feature. This will require manual cleaning of the sensor. When you activate this feature, it will raise the camera mirror and give you access to the sensor so that you can use a blower or other cleaning device to remove the stubborn dust speck. The camera will need to be turned off after cleaning to allow the mirror to reset.

If you choose to manually clean your sensor, use a device that has been made to clean sensors (not a cotton swab from your medicine cabinet). There are dozens of commercially available devices such as brushes, swabs, and blowers that will clean the sensor without damaging it. To keep the sensor clean, always store the camera with a body cap or lens attached.

The camera sensor is an electrically charged device. This means that when the camera is turned on, there is a current running through the sensor. This electric current can create static electricity, which will attract small dust particles to the sensor area. For this reason, it is always a good idea to turn off the camera prior to removing a lens. You should also consider having the lens mount facing down so that there is less opportunity for dust to fall into the inner workings of the camera.

USING THE CLEAN NOW FEATURE

1. Press the Menu button and use the Main dial to get to the second camera setup menu.

2. Use the down Cross key to highlight Sensor cleaning and then press the Set button (**A**).

3. Use the right Cross key to select Clean now and press the Set button again (**B**).

4. Press Set one more time to start the cleaning function.

5. To return to shooting mode, just lightly press the shutter release button.

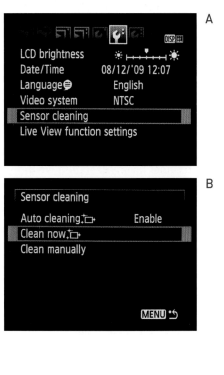

USING THE RIGHT FORMAT: RAW VS. JPEG

When shooting with your T1i, you have a choice of image formats that your camera will use to store the pictures on the memory card. JPEG is probably the most familiar format to anyone who has been using a digital camera. I touched on this topic briefly in Chapter 1, so you already have a little background on what JPEG and RAW files are.

There is nothing wrong with JPEG if you are taking casual shots. JPEG files are ready to use, right out of the camera. Why go through the process of adjusting RAW images of the kids opening presents when you are just going to email them to Grandma? Also, for journalists and sports photographers who are shooting nine frames per second and who need to transmit their images across the wire, again, JPEG is just fine. So what is wrong with JPEG? Absolutely nothing—unless you care about having complete creative control over all of your image data (as opposed to what a compression algorithm thinks is important).

As I mentioned in Chapter 1, JPEG is not actually an image format. It is a compression standard, and compression is where things go bad. When you have your camera set to JPEG—whether it is High, Medium, or Low—you are telling the camera to process the image however it sees fit and then throw away enough image data to make it shrink into a smaller space. In doing so, you give up subtle image details that you will never get back in postprocessing. That is an awfully simplified statement, but still fairly accurate.

SO WHAT DOES RAW HAVE TO OFFER?

First and foremost, RAW images are not compressed. (There are some cameras that have a compressed RAW format but it is lossless compression, which means there is no loss of actual image data.) Note that RAW image files will require you to perform post-processing on your photographs. This is not only necessary; it is the reason that most photographers use it.

RAW images have a greater dynamic range than JPEG-processed images. This means that you can recover image detail in the highlights and shadows that just aren't available in JPEG-processed images.

There is more color information in a RAW image because it is a 14-bit image, which means it contains more color information than a JPEG, which is almost always an 8-bit image. More color information means more to work with and smoother changes between tones—kind of like the difference between performing surgery with a scalpel as opposed to a butcher's knife. They'll both get the job done, but one will do less damage.

Regarding sharpening, a RAW image offers more control because you are the one who is applying the sharpening according to the effect you want to achieve. Once again, JPEG processing applies a standard amount of sharpening that you cannot change after the fact. Once it is done, it's done.

Finally, and most importantly, a RAW file is your negative. No matter what you do to it, you won't change it unless you save your file in a different format. This means that you can come back to that RAW file later and try different processing settings to achieve differing results and never harm the original image. By comparison, if you make a change to your JPEG and accidentally save the file, guess what? You have a new original file, and you will never get back to that first image. That alone should make you sit up and take notice.

ADVICE FOR NEW RAW SHOOTERS

Don't give up on shooting RAW just because it means more work. Hey, if it takes up more space on your card, buy bigger cards or more smaller ones. Will it take more time to download? Yes, but good things come to those who wait. Don't worry about needing to purchase expensive software to work with your RAW files; you already own a program that will allow you to work with your RAW files. Canon's Digital Photo Professional software comes bundled in the box with your camera and gives you the ability to work directly on the RAW files and then output the enhanced results.

My recommendation is to shoot in JPEG mode while you are using this book. This will allow you to quickly review your images and study the effects of future lessons. Once you have become comfortable with all of the camera features, you should switch to shooting in RAW mode so that you can start gaining more creative control over your image processing. After all, you took the photograph—shouldn't you be the one to decide how it looks in the end?

IMAGE RESOLUTION

When discussing digital cameras, image resolution is often used to describe pixel resolution or the number of pixels used to make an image. This can be displayed as a dimension such as 4752 x 3168. This is the physical number of pixels in width and height of the image sensor. Resolution can also be referred to in megapixels (MP) such as 15.1 MP. This number represents the number of total pixels on the sensor and is commonly used to describe the amount of image data that a digital camera can capture.

SELECTING RAW + JPEG

Your camera has the added benefit of being able to write two files for each picture you take, one in RAW and one in JPEG. This can be useful if you need a quick version to email but want a higher-quality version for more advanced processing.

Note that using both formats requires more space on the memory card. I recommend that you use only one format or the other unless you have a specific need to shoot both.

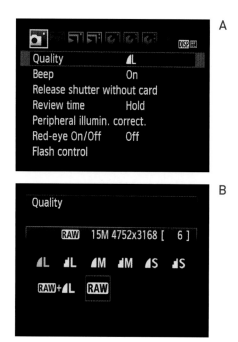

SELECTING YOUR IMAGE QUALITY SETTING

1. Press the Menu button and use the Main dial to select the first shooting menu tab.

2. Use the Cross keys to highlight the Quality setting and press the Set button to enter the Quality setting page (**A**).

3. Use the left/right Cross keys to change the quality setting (**B**).

4. Press the Menu button to lock in your changes.

LENSES AND FOCAL LENGTHS

If you ask most photographers what they believe to be their most critical piece of photographic equipment, they would undoubtedly tell you that it is their lens. The technology and engineering that goes into your camera is a marvel, but it isn't worth a darn if it can't get the light from the outside onto the sensor. The T1i, as a digital single lens reflex (dSLR) camera, uses the lens for a multitude of tasks, from focusing on a subject, to metering a scene, to delivering and focusing the light onto the camera sensor. The lens is also responsible for the amount of the scene that will be captured (the frame). With all of this riding on the lens, let's take a more in-depth look at the camera's eye on the world.

Lenses are composed of optical glass that is both concave and convex in shape. The alignment of the glass elements is designed to focus the light coming in from the front of the lens onto the camera sensor. The amount of light that enters the camera is also controlled by the lens, the size of the glass elements, and the aperture mechanism within the lens housing. The quality of the glass used in the lens will also have a direct effect on how well the lens can resolve details and the contrast of the image (the ability to deliver great highlights and shadows). Most lenses now routinely include things like the autofocus motor and, in some cases, an image-stabilization mechanism.

There is one other aspect of the camera lens that is often the first consideration of the photographer: lens length. Lenses are typically divided into three or four groups depending on the field of view they deliver.

Wide-angle lenses cover a field of view from around 110 degrees to about 60 degrees (**Figure 2.3**). There is also a tendency to get some distortion in your image when using extremely wide-angle lenses. This will be apparent toward the outer edges of the frame. As for which lenses would be considered wide angle, anything 35mm or smaller could be considered as wide.

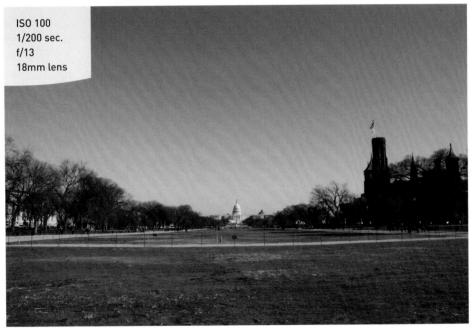

ISO 100
1/200 sec.
f/13
18mm lens

FIGURE 2.3
The 18mm lens setting provides a wide view of the scene but little detail of distant objects.

Wide-angle lenses can display a large depth of field, which allows you to keep the foreground and background in sharp focus. This makes them very useful for landscape photography. They also work well in tight spaces, such as indoors, where there isn't much elbow room available (**Figure 2.4**). They can also be handy for large group shots but due to the amount of distortion, not so great for close-up portrait work.

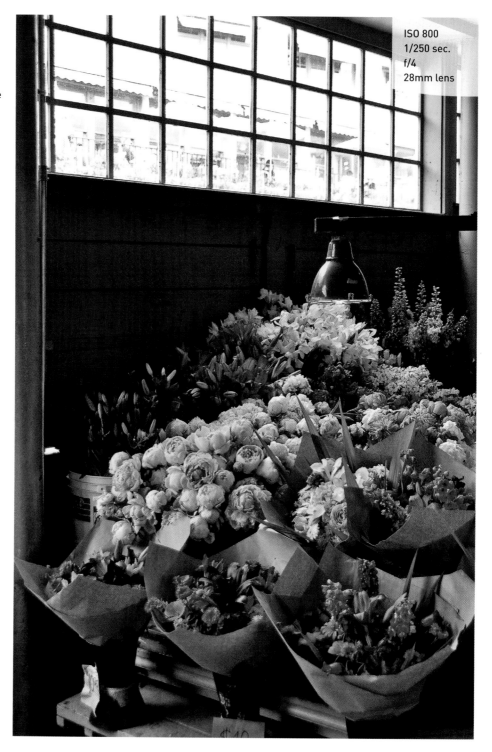

FIGURE 2.4

When shooting in tight spaces, such as indoors, a nice wide-angle lens helps capture more of the scene.

ISO 800
1/250 sec.
f/4
28mm lens

A *normal* lens has a field of view that is about 45 degrees and delivers approximately the same view as the human eye. The perspective is very natural and there is little distortion in objects. The normal lens for full-frame and 35mm cameras is the 50mm lens, but for the T1i it is more in the neighborhood of a 35mm lens (**Figure 2.5**).

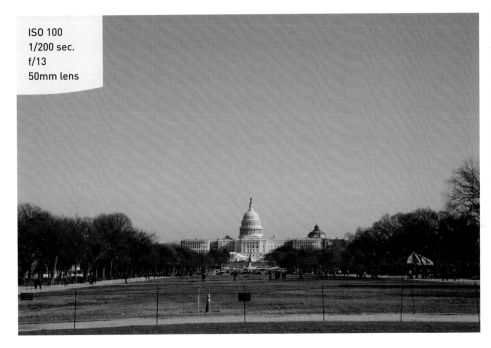

ISO 100
1/200 sec.
f/13
50mm lens

FIGURE 2.5

Long considered the "normal" lens for 35mm photography, the 50mm focal length can be considered somewhat of a telephoto lens on the T1i because it has the same angle of view and magnification as an 80mm lens on a 35mm camera body.

Normal focal length lenses are useful for photographing people, architecture, and most other general photographic needs. They have very little distortion and offer a moderate range of depth of field (**Figure 2.6**).

Most longer focal length lenses are referred to as *telephoto* lenses. They can range in length from 135mm up to 800mm or longer, and have a field of view that is about 35 degrees or smaller. These lenses have the ability to greatly magnify the scene, allowing you to capture details of distant objects, but the angle of view is greatly reduced (**Figure 2.7**). You will also find that you can achieve a much narrower depth of field. They also suffer from something called distance compression, which means they make objects at different distances appear to be much closer together than they really are.

FIGURE 2.6

The normal lens worked well in this image by providing enough coverage area while not distorting the lines of the fence.

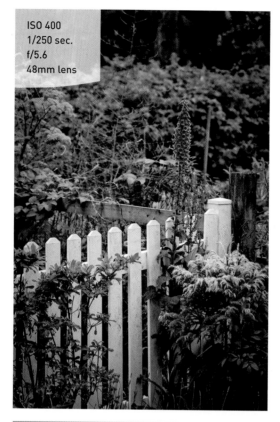

ISO 400
1/250 sec.
f/5.6
48mm lens

FIGURE 2.7

It would have been difficult for me to get this shot of the dome with anything less than a telephoto lens, since I was standing about a quarter of a mile away.

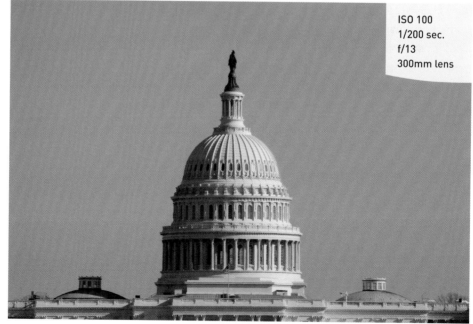

ISO 100
1/200 sec.
f/13
300mm lens

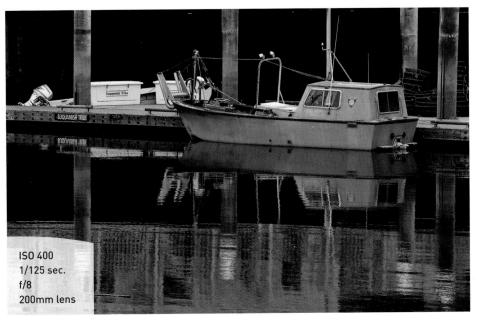

ISO 400
1/125 sec.
f/8
200mm lens

FIGURE 2.8
The long telephoto
helped me isolate
the boat from the
rest of the ships
in the area. The
smaller aperture
helped keep the
reflection from
becoming too soft.

Telephoto lenses are most useful for sports photography or any application where
you just need to get closer to your subject (**Figure 2.8**). They can have a compressing
effect—making objects look closer together than they actually are—and a very narrow depth of field when shot at their widest apertures.

A *zoom* lens is a great compromise to carrying a bunch of single focal-length lenses
(also referred to as "prime" lenses). They can cover a wide range of focal lengths
because of the configuration of their optics. However, because it takes more optical
elements to capture a scene at different focal lengths, the light must pass through
more glass on its way to the image sensor. The more glass, the lower the quality of
the image sharpness. The other sacrifice that is made is in aperture. Zoom lenses typically have smaller maximum apertures than prime lenses, which means they cannot
achieve a narrow depth of field or work in lower light levels without the assistance
of image stabilization, a tripod, or higher ISO settings. (We'll discuss all this in more
detail in later chapters.)

The T1i can be purchased with the body only, but many folks will purchase it with a
kit lens. The most common kit lens is the 18–55mm IS f/3.5–5.6. Another great lens
option for the T1i is the 18–200mm EF-S IS lens. It is a great all-around lens that provides a range of focal lengths from the very wide to the medium telephoto. Combine
that with some great image stabilization and you have what I like to call the perfect
vacation lens. Unfortunately, it is not available as a kit lens at the moment, but it should
definitely be considered if you are thinking of adding a new lens to your camera bag.

WHAT IS EXPOSURE?

In order for you to get the most out of this book, I need to briefly discuss the principles of exposure. Without this basic knowledge, it will be difficult for you to move forward in improving your photography. Granted, I could write an entire book on exposure and the photographic process—and many people have—but for our purposes I will just cover some of the basics. This will give you the essential tools to make educated decisions in determining how best to photograph a subject.

Exposure is the process whereby the light reflecting off a subject reflects through an opening in the camera lens for a defined period of time onto the camera sensor. The combination of the lens opening, shutter speed, and sensor sensitivity is used to achieve a proper exposure value (EV) for the scene. The EV is the sum of these components necessary to properly expose a scene. A relationship exists between these factors that is sometimes referred to as the "Exposure Triangle."

At each point of the triangle lies one of the factors of exposure:

- **ISO:** Determines the sensitivity of the camera sensor. ISO stands for the International Organization for Standardization, but the acronym is used as a term to describe the sensitivity of the camera sensor to light. The higher the sensitivity, the less light is required for a good exposure. These values are a carryover from the days of traditional color and black and white films.

- **Aperture:** Also referred to as the f-stop, this determines how much light passes through the lens at once.

- **Shutter Speed:** Controls the length of time that light is allowed to hit the sensor.

Here's how it works. The camera sensor has a level of sensitivity that is determined by the ISO setting. To get a proper exposure—not too much, not too little—the lens needs to adjust the aperture diaphragm (the size of the lens opening) to control the volume of light entering the camera. Then the shutter is opened for a relatively short period of time to allow the light to hit the sensor long enough for it to record on the sensor.

ISO numbers for the T1i start at 100 and then double in sensitivity as you double the number. So 200 is twice as sensitive as 100. The camera can be set to use 1/2- or 1/3-stop increments, but for ISO just remember that the base numbers double: 100, 200, 400, 800, and so on. There is also a wide variety of shutter speeds that you can use. The speeds on the T1i range from as long as 30 seconds to as short as 1/4000 of a second. When using the camera, you will not see the one over the number while looking through the viewfinder, so you will need to remember that anything shorter than a second will be a fraction. Typically, you will be working with a shutter speed range from around 1/30 of a second to about 1/2000, but these numbers will change depending on your circumstances and the effect that you are trying to achieve. The lens apertures will vary slightly depending on which lens you are using. This is because different lenses have different maximum apertures. The typical apertures that are at your disposal are f/4, f/5.6, f/8, f/11, f/16, and f/22.

When it comes to exposure, a change to any one of these factors requires changing one or more of the other two. This is referred to as a reciprocal change. If you let more light in the lens by choosing a larger aperture opening, you will need to shorten the amount of time the shutter is open. If the shutter is allowed to stay open for a longer period of time, the aperture needs to be smaller to restrict the amount of light coming in.

HOW IS EXPOSURE CALCULATED?

We now know about the exposure triangle—ISO, shutter speeds, and aperture—so it's time to put all three together to see how they relate to one another and how you can change them as needed.

STOP

You will hear the term *stop* thrown around all the time in photography. It relates back to the f-stop, which is a term used to describe the aperture opening of your lens. When you need to give some additional exposure, you might say that you are going to "add a stop." This doesn't just equate to the aperture; it could also be used to describe the shutter speed or even the ISO. So when your image is too light or dark or you have too much movement in your subject, you will probably be changing things by a "stop" or two.

When you point your camera at a scene, the light reflecting off your subject enters the lens and is allowed to pass through to the sensor for a period of time as dictated by the shutter speed. The amount and duration of the light needed for a proper exposure depends on how much light is being reflected and how sensitive the sensor is. To figure this out, your camera utilizes a built-in light meter that looks through the lens and measures the amount of light. That level is then calculated against the sensitivity of the ISO setting and an exposure value is rendered. Here is the tricky part: there is no single way to achieve a perfect exposure because the f-stop and shutter speed can be combined in different ways to allow the same amount of exposure. See, I told you it was tricky.

Here is a list of reciprocal settings that would all produce the same exposure result. Let's use the "sunny 16" rule, which states that, when using f/16 on a sunny day, you can use a shutter speed that is roughly equal to the ISO setting to achieve a proper exposure. For simplification purposes, we will use an ISO of 100.

RECIPROCAL EXPOSURES: ISO 100

F-STOP	2.8	4	5.6	8	11	16	22
SHUTTER SPEED	1/4000	1/2000	1/1000	1/500	1/250	1/125	1/60

If you were to use any one of these combinations, they would each have the same result in terms of the exposure (i.e., how much light hits the camera's sensor). Also take note that every time we cut the f-stop in half, we reciprocated by doubling our shutter speed. For those of you wondering why f/8 is half of f/5.6, it's because those numbers are actually fractions based on the opening of the lens in relation to its focal length. This means that a lot of math goes into figuring out just what the total area of a lens opening is, so you just have to take it on faith that f/8 is half of f/5.6 but twice as much as f/11. A good way to remember which opening is larger is to think of your camera lens as a pipe that controls the flow of water. If you had a pipe that was 1/2" in diameter (f/2) and one that was 1/8" (f/8), which would allow more water to flow through? It would be the 1/2" pipe. The same idea works here with the camera f-stops; f/2 is a larger opening than f/4 or f/8 or f/16.

Now that we know this, we can start using this information to make intelligent choices in terms of shutter speed and f-stop. Let's bring the third element into this by changing our ISO by one stop, from 100 to 200.

RECIPROCAL EXPOSURES: ISO 200

F-STOP	2.8	4	5.6	8	11	16	22
SHUTTER SPEED	–	1/4000	1/2000	1/1000	1/500	1/250	1/125

Notice that, since we doubled the sensitivity of the sensor, we now require half as much exposure as before. We have also reduced our maximum aperture from f/2.8 to f/4 because the camera can't use a shutter speed that is faster than 1/4000 of a second.

So why not just use the exposure setting of f/16 at 1/250 of a second? Why bother with all of these reciprocal values when this one setting will give us a properly exposed image? The answer is that the f-stop and shutter speed also control two other important aspects of our image: motion and depth of field.

MOTION AND DEPTH OF FIELD

There are distinct characteristics that are related to changes in aperture and shutter speed. Shutter speed controls the length of time the light has to strike the sensor; consequently, it also controls the blurriness (or lack of blurriness) of the image. The less time light has to hit the sensor, the less time your subjects have to move around and become blurry. This can let you control things like freezing the motion of a fast-moving subject (**Figure 2.9**) or intentionally blurring subjects to give the feel of energy and motion (**Figure 2.10**).

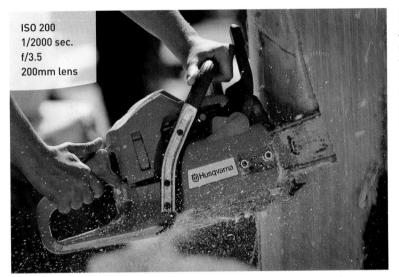

ISO 200
1/2000 sec.
f/3.5
200mm lens

FIGURE 2.9
A fast shutter speed was used to capture the cutting power of the saw as it chewed through the wood.

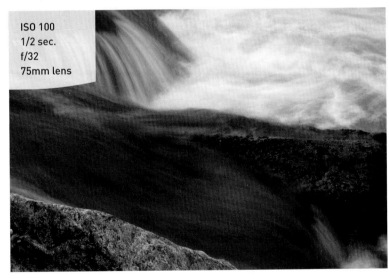

ISO 100
1/2 sec.
f/32
75mm lens

FIGURE 2.10
The slower shutter speed combined with the Monochrome picture style shows the flow of the water across the rocks.

The aperture controls the amount of light that comes through the lens, but also determines what areas of the image will be in focus. This is referred to as depth of field, and it is an extremely valuable creative tool. The smaller the opening (the larger the number, such as f/22), the greater the sharpness of objects from near to far (**Figure 2.11**).

A large opening (or small number, like f/2.8) means more blurring of objects that are not at the same distance as the subject you are focusing on (**Figure 2.12**).

As we further explore the features of the camera, we will learn not only how to utilize the elements of exposure to capture properly exposed photographs, but also how we can make adjustments to emphasize our subject. It is the manipulation of these elements—motion and focus—that will take your images to the next level.

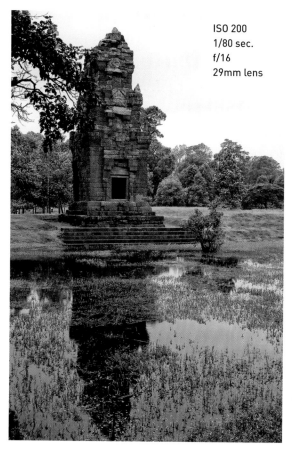

ISO 200
1/80 sec.
f/16
29mm lens

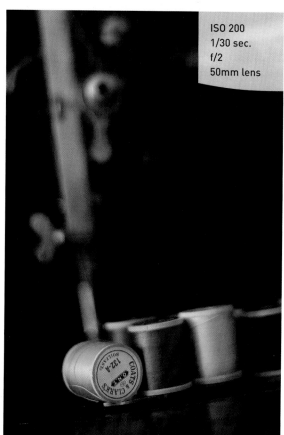

ISO 200
1/30 sec.
f/2
50mm lens

FIGURE 2.11
By using a small aperture, the area of sharp focus extends from a point that is near the camera all the way out to distant objects. In this instance, I wanted the reflection and grass, as well as the temple, to be in focus.

FIGURE 2.12
Isolating a subject is accomplished by using a large aperture, which produces a narrow area of sharp focus.

VIDEO AND THE T1i

One of the reasons you probably purchased the T1i instead of the competing cameras is its ability to capture video. Not just regular video, but high-definition video. As I discussed in the book's introduction, I am going to keep the focus of this book on the photography aspects of the camera but that doesn't mean I am going to simply ignore the video functions completely. In fact, I am dedicating a bonus chapter to some fun video tips. But I thought that I would at least cover the video basics here in Chapter 2 since we have already looked at a lot of other camera functions. First, let's cover some of the basic facts about the movie making features.

First, the video recording is a separate feature from the Live View capabilities of the camera. To shoot video, you will need to turn your Mode dial to the Movie shooting position.

Once Movie mode is active, you will need to focus the camera by placing the white focus box on the subject (**Figure 2.13**) and holding down the ✱ AF Lock button button until the focus operation is complete and the rectangle turns red.

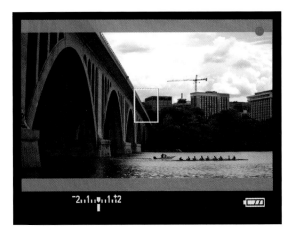

FIGURE 2.13
Recording high-def video with your T1i.

Once your subject is in focus, you can push the Live View/Record button to begin the recording process. When the camera begins recording, you will notice that the focus box disappears and a few new icons show up on the LCD. In the top right will be a red Record icon to let you know that the camera is in active record mode. In the bottom of the screen is an exposure compensation scale and the battery level indicator. To stop the video recording, simply press the Live View/Record button a second time.

VIDEO QUALITY

The highest quality video setting on your T1i will render high-definition video with a resolution of 1920 x 1080 or 1280 x 720 pixels. This is also referred to as 1080P and 720P. The "1080" and "720" represent the height of the video image in pixels, and the "P" stands for Progressive, which is how the camera actually records/draws the video on the screen. You can select a lower resolution video depending on your needs. The other video resolution is 640 x 480. For high-definition TV and computer/ media station viewing, you will be served best using the 1080 or 720 recording resolutions. If you plan on recording for the internet, iPods, or portable video players, you might want to consider using the 640 x 480 resolution. The benefit of 640 x 480 is that it requires less physical storage since it contains a smaller pixel count. This means that you will not only fit more video on your storage card, you will also require less time to upload the video to the internet.

PROGRESSIVE SCAN

When it comes to video, there are usually two terms associated with the quality of the video and how it is captured and displayed on a monitor/screen: *progressive* and *interlaced*. The two terms describe how the video is drawn by line for each frame. Video frames are not displayed all at once like a photograph. In progressive video, the lines are drawn in sequence from top to bottom. Interlaced video draws all of the odd-numbered lines and then all of the even-numbered lines. This odd-even drawing can present itself as screen flicker, which is why the progressive video standard is most preferred, especially when viewing high-definition images.

SETTING THE MOVIE QUALITY

1. To change the quality of your video recording, start by turning the Mode dial to the Movie shooting position.

2. Press the Disp. button to bring up the movie options.

3. Press the Set button to activate the cursor, and then use the Cross keys to highlight the resolution setting.

4. Once it is highlighted, use the Main dial to select the desired movie resolution and press the Set button again to return to Movie mode.

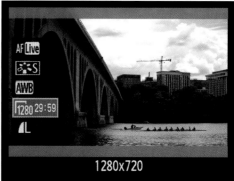

You can also use this method to adjust other settings such as white balance, picture style, Live View focus mode, and image quality for capturing still images.

SOUND

The T1i can record audio to go along with your video, but there are a couple of things to keep in mind when using it. The first is to make sure you don't block the microphone on the front of the camera. If you look closely at the front of the camera body you will notice four small holes right above the silver EOS nameplate, located just above the lens release button (**Figure 2.14**). This should not be a problem if you are holding the camera as instructed in Chapter 1.

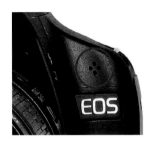

FIGURE 2.14
The T1i's built-in microphone.

The next thing you need to know about the sound is that it is mono, not stereo. There is no way to change this feature, so when you are watching your recorded video on your TV or computer, you might only hear the sound coming from one speaker. You also have the option of turning off the audio all together. This can be useful if the sound might be distracting or you plan on using your own soundtrack to be added to the video at a later time.

TURNING OFF THE SOUND

1. Turn the Mode dial to the Movie shooting position.

2. Press the Menu button and navigate to the Sound recording option using the Cross keys, then press the Set button (**A**).

3. Select the Off option and press Set to lock in the change (**B**). Press the Menu button to return to recording mode.

A

Grid display	Off
Metering timer	16 sec.
Movie rec. size	1920x1080
AF mode	Live mode
Sound recording	On
Remote control	Disable

B

Sound recording	On
	▸ Off

FOCUSING THE CAMERA

As previously mentioned, you must focus the camera using the ✱ AF Lock button before you will be able to start recording video. Once the video is recording, you can refocus using the same button. If your subject moves closer or farther from the camera position, it will be necessary for you to refocus in order to maintain sharp focus. You cannot follow-focus your subject, which means that it will appear out of focus as it moves farther from or closer to the camera position. You can manually focus your lens by setting the focus switch on the lens to the MF position.

You will also need to manually zoom your lens to provide the coverage that is appropriate for the scene you are recording. The more you zoom in to your subject, the more critical the focus will need to be.

TAKING PICTURES WHILE RECORDING

It is possible to capture a still image in the midst of a video recording session. To do this, simply press the shutter release button down completely. The image will be stored on the card as a separate file from the video. You will probably notice a small gap in your video where it was paused momentarily to allow the shutter to flip back into photo mode for a moment. Video recording will resume automatically after the picture has been taken.

WATCHING YOUR VIDEOS

There are a couple of different options for you to review your video once you have finished recording. The first is probably the easiest: press the Image Review button to bring up the recorded image on the LCD screen, and then use the Set button to start playing the video. The left/right Cross keys act as the video controller and allow you to rewind and fast-forward as well as stop the video altogether.

If you would like to get a larger look at things, you will need to either watch the video on your TV or move the video files to your computer. To watch on your TV, you can use the video cable that came with your camera and plug it into the small port on the side of the camera body (**Figure 2.15**). This will let you watch low-resolution video on your TV. To get the full effect from your HD videos you will need to purchase an HDMI cable (your TV needs to support at least 720 HD and have an HDMI port to use this option). Once you have the cable hooked up to your TV, simply use the same camera controls that you used for watching the video on the LCD screen.

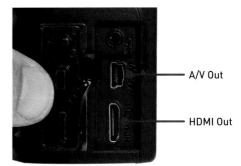

A/V Out

HDMI Out

FIGURE 2.15
The video ports on the T1i.

If you want to watch or use the videos on your computer, you will need to download the images using the Canon software or by using an SD card reader attached to your computer. The video files will have the extension ".mov" at the end of the file name.

These files should play on either a Mac or PC using software that came with your operating system or that can be downloaded for free (Apple's QuickTime for Mac and Windows is available at http://www.apple.com/quicktime/download/).

For even more information about using video with your T1i, be sure to download the bonus chapters from Peachpit.com.

MANUAL CALLOUT

You can check out all of the video features of your camera by turning to pages 121–128 of your owner's manual.

Chapter 2 Assignments

Formatting your card

Even if you have already begun using your camera, make sure you are familiar with formatting the SD card. If you haven't done so already, follow the directions given earlier in the chapter and format as described (make sure you save any images that you may have already taken). Then perform the format function every time you have downloaded or saved your images or use a new card.

Checking your firmware version

Using the most up-to-date version of the camera firmware will ensure that your camera is functioning properly. Use the menu to find your current firmware version and then update as necessary using the steps listed in this chapter.

Cleaning your sensor

You probably noticed the sensor-cleaning message the first time you turned your camera on. Make sure you are familiar with the Clean Now command so you can perform this function every time you change a lens.

Exploring your image formats

I want you to become familiar with all of the camera features before using the RAW format, but take a little time to explore the format menu so you can see what options are available to you.

Exploring your lens

If you are using a zoom lens, spend a little time shooting with all of the different focal lengths, from the widest to the longest. See just how much of an angle you can cover with your widest lens setting. How much magnification will you be able to get from the telephoto setting? Try shooting the same subject with a variety of different focal lengths to note the differences in how the subject looks, and also the relationship between the subject and the other elements in the photo.

Recording some video clips

Take a little time to discover how the video function works on your camera. Set the video quality to 1080 and record a short sequence, and then try it with some of the lower-resolution settings. Open the video clips on your computer or hook the camera up to your TV and review the different video clips to see how the quality settings effect the video.

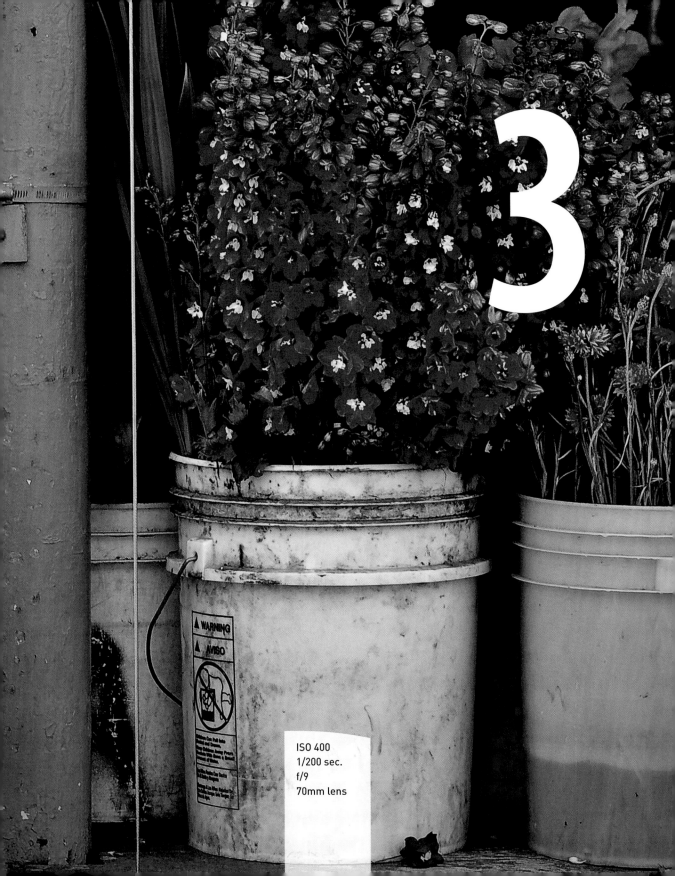

ISO 400
1/200 sec.
f/9
70mm lens

3

The Basic Zone

GET SHOOTING WITH THE AUTOMATIC CAMERA MODES

The Canon T1i is an amazing camera that has some incredible features. In fact, with all of the technology built into it, it can be pretty intimidating for the person new to dSLR photography. For that reason, the good folks at Canon have made it a little easier for you to get some great-looking photographs without having to do a lot of thinking. Enter the Basic zone. The camera modes that comprise the Basic zone side of the Mode dial are simple, icon-labeled modes that are set up to use specific features of the camera for various shooting situations. Let's take a look at the different modes and how and when to use them.

PORING OVER THE PICTURE

The camera was positioned so that the tree line would not intersect with her head.

I chose a lens with a slightly wide angle so that I could capture some of the scenery.

It was late in the day but the sky was still bright, so there was ample light to help keep the ISO low.

The composition for the portrait is a simple "rule of thirds," with the horizon placed at the top third of the image.

A short time back my nieces came up for a visit, so naturally I had to break out the camera. My oldest niece is quite the model and never passes up a chance to pose for me. We were down by the stables so I had her jump up on the fence and pose for a few shots. I wish all my kids were this cooperative.

ISO 200
1/250 sec.
f/9
32mm lens

Madison, Wisconsin, is not where I would normally want to spend the spring. Not because it's not a great town, but because their spring usually comes pretty late in the season. That wasn't the case this year, and I was blessed with beautiful weather and blossoming flowers at every turn. This group of tulips had been planted on the grounds of the state capitol and were at the peak of their color.

A cloud passing over provided a soft, shadow-free light source.

I chose a low camera angle to get more of the flowers in view and to give a feeling of depth.

To get a sharp focus throughout the image, the camera was focused about a third of the way into the scene.

I used the longest focal length available on my lens to get tight to the flowers.

ISO 100
1/800 sec.
f/5.6
55mm lens

FULL AUTO MODE

 Full Auto mode is all about thought-free photography. There is little to nothing for you to do in this mode except point and shoot. Your biggest concern when using Full Auto mode is focusing. The camera will utilize the automatic focusing modes to achieve the best possible focus for your picture. Naturally, the camera is going to assume that the object that is closest to the camera is the one that you want to have the sharpest focus. Simply press the shutter button down halfway while looking through the viewfinder and you should see one of the focus points light up over the subject. Of course, you know that putting your subject in the middle of the picture is not the best way to compose your shot. So wait for the chirp to confirm that the focus has been set, and then, while still holding down the button, recompose your shot. Now just press down the shutter button the rest of the way to take the photo. It's just that easy (**Figure 3.1**). The camera will take care of all your exposure decisions, including when to use flash.

Let's face it: This is the lazy man's mode. But sometimes it's just nice to be lazy and click away without giving thought to anything but preserving a memory. There are times, though, when you will want to start using your camera's advanced features to improve your shots.

FIGURE 3.1
Full Auto works great when you don't want to think too much and just snap some shots. This picture was taken while walking a trail in Arizona.

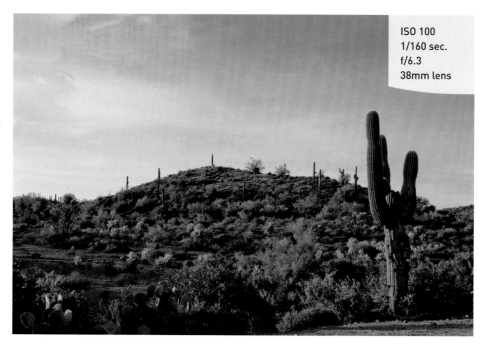

ISO 100
1/160 sec.
f/6.3
38mm lens

PORTRAIT MODE

 One problem with Full Auto mode is that it has no idea what type of subject you are photographing and, therefore, uses the same settings for each situation. Shooting portraits is a perfect example. Typically, when you are taking a photograph of someone, you want the emphasis of the picture to be on them, not necessarily on the stuff going on in the background.

This is what Portrait mode is for. When you set your camera to this mode, you are telling the camera to select a larger aperture so that the depth of field is much narrower and will give more blur to objects in the background. This blurry background places the attention on your subject (**Figure 3.2**). The other feature of this mode is the automatic selection of the T1i's built-in Portrait picture style (we'll go into more detail about picture styles in later chapters). This style is optimized for skin tones and will also be a little softer to improve the look of skin.

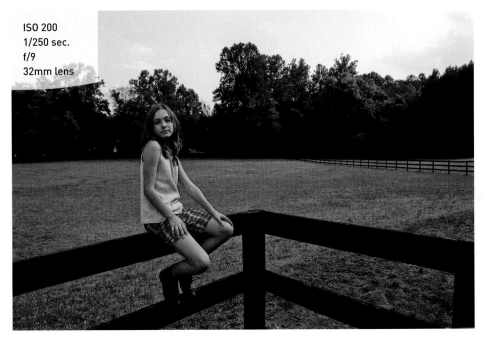

ISO 200
1/250 sec.
f/9
32mm lens

FIGURE 3.2
Portrait mode is a great choice for shots like this one of my niece. She was placed to the side of the frame to make the composition a little more interesting.

USING THE BEST LENS FOR GREAT PORTRAITS

Though I used a wider lens in Figure 3.2, when using Portrait mode it's usually best to use a lens length that is 50mm or longer. The longer lens will give you a natural view of the subject, as well as aid in keeping the depth of field narrow.

LANDSCAPE MODE

 As you might have guessed, Landscape mode has been optimized for shooting landscape images. Particular emphasis is placed on the picture style, with the camera trying to boost the greens and blues in the image (**Figure 3.3**). This makes sense, since the typical landscape would be outdoors where grass, trees, and skies should look more colorful. This picture style also boosts the sharpness that is applied during processing. The camera also utilizes the lowest ISO settings possible in order to keep digital noise to a minimum. The downfall to this setting is that, once again, there is no control over any settings other than the file type and the ability to use the self-timer in 10-second mode.

FIGURE 3.3
This type of scene just calls out for the Landscape mode. The vegetation and sky were given more saturation and a small aperture was used for greater depth of field.

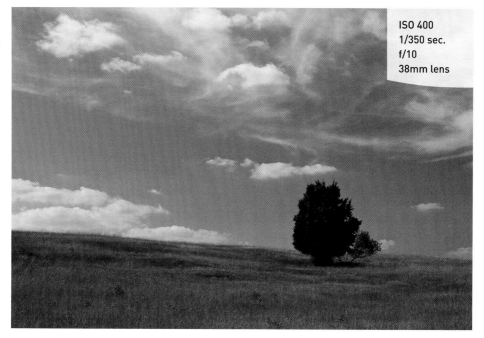

ISO 400
1/350 sec.
f/10
38mm lens

CLOSE-UP MODE

 Although most zoom lenses don't support true "macro" settings, that doesn't mean you can't shoot some great close-up photos. The key here is to use your camera-to-subject distance to fill the frame while still being able to achieve sharp focus. This means that you move yourself as close as possible to your subject while still being able to get a good sharp focus. Oftentimes, your lens will be marked with the minimum focusing distance. On my 18–55mm zoom it is .8

feet. To help get the best focus in the picture, Close-up mode will use the smallest aperture it can while keeping the shutter speed fast enough to get a sharp shot (**Figure 3.4**). It does this by raising the ISO or turning on the built-in flash—or a combination of the two. Unfortunately, we have no way to turn off or alter these adjustments, so the possibility exists of getting more digital noise (from a high ISO) or harsh shadows (from the flash) in your picture.

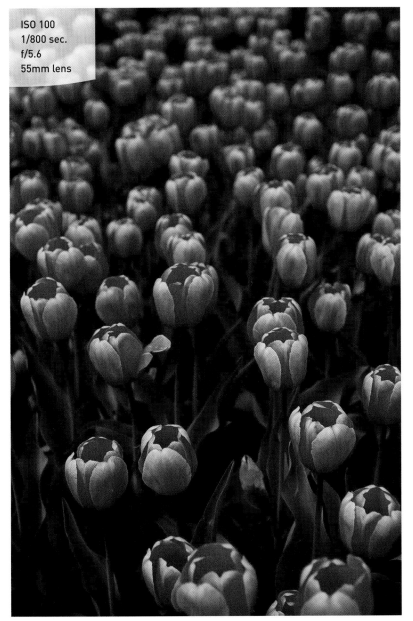

ISO 100
1/800 sec.
f/5.6
55mm lens

FIGURE 3.4
Close-up mode provided the proper exposure for this field of tulips.

SPORTS MODE

 While this is called Sports mode, you can use it for any moving subject that you are photographing. The mode is built on the principles of sports photography: continuous focusing, large apertures, and fast shutter speeds **(Figure 3.5)**. To handle these requirements, the camera sets the drive mode to Continuous shooting, the aperture to a very large opening, and the ISO to Auto. Overall, these are sound settings that will capture most moving subjects well. We will take an in-depth look at all of these features, like Continuous drive mode, in Chapter 5.

You can, however, run the risk of too much digital noise in your picture if the camera decides that you need a very high ISO (such as 1600). Also, when using Sports mode, you will need to frame your subject in the middle of the viewfinder so that the center focus point is on them. You won't hear the familiar chirp or see the focus points illuminate in this mode because, as long as you are holding down the shutter button halfway, the camera will continue to focus on the subject. The only problem with this is that you won't be able to recompose while shooting.

FIGURE 3.5
This is the type of shot that was made for Sports mode, where action-freezing shutter speeds and continuous focusing capture the moment.

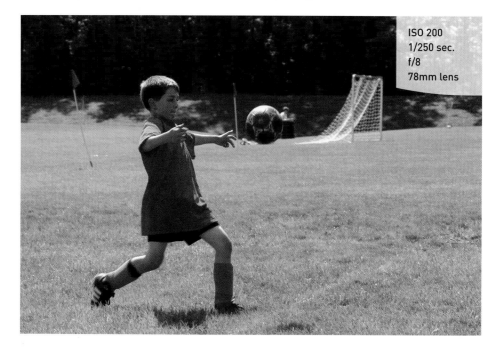

ISO 200
1/250 sec.
f/8
78mm lens

NIGHT PORTRAIT MODE

 You're out on the town at night and you want to take a nice picture of someone, but you want to show some of the interesting scenery in the background as well. You could use Full Auto mode, which would probably turn on the flash and take the photo. The problem is that, while it would give you a decent exposure for your subject, the background would be completely dark. The solution is to use Night Portrait mode. When you set the dial to this mode, you are telling the camera that you want to use a slower-than-normal shutter speed so that the background is getting more time (and, thus, more light) to achieve a proper exposure.

The typical shutter speed for using flash is about 1/60 of a second or faster (but not faster than 1/250 of a second). By leaving the shutter open for a longer duration, the camera allows more of the background to be exposed so that you get a much more balanced scene (**Figure 3.6**). This is also a great mode for taking portraits during sunset. Once again, the camera uses an automatic ISO setting, so you will want to keep an eye on it to make sure that setting isn't so high that the noise levels ruin your photo.

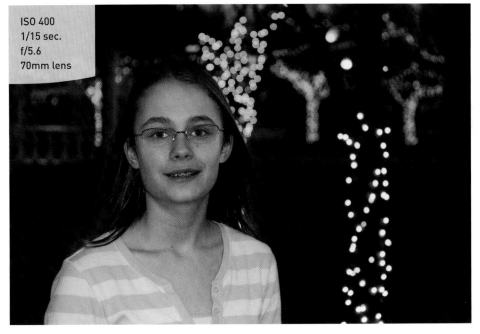

ISO 400
1/15 sec.
f/5.6
70mm lens

FIGURE 3.6
Night Portrait mode uses a slower shutter speed, higher ISO, and larger aperture to balance the background lights with the flash exposure.

FLASH OFF MODE

 Sometimes you will be in a situation where the light levels are low but you don't want to use the flash. It could be that you are shooting in a place that restricts flash photography, such as a museum, or it could be a situation where you want to take advantage of the available light, as when shooting candles on a birthday cake. This is where Flash Off mode comes into play.

By keeping the flash from firing, you will be able to use just the available ambient light while the camera modifies the ISO setting to assist you in getting good exposures (**Figure 3.7**). If the camera feels that the shutter speed is going to be slow enough to introduce camera shake, it will make the shutter speed indicator blink in the view-finder. Fortunately, most of the new image stabilization (IS) lenses being sold today allow you to handhold the camera at much slower shutter speeds and still get great results. The two downfalls to this mode are the Auto ISO setting, which can quickly raise your ISO setting, and the possibility of getting blur from subject movement.

FIGURE 3.7
Flash would have ruined this shot of the Christmas sculpture being displayed in a museum. Flash Off mode made sure the pop-up flash stayed disabled in the low-light environment.

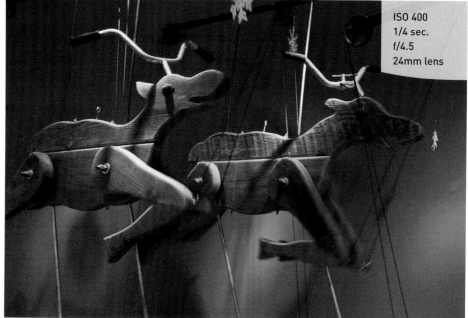

ISO 400
1/4 sec.
f/4.5
24mm lens

CREATIVE AUTO MODE

Let's face it—there will be times when these automatic modes in the Basic zone are nice, but you will want more control over what the camera is doing and how your pictures look. In the Basic zone, this is where the Creative Auto (CA) mode comes in. You won't have total control over the picture-making process, but you will be able to make some adjustments to gain a little more creative control over things like image brightness, use of flash, and background sharpness (**Figure 3.8**). To make these adjustments, the camera will display a series of adjustable settings on the LCD screen that can be changed by using the Cross keys and the Main dial (**Figure 3.9**).

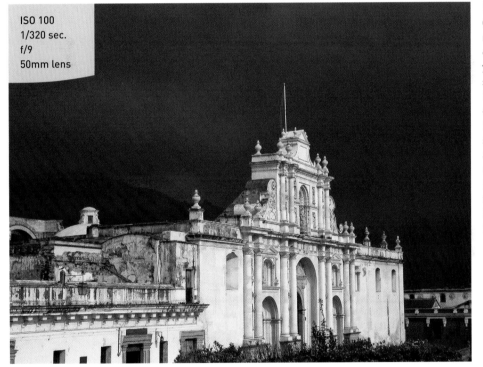

ISO 100
1/320 sec.
f/9
50mm lens

FIGURE 3.8
Creative Auto mode means you can change how your picture looks, such as making the image lighter or darker. This shot benefited from some darkening, as the normal auto exposure would have tried to make the sky too bright. (Photo: Suzanne Revell)

To make changes to your settings, press the Set button and then use the Cross keys to highlight the item that you want to change. Once highlighted, use the Main dial to select your new setting.

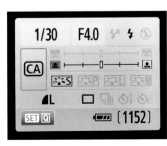

FIGURE 3.9
All of the basic shooting information in one easy-to-read screen.

FLASH

This option allows you to set the flash to one of three positions: Auto, On, or Off. In Auto, the flash will automatically pop up whenever the camera determines that there isn't enough light in the scene for a proper exposure. If you want to force the flash to come on no matter what (as when you want to fill in some shadows), set the option to On (**Figure 3.10**). The Off setting will keep the flash from firing, just as it does in Flash Off mode.

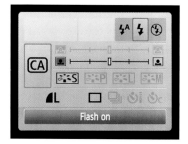

FIGURE 3.10
This setting shows the flash being turned on.

BACKGROUND SHARPNESS

This setting forces the camera to use either a larger or smaller aperture setting to change the depth of field in your image: the smaller the aperture (which means a larger number such as f/16 or f/22), the greater the sharpness in your background. To change this setting, highlight the Background scale. Then move the index point to the right for a sharper background or to the left for more blur (**Figure 3.11**). Each step will change the exposure by about one f-stop.

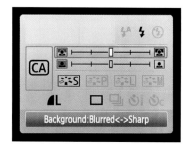

FIGURE 3.11
Moving to the right uses a smaller aperture for greater depth of field.

EXPOSURE

If you notice that your pictures are turning out a little lighter or darker than you wanted, highlight the Exposure setting. Each step that you move the index point will adjust the camera in 2/3-stop increments (**Figure 3.12**). Move it to the right for increased exposure (brighter) or to the left for decreased exposure (darker). The camera will use a mix of shutter speed and aperture to achieve the desired setting. This could also include using the flash if you have the Flash set to Auto.

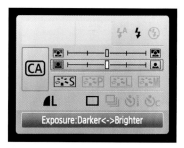

FIGURE 3.12
The Exposure slider will increase or decrease the amount of exposure, resulting in lighter or darker images.

PICTURE STYLE

You can change the look of your image by using a different picture style to affect the sharpness, contrast, and color saturation (**Figure 3.13**). You can even select the Monochrome style to shoot in black and white. Four different styles are available: Standard, which is commonly used for sharp, vivid pictures; Portrait, which gives you smoother skin tones; Landscape, which gives you more vivid blues and greens; and Monochrome, used for black and whites. Note that, unlike with the modes in the Creative zone (see Chapter 4), you cannot change the parameters in the picture styles here; you must use their default values.

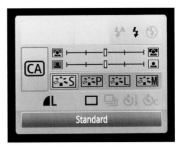

FIGURE 3.13
To add a little zip to your image, try changing the picture style.

QUALITY

The Quality setting allows you to change the JPEG quality of your image and the image size, and it even allows you to select the RAW format for ultimate quality (**Figure 3.14**). Simply highlight this section of the Creative Auto screen and then scroll with the dial until you find your desired quality setting.

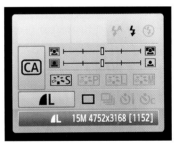

FIGURE 3.14
The L setting is for the large, high-quality JPEG file.

DRIVE MODE

Three different drive modes are available in the Creative Auto mode: Single shooting, Continuous shooting, and Self-Timer (**Figure 3.15**). In Single shooting, the camera takes only one picture when the shutter button is depressed all the way. Taking another picture requires releasing the button and then pressing it again. In Continuous, the camera continually takes photographs at about three frames per second until you release the button. You will probably want to use this setting for capturing action. The third setting available here

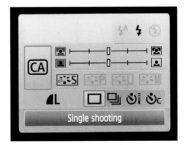

FIGURE 3.15
You can decide if you want to take one shot at a time or use a more rapid-fire approach.

is the Self-Timer option. Using this setting allows you to depress the shutter button and have the camera automatically fire 10 seconds later. The obvious use for this setting is to run around and get yourself in the picture. You might also consider using it for macro (close-up) or landscape photography, when you can set your camera on a tripod or a stable surface. The self-timer will let you take the picture without having to worry about camera shake from physically having your hands on the camera while activating the shutter.

There is one small annoyance with using the Creative Auto mode. Every time you make changes to any of the settings, they will remain active only during the time that the camera is "awake." As soon as the camera goes into Auto Off mode, all of the Creative Auto settings return to their defaults. One way to combat this is to go into the camera menu and change the Auto Off setting to a longer period. The default is one minute, but it can be set to as long as 30 minutes. There is even an option to turn it off completely, but I highly advise against using this setting as it will drain your camera battery much faster.

CHANGING THE AUTO POWER OFF

1. Press the Menu button and then use the Main dial to navigate to the first camera setup menu (**A**).

2. Use the Cross keys to highlight the Auto power off menu item and press the Set button.

3. Use the up/down Cross keys to select the duration of your choice and press the Set button to lock in the change (**B**).

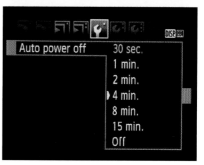

WHY YOU WILL NEVER WANT TO USE THE BASIC ZONE AGAIN

With so many easy-to-use camera modes, why would anyone ever want to use anything else? Well, the first thing that comes to my mind is control. It is the number one reason for using a digital SLR camera. The ability to control every aspect of your photography will open up creative avenues that just aren't available in the Basic zone. Let's face it: there is a reason that the Mode dial is split into two different categories. Let's look at what we are giving up when we work in the Basic zone.

- **ISO.** No options are available in any of the automatic modes in the Basic zone to change the ISO setting from the default Auto ISO setting. This will undoubtedly lead to unwanted digital noise in your images when the ISO begins to reach up into the higher settings.

- **Picture style.** If you are using anything but the Creative Auto mode, you cannot change the picture style or any of its attributes to fine-tune your images.

- **Color space.** The default is set to sRGB, and there is no way to change it. If you plan on printing any of your pictures, the preferred yet unavailable setting is Adobe RGB.

- **White balance.** There is no choice available for white balance. You are simply stuck with the Auto setting. This isn't always a bad thing, but your camera doesn't always get it right. And in the Basic zone, there is just no way to change it.

- **Auto focus.** Each of the modes uses a specific focus type. CA, Full Auto, and No Flash modes use AI Focus; Sports uses the AI Servo; and the four remaining modes utilize the One Shot focus mode. There is no way to change these. Even more frustrating is the fact that they all use the Auto Focus Point selection. This means that you can't manually select a focus point, so you must constantly recompose your image.

FOCUS MODES ON THE CANON T1i

Three focus modes are available on the T1i. Depending on the type of photography you are doing, you can easily select the mode that will be most beneficial. The standard mode is called One Shot, which allows you to focus on one spot and hold the focus until you take the picture or release the shutter button. The AI Servo mode will constantly refocus the camera on your subject the entire time you are depressing the shutter release button. This is great for sports and action photography. The AI Focus mode is a combination of both of the previous modes, using One Shot mode unless it senses that the subject is moving, when it will switch to AI Servo mode.

Another thing you will find when using any of the automatic modes in the Basic zone is that the options in the main camera menu have been reduced to just a few user-friendly choices. And yet another missing camera feature in the Basic zone is Live View. It is disabled in the Basic zone, so to use it you have no choice but to move on over to the Creative zone (see the next chapter). These aren't the only restrictions to using the Basic zone, but they should be enough to make you want to explore the Creative side of the dial.

LIVE VIEW

Live View is the feature on your T1i that allows you to see a real-time view of what the camera is looking at via the LCD display. Using Live View can be helpful when you want to see shoot from an angle that doesn't allow you to place your eye to the viewfinder. It is also an excellent way of previewing any changes to white balance or the picture style because their effects will be visible on the screen. More on Live View is in Chapters 6 and 7.

Chapter 3 Assignments

These assignments will have you shooting in the various Basic modes so that you can experience the advantages and disadvantages of using them in your daily photography.

Shooting in Full Auto mode

It's time to give up complete control and just concentrate on what you see in the viewfinder. Set your camera to Full Auto and practice shooting in a variety of conditions, both indoors and outside. Take notice of the camera settings when you are reviewing your pictures. Try using the One Shot focus to pick a focus and then recompose before taking the picture.

Checking out Portrait mode

Grab your favorite photogenic person and start shooting in Portrait mode. Try switching between Full Auto and Portrait mode while photographing the same person in the same setting. You should see a difference in the sharpness of the background as well as the skin tones. If you are using a zoom lens, set it to about 50mm if available.

Capturing the scenery with Landscape and Close-up modes

Take your camera outside for some landscape and macro work. First, find a nice scene and then, with your widest available lens, take some pictures using Landscape mode and then switch back to Full Auto so that you can compare the settings used for each image as well as the changes to colors and sharpness. Now, while you are still outside, find something in the foreground—a leaf or a flower—and switch the camera to Close-up mode. See how close you can get and take note of the f-stop that the mode uses. Then switch to Full Auto and shoot the same subject.

Stopping the action with Sports mode

This assignment will require that you find a subject that is in motion. That could be the traffic in front of your home or your child at play. The only real requirement is that the subject be moving. This will be your opportunity to test out Sports mode. There isn't a lot to worry about here. Just point and shoot. Try shooting a few frames one at a time and then go ahead and hold down the shutter button and shoot a burst of about five or six frames. It will help if your subject is in good available light to start with so that the camera won't be forced to use high ISOs.

Capturing the mood with Night Portrait mode

This time, wait for it to get dark outside and have a friend sit in a location that has an incandescent lamp in the background (not too bright, though). Switch the camera to Night Portrait and then, using a wide enough angle to see the subject and some of the room in the background, take a photo. The goal is to get a well-lit picture of your subject and balance that with the light from the lamp in the background. For a comparison, switch the camera back to Full Auto and shoot the same subject. Take notice of the difference in the brightness of the background. Now, take another picture with the camera set to Flash Off, but this time, have your subject sit near the lamp so that it lights up their face. Ask them to sit as still as possible while you hold the camera as still as possible.

Getting a little more creative with Creative Auto mode

Now it's time to have a little fun exploring the options that are available to you using the Creative Auto shooting mode. Get a feel for navigating through the options. Then, working your way down the screen, start making adjustments to each option, taking a picture with each to see how it impacts the final photo. The key here is to select one scene and then use it for each change in your settings. This will give you reference to see how each of the images (minus the picture quality and image format) will be affected by changing the options. Try using more than one option to fine-tune your photos.

4

ISO 400
1/160 sec.
f/5.6
55mm lens

The Creative Zone

TAKING YOUR PHOTOGRAPHY TO THE NEXT LEVEL

The Creative zone is the name given by Canon to the shooting modes that offer you the greatest amount of control over your photography. To anyone who has been involved with photography for any period of time, these modes are known as the backbones of photography. They allow you to influence two of the most important factors in taking great photographs: *aperture* and *shutter speed*. To access these modes, you simply turn the Mode dial to the Creative mode of your choice and begin shooting. But wouldn't it be nice to know exactly what those modes control and how to make them do our bidding? Well, if you really want to take that next step in controlling your photography, it is essential that you understand not only how to control these modes, but why you are controlling them. So let's move that Mode dial to the first of our Creative modes: Program mode.

The camera was positioned so that I could capture elements in the foreground and background to give a feeling of depth.

One of my favorite local hiking spots is the area around Great Falls on the Potomac River. There is such a diversity of subjects that I never seem to run out of things to shoot. On this particular day I was exploring a small tributary called Difficult Run, which offered this great vantage point of the stream flowing through the rocks towards the Potomac River.

Because the camera was on a tripod, manual focus was used to focus on the rock in the stream.

ISO 100
10 sec.
f/22
18mm lens

A low ISO of 100 was selected to keep the image free of digital noise.

To achieve sharpness from the closest rocks to the distant waterfall, a very small aperture was used.

PORING OVER THE PICTURE

I know what you're thinking: "Hey, it's just a squirrel picture." And you're right. But it's a really nice squirrel picture. Shooting wildlife doesn't mean that you have to head out to some exotic location. In fact, you will get better shots of animals if you practice your techniques on the critters that are running around your backyard.

Image Stabilization helped maintain a sharp image while shooting at 1/50 sec.

The canopy of leaves forced me to increase my ISO so that I could get the desired exposure.

Aperture Priority mode was selected so that a large-enough aperture could be used blur the leaves in the background.

I used the One Shot focusing mode to focus on the squirrel and then recompose the image.

ISO 800
1/50 sec.
f/5.6
200mm lens

P: PROGRAM MODE

 There is a reason that Program mode is only one click away from the Basic modes: with respect to apertures and shutter speeds, the camera is doing most of the thinking for you. So, if that is the case, why even bother with Program mode? First, let me say that it is very rare that I will use Program mode because it just doesn't give as much control over the image-making process as the other Creative modes. There are occasions, however, when it comes in handy, like when I am shooting in widely changing lighting conditions and I don't have the time to think through all of my options, or I'm not very concerned with having ultimate control of the scene. Think of a picnic outdoors in a partial shade/sun environment. I want great-looking pictures, but I'm not looking for anything to hang in a museum. If that's the scenario, why choose Program over one of the Basic modes? Because it gives me choices and control that none of the Basic modes, including Creative Auto, can deliver.

Manual Callout

To see a comparison of all of the different modes in the Basic and Creative zones, check out the tables on pages 198–199 of your owner's manual.

WHEN TO USE PROGRAM (P) MODE INSTEAD OF THE BASIC ZONE MODES

- When shooting in a casual environment where quick adjustments are needed

- When you want control over the ISO

- If you want or need to shoot in the Adobe RGB color space

- If you want to make corrections to the white balance

- If you want shoot using Live View

Let's go back to our picnic scenario. As I said, the light is moving from deep shadow to bright sunlight, which means that the camera is trying to balance our three photo factors (ISO, aperture, and shutter speed) to make a good exposure. From Chapter 1, we know that Auto ISO is just not a consideration, so we have already turned that feature off (you did turn it off, didn't you?). Well, in Program mode, you can choose which ISO you would like the camera to base its exposure on. The lower the ISO number, the better the quality of our photographs, but the less light sensitive the camera becomes. It's a balancing act with the main goal always being to keep the ISO as low as possible—too low an ISO, and we will get camera shake in our images from a long

STARTING POINTS FOR ISO SELECTION

There is a lot of discussion concerning ISO in this and other chapters, but it might be helpful if you know where your starting points should be for your ISO settings. The first thing you should always try to do is use the lowest possible ISO setting. That being said, here are good starting points for your ISO settings:

- 100: Bright sunny day

- 200: Hazy or outdoor shade on a sunny day

- 400: Indoor lighting at night or cloudy conditions outside

- 800: Late night, low-light conditions or sporting arenas at night

These are just suggestions and your ISO selection will depend on a number of factors that will be discussed later in the book. You might have to push your ISO even higher as needed, but at least now you know where to start.

shutter speed; and too high an ISO means we will have an unacceptable amount of digital noise. For our purposes, let's go ahead and select ISO 400 so that we provide enough sensitivity for those shadows while allowing the camera to use shutter speeds that are fast enough to stop motion.

With the ISO selected, we can now make use of the other controls built into Program mode. By rotating the Main dial, we now have the ability to shift the program settings. Remember, your camera is using the internal meter to pick what it believes are suitable exposure values, but sometimes it doesn't know what it's looking at and how you want those values applied (**Figures 4.1** and **4.2**). With the program shift, you can influence what the shot will look like. Do you need faster shutter speeds in order to stop the action? Just turn the Main dial clockwise. Do you want a smaller aperture so that you get a narrow depth of field? Then turn the dial counterclockwise until you get the desired aperture. The camera shifts the shutter speed and aperture accordingly in order to get a proper exposure, and you will get the benefit of your choice as a result.

FIGURE 4.1
(left) This is my first shot using Program mode. The camera settings are affected by the bright sky as well as the light color of the paint on the front of the building.

FIGURE 4.2
(right) By zooming in, there was less of the front of the building to influence the light meter, resulting in a change of exposure.

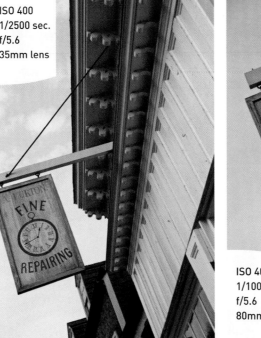

ISO 400
1/2500 sec.
f/5.6
35mm lens

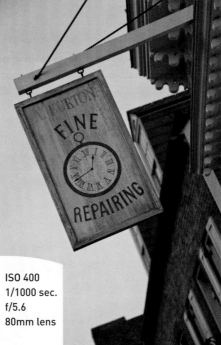

ISO 400
1/1000 sec.
f/5.6
80mm lens

Let's set up the camera for Program mode and see how we can make all of this come together.

SETTING UP AND SHOOTING IN PROGRAM MODE

1. Turn your camera on and then turn the Mode dial to align the P with the indicator line.

2. Select your ISO by pressing the ISO button on the top of the camera, and then turning the Main dial (the ISO selection will appear in the rear LCD panel).

3. Point the camera at your subject and then activate the camera meter by depressing the shutter button halfway.

4. View the exposure information in the bottom of the viewfinder or by looking at the display panel on the back of the camera.

5. While the meter is activated, use your index finger to roll the Main dial left and right to see the changed exposure values.

6. Select the exposure that is right for you and start clicking. (Don't worry if you aren't sure what the right exposure is. We will start working on making the right choices for those great shots beginning with the next chapter.)

TV: SHUTTER PRIORITY MODE

 Tv mode is what we photographers commonly refer to as Shutter Priority mode. If you dig deep in your manual, you will actually see that Tv stands for "Time Value." I'm not sure who came up with this term, but I can tell you that it wasn't a photographer. In all my years of shooting, I don't ever recall thinking, "Hey, this would be a great situation to use the Time Value mode." However, you don't need to know why it is called Tv mode; the important thing is to know why and when to use it.

Just as with Program mode, Tv mode gives us more freedom to control certain aspects of our photography. In this case, we are talking about shutter speed. The selected shutter speed determines just how long you expose your camera's sensor to light. The longer it remains open, the more time your sensor has to gather light. The shutter speed also, to a large degree, determines how sharp your photographs are. This is different from the image being sharply in focus. One of the major influences on the sharpness of an image is just how sharp it is based on camera shake and the subject's movement. Because a slower shutter speed means that light from your subject is hitting the sensor for a longer period of time, any movement by you or your subject will show up in your photos as blur.

SHUTTER SPEEDS

A *slow* shutter speed refers to leaving the shutter open for a long period of time—like 1/30 of a second or less. A *fast* shutter speed means that the shutter is open for a very short period of time—like 1/250 of a second or more.

WHEN TO USE SHUTTER PRIORITY (TV) MODE

- When working with fast-moving subjects where you want to freeze the action (**Figure 4.3**); much more on this is in Chapter 5

- When you want to emphasize movement in your subject with motion blur (**Figure 4.4**)

- When you want to use a long exposure to gather light over a long period of time (**Figure 4.5**); more on this is in Chapter 8

- When you want to create that silky-looking water in a waterfall (**Figure 4.6**)

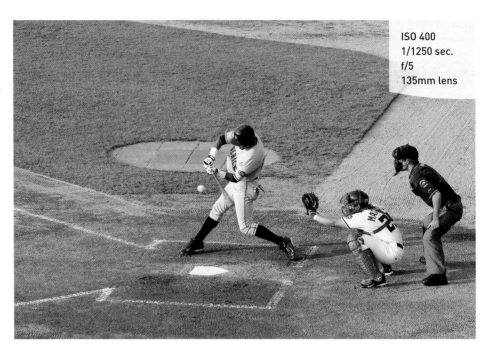

FIGURE 4.3
Even the fastest
of subjects can be
frozen with the
right shutter speed.

ISO 400
1/1250 sec.
f/5
135mm lens

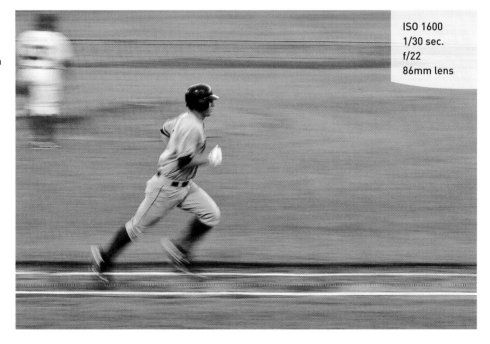

FIGURE 4.4
Slowing down the
shutter speed and
following the action
conveys a sense
of movement in
the shot.

ISO 1600
1/30 sec.
f/22
86mm lens

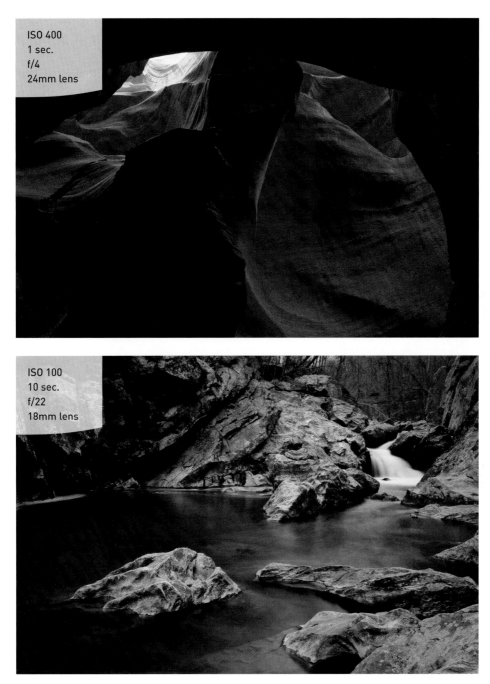

ISO 400
1 sec.
f/4
24mm lens

FIGURE 4.5
A long exposure
coupled with a
steady tripod
helped capture
this shot of the
Antelope Slots.

ISO 100
10 sec.
f/22
18mm lens

FIGURE 4.6
Increasing the
length of the
exposure time
gives flowing
water a silky look.

As you can see, the subject of your photo usually determines whether or not you will use Tv mode. It is important that you be able to visualize the result of using a particular shutter speed. The great thing about shooting with digital cameras is that you get instant feedback by checking your shot on the LCD screen. But what if your subject won't give you a do-over? Such is often the case when shooting sporting events. It's not like you can go ask the quarterback to throw that touchdown pass again because your last shot was blurry from a slow shutter speed. This is why it's important to know what those speeds represent in terms of their capabilities to stop the action and deliver a blur-free shot.

First, let's examine just how much control you have over the shutter speeds. The T1i has a shutter speed range from 1/4000 of a second all the way down to 30 seconds. With that much latitude, you should have enough control to capture almost any subject. The other thing to think about is that Tv mode is considered a "semiautomatic" mode. This means that you are taking control over one aspect of the total exposure while the camera handles the other. In this instance, you are controlling the shutter speed and the camera is controlling the aperture. This is important because there will be times that you want to use a particular shutter speed but your lens won't be able to accommodate your request.

For example, you might encounter this problem when shooting in low-light situations: if you are shooting a fast-moving subject that will blur at a shutter speed slower than 1/125 of a second but your lens's largest aperture is f/3.5, you might find your aperture display in your viewfinder and the rear LCD panel will begin to blink. This is your warning that there won't be enough light available for the shot—due to the limitations of the lens—so your picture will be underexposed.

Another case where you might run into this situation is when you are shooting moving water. To get that look of silky, flowing water, it's usually necessary to use a shutter speed of at least 1/15 of a second. If your waterfall is in full sunlight, you may get that blinking aperture display once again because the lens you are using only closes down to f/22 at its smallest opening. In this instance, your camera is warning you that you will be overexposing your image. There are workarounds for these problems, which we will discuss later (see Chapter 7), but it is important to know that there can be limitations when using Tv mode.

SETTING UP AND SHOOTING IN TV MODE

1. Turn your camera on and then turn the Mode dial to align the Tv with the indicator line.
2. Select your ISO by pressing the ISO button on the top of the camera, and then turning the Main dial (the ISO selection will appear in the rear LCD panel).

3. Point the camera at your subject and then activate the camera meter by depressing the shutter button halfway.

4. View the exposure information in the bottom area of the viewfinder or by looking at the rear LCD panel.

5. While the meter is activated, use your index finger to roll the Main dial left and right to see the changed exposure values. Roll the dial to the right for faster shutter speeds and to the left for slower speeds.

AV: APERTURE PRIORITY MODE

 You wouldn't know it from its name, but Av mode is one of the most useful and popular modes in the Creative zone. Av stands for Aperture Value and, like Time Value, it's another term that you'll never hear a photographer toss around. The mode, however, is one of my personal favorites, and I believe that it will quickly become one of yours, as well. Av, more commonly referred to as Aperture Priority mode, is also deemed a semiautomatic mode because it allows you to once again control one factor of exposure while the camera adjusts for the other.

Why, you may ask, is this one of my favorite modes? It's because the aperture of your lens dictates depth of field. Depth of field, along with composition, is a major factor in how you direct attention to what is important in your image. It is the controlling factor of how much area in your image is sharp. If you want to isolate a subject from the background, such as when shooting a portrait, you can use a large aperture to keep the focus on your subject and make both the foreground and background blurry. If you want to keep the entire scene sharply focused, such as with a landscape scene, then using a small aperture will render the greatest amount of depth of field possible.

WHEN TO USE APERTURE PRIORITY (AV) MODE

- When shooting portraits or wildlife (**Figure 4.7**)
- When shooting most landscape photography (**Figure 4.8**)
- When shooting macro, or close-up, photography (**Figure 4.9**)
- When shooting architectural photography, which often benefits from a large depth of field (**Figure 4.10**)

FIGURE 4.7
A large aperture
created a very
blurry background
so all the emphasis
was left on the
subject.

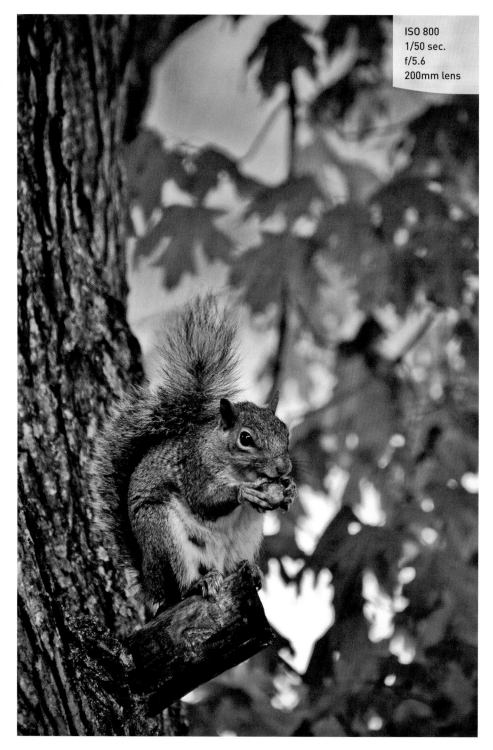

ISO 800
1/50 sec.
f/5.6
200mm lens

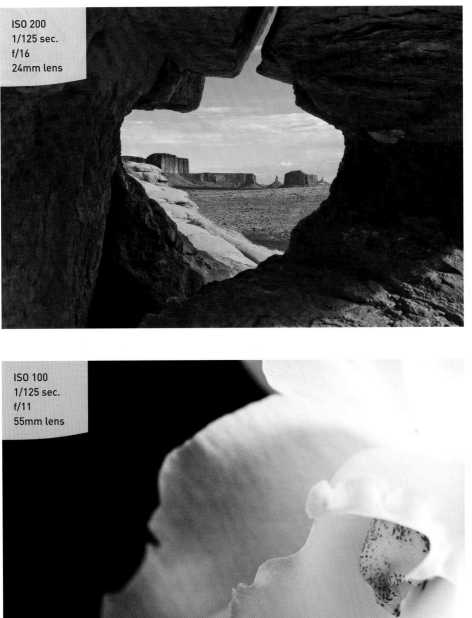

ISO 200
1/125 sec.
f/16
24mm lens

FIGURE 4.8
The smaller aperture setting brings sharpness to near and far objects.

ISO 100
1/125 sec.
f/11
55mm lens

FIGURE 4.9
Small apertures give more sharpness in macro images.

FIGURE 4.10
A wide-angle
lens combined
with a fairly small
aperture makes
for a lot of depth
of field.

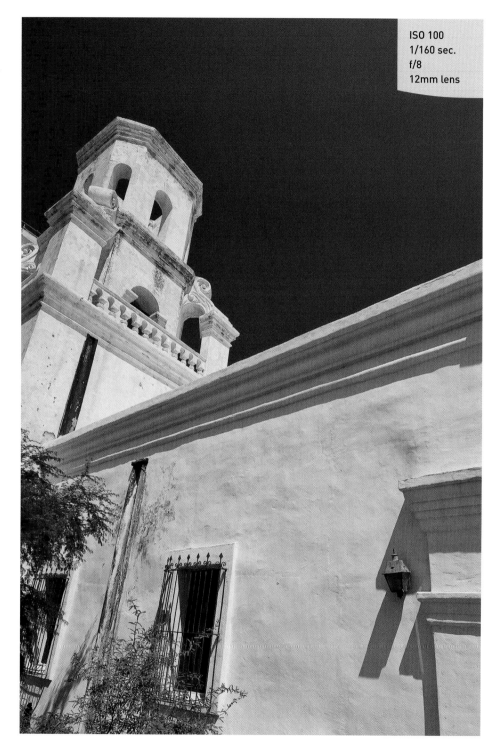

ISO 100
1/160 sec.
f/8
12mm lens

F-STOPS AND APERTURE

As discussed earlier, when referring to the numeric value of your lens aperture, you will find it described as an *f-stop*. The f-stop is one of those old photography terms that, technically, relates to the focal length of the lens (e.g., 200mm) divided by the effective aperture diameter. These measurements are defined as "stops" and work incrementally with your shutter speed to determine proper exposure. Older camera lenses used one-stop increments to assist in exposure adjustments, such as 1.4, 2, 2.8, 4, 5.6, 8, 11, 16, and 22. Each stop represents about half the amount of light entering the lens iris as the larger stop before it. Today, most lenses don't have f-stop markings since all adjustments to this setting are performed via the camera's electronics. The stops are also now typically divided into 1/3-stop increments to allow much finer adjustments to exposures, as well as to match the incremental values of your camera's ISO settings, which are also adjusted in 1/3-stop increments.

So we have established that Aperture Priority (Av) mode is highly useful in control-ling the depth of field in your image. But it's also pivotal in determining the limits of available light that you can shoot in. Different lenses have different maximum aper-tures. The larger the maximum aperture, the less light you need in order to achieve an acceptably sharp image. You will recall that, when in Tv mode, there is a limit at which you can handhold your camera without introducing movement or hand shake, which causes blurriness in the final picture. If your lens has a larger aperture, you can let in more light all at once, which means that you can use faster shutter speeds. This is why lenses with large maximum apertures, such as f/1.4, are called "fast" lenses.

On the other hand, bright scenes require the use of a small aperture (such as f/16 or f/22), especially if you want to use a slower shutter speed. That small opening reduces the amount of incoming light, and this reduction of light requires that the shutter stay open longer.

SETTING UP AND SHOOTING IN AV MODE

1. Turn your camera on and then turn the Mode dial to align the Av with the indicator line.
2. Select your ISO by pressing the ISO button on the top of the camera, and then turning the Main dial.
3. Point the camera at your subject and then activate the camera meter by depressing the shutter button halfway.
4. View the exposure information in the bottom area of the viewfinder or by look-ing at the rear display panel.

5. While the meter is activated, use your index finger to roll the Main dial left and right to see the changed exposure values. Roll the dial to the right for a smaller aperture (higher f-stop number) and to the left for a larger aperture (smaller f-stop number).

ZOOM LENSES AND MAXIMUM APERTURES

Some zoom lenses (like the 18–55mm kit lens) have a variable maximum aperture. This means that the largest opening will change depending on the zoom setting. In the example of the 18–55mm zoom, the lens has a maximum aperture of f/3.5 at 18mm and only f/5.6 when the lens is zoomed out to 55mm.

M: MANUAL MODE

 Once upon a time, long before digital cameras and program modes, there was manual mode. In those days it wasn't called "manual mode" because there were no other modes. It was just photography. In fact, many photographers cut their teeth on completely manual cameras. Let's face it—if you want to learn the effects of aperture and shutter speed on your photography, there is no better way to learn than by setting these adjustments yourself. However, today, with the advancement of camera technology, many new photographers never give this mode a second thought. That's truly a shame, as not only is it an excellent way to learn your photography basics, but it's also an essential tool to have in your photographic bag of tricks.

When you have your camera set to Manual (M) mode, the camera meter will give you a reading of the scene you are photographing. It's your job, though, to set both the f-stop (aperture) and the shutter speed to achieve a correct exposure. If you need a faster shutter speed, you will have to make the reciprocal change to your f-stop. Using any other mode, such as Tv or Av, would mean that you just have to worry about one of these changes, but Manual mode means you have to do it all yourself. This can be a little challenging at first, but after a while you will have a complete understanding of how each change affects your exposure, which will, in turn, improve the way that you use the other modes.

WHEN TO USE MANUAL (M) MODE

- When learning how each exposure element interacts with the others (**Figure 4.11**)

- When your environment is fooling your light meter and you need to maintain a certain exposure setting (**Figure 4.12**)

- When shooting silhouetted subjects, which requires overriding the camera's meter readings (**Figure 4.13**)

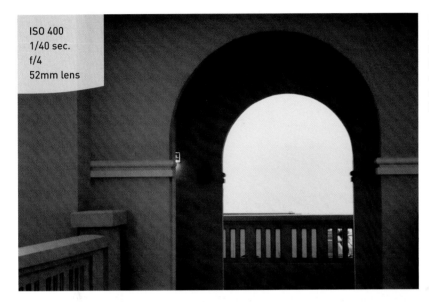

ISO 400
1/40 sec.
f/4
52mm lens

FIGURE 4.11
Manual mode allowed the sky to be balanced with shadows of the archway, even though the camera meter was calling for a bit more underexposure because of the brighter sky.

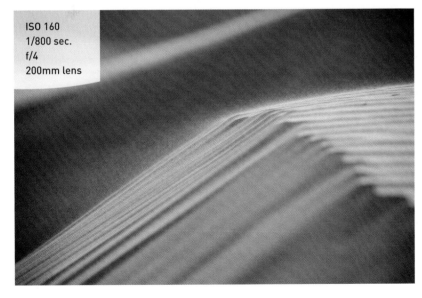

ISO 160
1/800 sec.
f/4
200mm lens

FIGURE 4.12
Beaches and snow are always a challenge for light meters. Add to that the desire to have a narrow depth of field and a fast enough shutter speed to freeze the blowing sand and you have a perfect scenario for Manual mode.

FIGURE 4.13
Although the meter was doing a pretty good job of exposing for the sky, I used Manual mode to push the skyline elements into complete black silhouette.

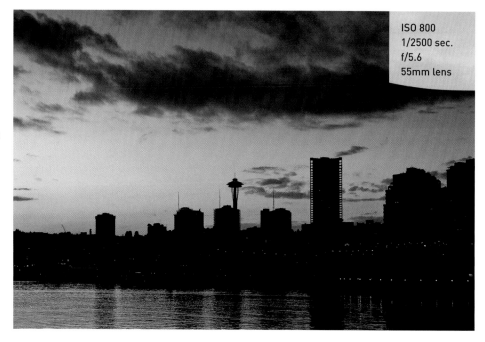

ISO 800
1/2500 sec.
f/5.6
55mm lens

SETTING UP AND SHOOTING IN MANUAL MODE

1. Turn the Mode dial to align the M with the indicator line.

2. Select your ISO by pressing the ISO button on the top of the camera, and then turning the Main dial.

3. Point the camera at your subject and then activate the camera meter by depressing the shutter button halfway.

4. View the exposure information in the bottom area of the viewfinder or by looking at the rear display panel.

5. While the meter is activated, use your index finger to roll the Main dial left and right to change your shutter speed value until the exposure mark is lined up with the zero mark. The exposure information is displayed by a scale with marks that run from –2 to +2 stops. A proper exposure will line up with the arrow mark in the middle. As the indicator moves to the left, it is a sign that you will be underexposing (there is not enough light on the sensor to provide adequate exposure). Move the indicator to the right and you will be providing more exposure than the camera meter calls for. This is overexposure.

6. To set your exposure using the aperture, depress the shutter release button until the meter is activated. Then, using your thumb, hold in on the Av button and then use your index finger to turn the Main dial, right for a smaller aperture (large f-stop number), left for a larger aperture (small f-stop number).

A-DEP: AUTO DEPTH OF FIELD MODE

 The A-DEP, or Auto Depth of Field, setting is on the Creative zone side of the dial, but in my opinion it should be over in the Basic zone. The mode works this way: As you depress the shutter release button to focus on your subject, the camera will use the other focus points to measure the distance of the other objects in the viewfinder. Then, it will determine what the appropriate aperture setting is to render all of the objects in focus (**Figure 4.14**). The only way to adjust your exposure is to change the ISO. There will be more discussion of the A-DEP mode and how to use it in Chapter 7.

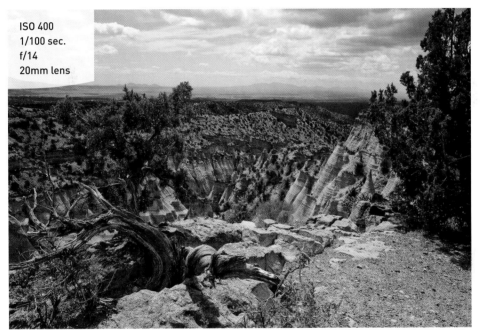

ISO 400
1/100 sec.
f/14
20mm lens

FIGURE 4.14
Landscapes with subjects that are at differing distances could benefit from the A-DEP mode.

HOW I SHOOT: A CLOSER LOOK AT THE CAMERA SETTINGS I USE

The great thing about working with a dSLR camera is that I can always feel confident that some things will remain unchanged from camera to camera. For me, these are the Aperture Priority (Av) and Shutter Priority (Tv) shooting modes. Although I like to think of myself as a generalist in terms of my photography, I do tend to lean heavily on the landscape and urban photography genres. Working in these areas means that

I am almost always going to be concerned with my depth of field. Whether it's isolating my subject with a large aperture or trying to maximize the overall sharpness of a sweeping landscape, I always keep an eye on my aperture setting. If I do have a need to control the action, I use Shutter Priority. If I am trying to create a silky waterfall effect, I can depend on Tv to provide that long shutter speed that will deliver. Maybe I am shooting a motocross jumper. I definitely need the fast shutter speeds that will freeze the fast-moving action. While the other camera modes have their place, I think you will find that, like myself and most other working pros, you will use the Av and Tv modes for 90 percent of your shooting.

The other concern that I have when I am setting up my camera is just how low I can keep my ISO. I raise the ISO only as a last resort because each increase in sensitivity is an opportunity for more digital noise to enter my image. To that end, I always have the High ISO Noise Reduction feature turned on (see Chapter 7).

To make quick changes while I shoot, I often use the Exposure Compensation feature (covered in Chapter 7) so that I can make small over- and underexposure changes. This is different than changing the aperture or shutter; it is more like fooling the camera meter into thinking the scene is brighter or darker than it actually is.

One of the reasons I change my exposure is to make corrections when I see the "blinkies" while looking at my images on the rear LCD. Blinkies are the warning signal that part of my image has been overexposed to the point that I no longer have any detail in the highlights. The highlight alert will flash wherever the potential exists for overexposure. The only unfortunate thing about this feature is that it doesn't work with the full-screen preview mode. You have to set your camera display for the Histogram mode and then you will see the highlight alert (**Figure 4.15**).

FIGURE 4.15
The T1i's highlight alert screen.

The flashing black areas are alerting me that these highlights are overexposed and will lose detail.

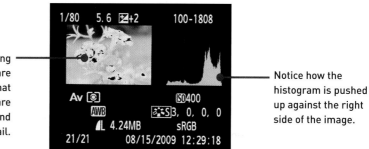

Notice how the histogram is pushed up against the right side of the image.

As you work your way through the coming chapters, you will see other tips and tricks I use in my daily photography, but the most important tip I can give is to understand the features of your camera so that you can leverage the technology in a knowledgeable way. This will result in better photographs.

Chapter 4 Assignments

The information covered in this chapter will define how you work with your camera from this point on. Granted, there may be times that you just want to grab some quick pictures and will resort to the Basic zone, but to get serious with your photography, you should learn the modes in the Creative zone.

Starting off with Program mode

Set your camera on Program mode and start shooting. Become familiar with the adjustments you can make to your exposure by turning the Main dial. While shooting, make sure that you keep an eye on your ISO.

Learning to control time with the Tv mode

Find some moving subjects and then set your camera to Tv mode. Have someone ride their bike back and forth or even just photograph cars as they go by. Start with a slow shutter speed of around 1/30 of a second and then start shooting with faster and faster shutter speeds. Keep shooting until you can freeze the action. Now find something that isn't moving, like a flower, and work your shutter speed from something fast like 1/500 of a second and then work your way down to about 1/4 of a second. The point is to see how well you can handhold your camera before you start introducing hand shake into the image.

Controlling depth of field with the Av mode

The name of the game with Av mode is depth of field. Set up three items in equal distance from you. I would use chess pieces or something similar. Now focus on the middle item and set your camera to the largest aperture that your lens allows (remember, large aperture means a small number like f/3.5). Now, while still focusing on the middle subject, start shooting with ever-smaller apertures until you are at the smallest f-stop for your lens. If you have a zoom lens, try doing this exercise with the lens at the widest and then the most telephoto settings. Now move up to subjects that are farther away, like telephone poles, and shoot them in the same way. The idea is to get a feel for how each aperture setting affects your depth of field.

Giving and taking with Manual mode

Go outside on a sunny day and, using the camera in Manual mode, set your ISO to 100, your shutter speed to 1/125 of a second, and your aperture to f/16. Now press your shutter release button to get a meter reading. You should be pretty close to that zero mark. If not, make small adjustments to one of your settings until it hits that mark. Now is where the fun begins. Start moving your shutter speed slower, to 1/60, and then set your aperture to f/22. Now go the other way. Set your aperture on f/8 and your shutter speed to 1/500. Now review your images. If all went well, all the exposures should look the same. This is because you balanced the light with reciprocal changes to the aperture and shutter speed. Now go back to our original setting of 1/125 at f/16 and try just moving the shutter speed without changing the aperture. Just make 1/3-stop changes (1/125 to 1/100 to 1/80 to 1/60), and then review your images to see what a 1/3 stop of overexposure looks like. Then do the same thing going in the opposite way. It's hard to know if you want to over- or underexpose a scene until you have actually done it and seen the results.

5

ISO 1000
1/320 sec.
f/4.5
200mm lens

Moving Target

THE TRICKS TO SHOOTING SPORTS AND MORE

Now that you have learned about the Creative zone, it's time to put your newfound knowledge to good use. Whether you are shooting the action at a professional sporting event or a child on a merry-go-round, you'll learn techniques that will help you bring out the best in your photography when your subject is in motion.

The number one thing to know when trying to capture a moving target is that speed is king! I'm not talking about how fast your subject is moving, but rather how fast your shutter is opening and closing. Shutter speed is the key to freezing a moment in time—but also to conveying movement. It's all in how you turn the dial. There are also some other considerations for taking your shot to the next level: composition, lens selection, and a few more items that we will explore in this chapter. So strap on your seatbelt and hit the gas, because here we go!

The wide-angle lens allowed me to capture the entire width of the ride from a very close distance.

A small aperture gave great depth of field and also allowed me to use a longer exposure time.

ISO 500
0.6 sec.
f/22
18mm lens

To get all the great lights looking close to their true colors I set the white balance to Tungsten.

I can always depend on my local county fair for some unique photo opportunities. Each year I grab my camera and a couple of lenses and head off to the midway to capture some great images. This year I happened to be walking by the merry-go-round when I saw the operator standing vigil in the center of the ride. As the carousel started to turn, I set my camera on a fence and took several images in an attempt to show the spinning motion of the ride as it swirled around the operator. Luckily he cooperated by standing still, and I got the shot I was after.

Due to the long exposure, the camera was placed on a solid surface to eliminate the possibility of camera shake.

PORING OVER THE PICTURE

To capture the horse and rider as they cleared the jump, I had to position myself so that the action would be coming towards me. Because the jump was so high I couldn't focus on the horse as it came toward the jump, so I decided to pre-focus on the front of the hedge. I was already set up to shoot in Continuous shooting mode so I waited until just before they jumped and then held my finger down and let it rip.

The large aperture helps to blur the trees in the background, keeping the emphasis on the horses and rider.

The fast shutter speed froze the action.

I began shooting just before the horse and rider started the jump so that the camera would be firing as they entered the plane of focus.

ISO 800 was selected to allow for the faster shutter speeds and a wide-open aperture setting.

ISO 800
1/1000 sec.
f/5.6
300mm lens

STOP RIGHT THERE!

Shutter speed is the main tool in the photographer's arsenal for capturing great action shots. The ability to freeze a moment in time often makes the difference between a good shot and a great one. To take advantage of this concept, you should have a good grasp of the relationship between shutter speed and movement. When you press the shutter release button, your camera goes into action by opening the shutter curtain and then closing it after a predetermined length of time. The longer you leave your shutter open, the more your subject will move across the frame, so commonsense dictates that the first thing to consider is just how fast your subject is moving.

Typically, you will be working in fractions of a second. How many fractions depends on several factors. Subject movement, while simple in concept, is actually based on three factors. The first is the direction of travel. Is the subject moving across your field of view (left to right) or traveling toward or away from you? The second consideration is the actual speed at which the subject is moving. There is a big difference between a moving sports car and child on a bicycle. Finally, the distance from you to the subject has a direct bearing on how fast the action seems to be taking place. Let's take a brief look at each of these factors to see how they might affect your shooting.

DIRECTION OF TRAVEL

Typically, the first thing that people think about when taking an action shot is how fast the subject is moving, but in reality the first consideration should be the direction of travel. Where you are positioned in relation to the subject's direction of travel is critically important in selecting the proper shutter speed. When you open your shutter, the lens gathers light from your subject and records it on the camera sensor. If the subject is moving across your viewfinder, you need a faster shutter speed to keep that lateral movement from being recorded as a streak across your image. Subjects that are moving perpendicular to your shooting location do not move across your viewfinder and appear to be more stationary. This allows you to use a slightly slower shutter speed (**Figure 5.1**). A subject that is moving in a diagonal direction—both across the frame and toward or away from you—requires a shutter speed in between the two.

SUBJECT SPEED

Once the angle of motion has been determined, you can then assess the speed at which the subject is traveling. The faster your subject moves, the faster your shutter speed needs to be in order to "freeze" that subject (**Figure 5.2**). A person walking across your frame might only require a shutter speed of 1/60 of a second, while a cyclist traveling in the same direction would call for 1/500 of a second. That same cyclist traveling toward you at the same rate of speed, rather than across the frame, might only require a shutter speed of 1/125 of a second. You can start to see how the relationship of speed and direction comes into play in your decision-making process.

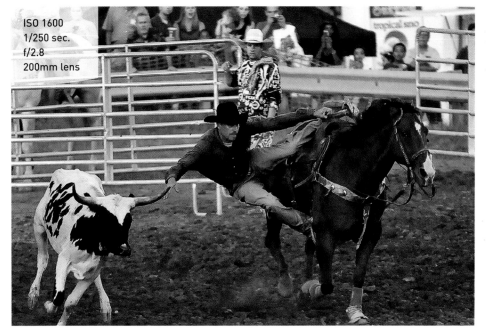

ISO 1600
1/250 sec.
f/2.8
200mm lens

FIGURE 5.1
Action coming toward the camera can be captured with slower shutter speeds.

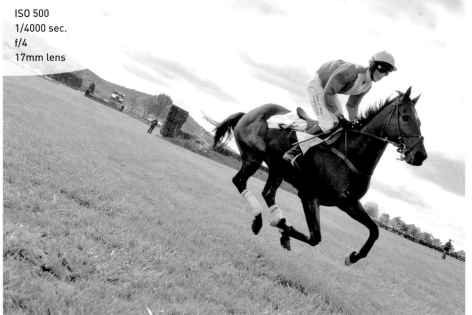

ISO 500
1/4000 sec.
f/4
17mm lens

FIGURE 5.2
A fast-moving subject that is crossing your path will require a faster shutter speed.

SUBJECT-TO-CAMERA DISTANCE

So now we know both the direction and the speed of your subject. The final factor to address is the distance between you and the action. Picture yourself looking at a highway full of cars from up in a tall building a quarter of a mile from the road. As you stare down at the traffic moving along at 55 miles per hour, the cars and trucks seem to be slowly moving along the roadway. Now picture yourself standing in the median of that same road as the same traffic flies by at the same rate of speed.

Although the traffic is moving at the same speed, the shorter distance between you and the traffic makes the cars look like they are moving much faster. This is because your field of view is much narrower; therefore, the subjects are not going to present themselves within the frame for the same length of time. The concept of distance applies to the length of your lens as well (**Figure 5.3**). If you are using a wide-angle lens, you can probably get away with a slower shutter speed than if you were using a telephoto, which puts you in the heart of the action. It all has to do with your field of view. That telephoto gets you "closer" to the action—and the closer you are, the faster your subject will be moving across your viewfinder.

FIGURE 5.3
Due to the distance from the camera, a slower shutter speed could be used to capture this action.

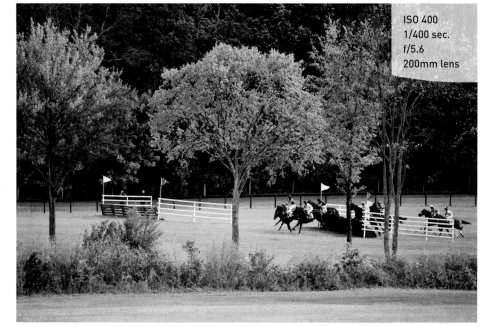

ISO 400
1/400 sec.
f/5.6
200mm lens

ZOOM IN TO BE SURE

When reviewing your shots on the LCD, don't be fooled by the display. The smaller your image is, the sharper it will look. To ensure that you are getting sharp, blur-free images, make sure that you zoom in on your LCD display.

To zoom in on your images, press the Image Review button located to the lower-right of the LCD display and then press the Magnify Image button to zoom (**Figure 5.4**). Continue pressing the Magnify Image button to increase the zoom ratio.

To zoom back out, simply press the Reduce Image button (the magnifying glass with the minus sign on it) or press the Image Review button again.

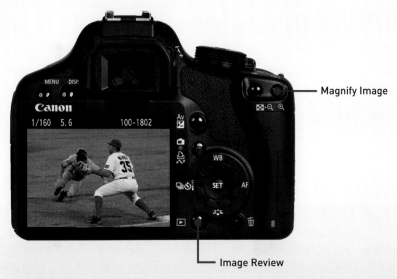

Magnify Image

Image Review

FIGURE 5.4
Zooming in on your image helps you confirm that the image is really sharp.

USING SHUTTER PRIORITY (TV) MODE TO STOP MOTION

In Chapter 4, you were introduced to the Creative zone's shooting modes. You'll remember that the mode that gives you ultimate control over shutter speed is Tv mode, where you are responsible for selecting the shutter speed while handing over the aperture selection to the camera. The ability to concentrate on just one exposure factor helps you quickly make changes on the fly while staying glued to your view-finder and your subject.

There are a couple of things to consider when using Tv mode, both of which have to do with the amount of light that is available when shooting. While you have control over which shutter speed you select in Tv mode, the range of shutter speeds that is available to you depends largely on how well your subject is lit.

Typically, when shooting fast-paced action, you will be working with very fast shutter speeds. This means that your lens will probably be set to its largest aperture. If the light is not sufficient for the shutter speed selected, you will need to do one of two things: select a lens that offers a larger working aperture, or raise the ISO of the camera. Working off the assumption that you have only one lens available, let's concentrate on balancing your exposure using the ISO.

Let's say that you are shooting a baseball game at night, and you want to get some great action shots. You set your camera to Tv mode and, after testing out some shutter speeds, determine that you need to shoot at 1/500 of a second to freeze the action on the field. When you place the viewfinder to your eye and press the shutter button halfway, you notice that the f-stop readout is blinking at f/4.5. This is your camera's way of telling you that the lens has now reached its maximum aperture and you are going to be underexposed if you shoot your pictures at the currently selected shutter speed. You could slow your shutter speed down until the aperture reading stops blinking, but then you would get images with too much motion blur.

The alternative is to raise your ISO to a level that is fast enough for a proper exposure. The key here is to always use the lowest ISO that you can get away with. That might mean ISO 200 in bright sunny conditions or ISO 1600 for an indoor or night situation (**Figure 5.5**). Just remember that the higher the ISO, the greater the amount of noise in your image. This is the reason that you see professional sports photographers using those mammoth lenses perched atop a monopod: they could use a smaller lens, but to get those very large apertures they need a huge piece of glass on the front of the lens. The larger the glass on the front of the lens, the more light it gathers, and the larger the aperture for shooting. For the working pro, the large aperture translates into low ISO (and thus low noise), fast shutter speeds, and razor-sharp action.

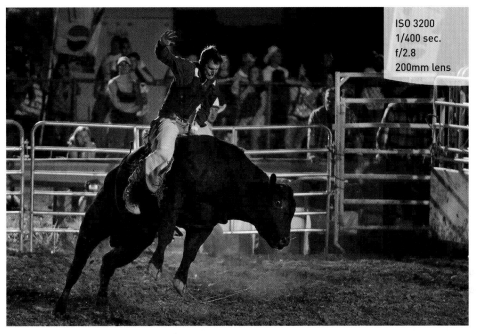

ISO 3200
1/400 sec.
f/2.8
200mm lens

FIGURE 5.5
The only way to stop action under the dim lights of this arena and still get a decent shutter speed was to crank up the ISO.

ADJUSTING YOUR ISO ON THE FLY

1. Check for the blinking aperture readout in the bottom-right portion of your viewfinder.

2. If it is blinking, move your index finger back from the shutter button and press the ISO button.

3. Now move your finger forward to the Main dial and raise the ISO to the next highest level by rotating it right.

4. Lightly press the shutter button and check to see if the aperture is still blinking.

5. If it's not blinking, shoot away. If it is, repeat steps 2–4 until it is set correctly.

USING APERTURE PRIORITY (AV) MODE TO ISOLATE YOUR SUBJECT

One of the benefits of working in Tv mode with fast shutter speeds is that, more often than not, you will be shooting with the largest aperture available on your lens. Shooting with a large aperture allows you to use faster shutter speeds, but it also narrows your depth of field.

To isolate your subject in order to focus your viewer's attention on it, a larger aperture is required. The larger aperture reduces the foreground and background sharpness: the larger the aperture, the more blurred they will be.

The reason that I bring this up here is that when you are shooting most sporting events, the idea is to isolate your main subject by having it in focus while the rest of the image has some amount of blur. This sharp focus draws your viewer right to the subject. Studies have shown that the eye is drawn to sharp areas before moving on to the blurry areas. Also, depending on what your subject matter is, there can be a tendency to get distracted by a busy background if everything in the photo is equally sharp. Without a narrow depth of field, it might be difficult for the viewer to establish exactly what the main subject is in your picture.

Let's look at how to use depth of field to bring focus to your subject. In the previous section, I told you that you should use Tv mode for getting those really fast shutter speeds to stop action. Generally speaking, Tv mode will be the mode you most often use for shooting sports and other action, but there will be times when you want to ensure that you are getting the narrowest depth of field possible in your image. The way to do this is by using Aperture Priority mode.

So how do you know when you should use Av mode as opposed to Tv mode? It's not a simple answer, but your LCD screen can help you make this determination. The best scenario for using Av mode is a brightly lit scene where maximum apertures will still give you plenty of shutter speed to stop the action.

Let's say that you are shooting a soccer game in the midday sun. If you have determined that you need something between 1/500 and 1/1250 of a second for stopping the action, you could just set your camera to a high shutter speed in Tv mode and just start shooting. But you also want to be using an aperture of, say, f/4.5 to get that narrow depth of field. Here's the problem: if you set your camera to Tv and select 1/1000 of a second as a nice compromise, you might get that desired f/stop—but you might not. As the meter is trained on your moving subject, the light levels could rise or fall, which might actually change that desired f-stop to something higher like f/5.6 or even f/8. Now the depth of field is extended, and you will no longer get that nice isolation and separation that you wanted.

To rectify this, switch the camera to Av mode and select f/4.5 as your aperture. Now, as you begin shooting, the camera holds that aperture and makes exposure adjustments with the shutter speed (**Figure 5.6**). As I said before, this works well when you have lots of light—enough light so that you can have a high-enough shutter speed without introducing motion blur.

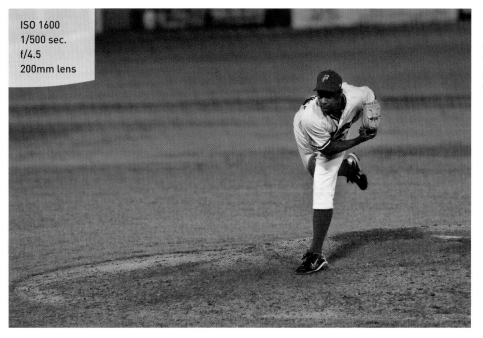

ISO 1600
1/500 sec.
f/4.5
200mm lens

FIGURE 5.6
By selecting a large
aperture setting,
the player is nicely
separated from the
field behind him.

KEEP THEM IN FOCUS WITH AI SERVO AND AUTO AF FOCUS POINT SELECTION

With the exposure issue handled for the moment, let's move on to an area that is equally important: focusing. If you have browsed your manual, you know that there are several focus modes to choose from in the T1i. To get the greatest benefit from each of them, it is important to understand how they work and the situations where each mode will give you the best opportunity to grab a great shot. Because we are discussing subject movement, our first choice is going to be AI Servo mode (the AI stands for Artificial Intelligence). AI Servo uses all of the focus points in the camera to find a moving subject and then lock in the focus when the shutter button is completely depressed. Unlike One Shot, which works best for stationary subjects such as in macro or photography portraits, AI Servo mode will help track your subject in the frame and give you better focus results.

SELECTING AND SHOOTING IN AI SERVO FOCUS MODE

1. Press the right Cross key button on the back of the camera.

2. Use your index finger to rotate the Main dial until AI SERVO appears on the rear LCD panel. You can also use the left and right Cross keys to make the selection. Press the Set button to lock in your change.

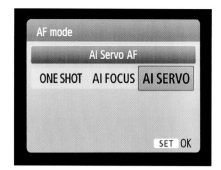

3. Locate your subject in the viewfinder, then press and hold the shutter button halfway to activate the focus mechanism.

4. The camera will maintain focus on your subject, as long as the subject remains within one of the focus points in the viewfinder or until you take a picture.

You should also note that the AF mode is used to select the method with which the camera will focus the lens. This is different from the AF point mode, which is a cluster of small points that are visible in the viewfinder and are used to determine where you want the lens to focus (**Figure 5.7**).

When using AI Servo mode, you have the choice of using the Automatic Focus (AF) point mode in automatic, which uses the center point in the viewfinder, or you can select one of the autofocus points as your starting point.

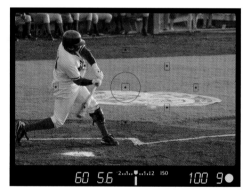

FIGURE 5.7
The Automatic Focus (AF) points are the nine small rectangular boxes arranged in a diamond pattern in your viewfinder.

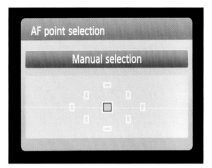

1. Press the Focus Point Selection button on the back of the camera. It is the same button you use to zoom in on your image in Preview mode.

2. Rotate the Main dial to move the focus point (you can also use the Cross keys on the back of the camera to quickly jump from one point to the next).

3. You can tell which point is selected by looking at either the rear LCD panel or the illuminated focus points in the viewfinder.

4. To select the Automatic Focus (AF) point mode, rotate the dial until all of the points are either displayed (on the rear LCD panel) or illuminated (in the viewfinder). If you are looking at the rear LCD, you will see the words "Automatic Selection" above the focus points when the camera is set to auto mode. If a single point has been selected, you will see the words "Manual Selection."

5. When you have an individual point selected, the camera will use that specific location to focus the lens. If all the points are selected, the camera will determine what the best source is for focus. The point or points must be on your subject for the autofocus to function properly.

STOP AND GO WITH AI FOCUS AF

If you are going to be changing between a moving target and one that is still, you should consider using the AI Focus AF mode. This mode mixes both the One Shot and AI Servo modes for shooting a subject that goes from stationary to moving without having to adjust your focus mode.

When you have a stationary subject, simply place your selected focus point on your subject and the camera will focus on it. If your subject begins to move out of focus, the camera will switch to AI Servo mode and track the movement, keeping a sharp focus.

For example, suppose you are shooting a football game. The quarterback has brought the team to the line and he is standing behind the center, waiting for the ball to be hiked. If you are using the AI Focus AF mode, you can place your focus point on the quarterback and start taking pictures of him as he stands at the line. As soon as the ball is hiked and the action starts, the camera will switch to AI Servo mode and track his movement within the frame. This can be a little tricky at first, but once you master it, it will make your action shooting effortless. Using this mode, you can identify your subject for the camera so that it knows exactly which subject to maintain as the priority for your focus selection.

To select AI Focus, simply follow the same steps listed for selecting AI Servo but instead select the AI Focus mode (**Figure 5.8**).

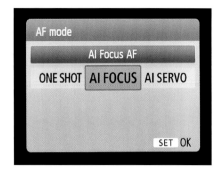

FIGURE 5.8
Setting your focus mode to AI Focus.

CHOOSING A FOCUS MODE

Selecting the proper focus mode depends largely on what type of subject you are photographing. One Shot is typically best for stationary subjects. It allows you to determine exactly where you want your focus to be and then recompose your image while holding the focus in place. If you are taking pictures of an active subject that is moving quickly, trying to set a focus point with One Shot can be difficult, if not impossible. This is when you will want to rely on the AI modes to quickly assess the subject distance and set your lens focus.

MANUAL FOCUS FOR ANTICIPATED ACTION

While I utilize the automatic focus modes for the majority of my shooting, there are times when I like to fall back on manual focus. This is usually when I know when and where the action will occur and I want to capture the subject as it crosses a certain plane of focus. This is useful in sports like motocross or auto racing, where the subjects are on a defined track. By pre-focusing the camera, all I have to do is wait for the subject to approach my point of focus and then start firing the camera.

In **Figure 5.9**, the horses in the steeplechase race were traveling directly towards me from behind the hedge jump, so tracking them with AI Servo would have been difficult, if not impossible. To get my shot, I simply focused on the front of the hedge and waited for the horses to come into range. As they began their jump over the hedge, I captured the horses and riders at the height of the action.

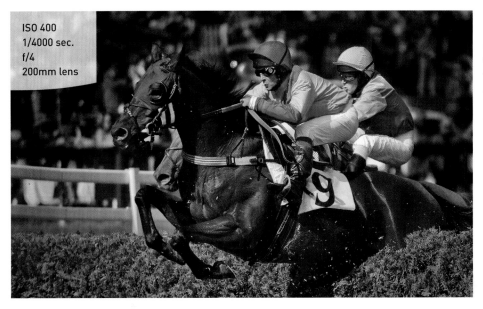

ISO 400
1/4000 sec.
f/4
200mm lens

FIGURE 5.9
Pre-focus the
camera to a point
where you know
the subject will be
and start shooting
right before they
get there.

DRIVE MODES

The drive mode determines how fast your camera will take pictures. Single Shot is for taking one photograph at a time. With every full press of the shutter, the camera will take a single image. The Continuous mode allows for a more rapid capture rate. Think of it like a machine gun. When you are using the Continuous mode, the camera continues to take pictures as long as the shutter release button is held down (or until the buffer fills up).

KEEPING UP WITH THE CONTINUOUS SHOOTING MODE

Getting great focus is one thing, but capturing the best moment on the sensor can be difficult if you are shooting just one frame at a time. In the world of sports, and in life in general, things move pretty fast. If you blink, you might miss it. The same can be said for shooting in Single shooting drive mode. Fortunately, your T1i comes equipped with a Continuous shooting—or "burst"—mode that lets you capture a series of images at up to 3.4 frames a second. (No, you can't actually capture .4 frames—it's an average.) See **Figure 5.10**.

Manual Callout

The number of actual frames that you can capture varies depending on the image format that you are using (JPEG, RAW, RAW+JPEG). To find out the frame rates, as well as the maximum number of frames that you can take in one continuous burst, check out page 70 of your camera manual.

FIGURE 5.10
Using the Continuous drive mode means that you are sure to capture the peak of the action.

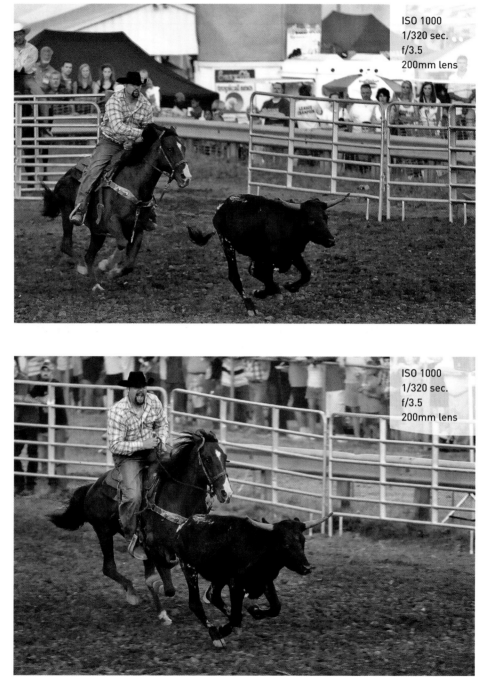

ISO 1000
1/320 sec.
f/3.5
200mm lens

ISO 1000
1/320 sec.
f/3.5
200mm lens

SETTING UP AND SHOOTING IN THE CONTINUOUS DRIVE MODE

1. Press the left Cross key button on the back of the camera.

2. Rotate the Main dial while looking at the rear LCD screen to select the desired mode. The icon that looks like stacked-up little rectangles is the Continuous mode. Press the Set button to lock in your change.

3. To shoot, just depress the shutter button and hold until the desired number of frames has been captured.

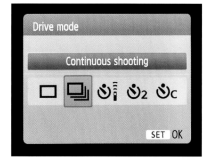

Your camera has an internal memory, called a "buffer," where images are stored while they are being processed prior to being moved to your memory card. Depending on the image format you are using, the buffer might fill up, and the camera will stop shooting until space is made in the buffer for new images. If this happens, you will see the word "Busy" appear in the viewfinder and on the rear LCD panel. The camera readout in the viewfinder tells you how many frames you have available.

A SENSE OF MOTION

Shooting action isn't always about freezing the action. There are times when you want to convey a sense of motion so that the viewer can get a feel for the movement and flow of an event. Two techniques you can use to achieve this effect are panning and motion blur.

PANNING

Panning has been used for decades to capture the speed of a moving object as it moves across the frame. It doesn't work well for subjects that are moving toward or away from you. Panning is achieved by following your subject across your frame, moving your camera along with the subject, and using a slower-than-normal shutter speed so that the background (and sometimes even a bit of the subject) has a sideways blur but the main portion of your subject is sharp and blur-free. The key to a great panning shot is selecting the right shutter speed: too fast and you won't get the desired blurring of the background; too slow and the subject will have too much blur and will not be recognizable. Practice the technique until you can achieve a smooth motion with your camera that follows along with your subject. The other thing to remember when panning is to follow through even after the shutter has closed. This will keep the motion smooth and give you better images.

In **Figure 5.11**, I used the panning technique to follow this ball player as he ran in front of me. I set the camera drive mode to Continuous drive, and I used Tv mode to select a shutter speed of 1/30 of a second while the focus mode was on AI Servo.

FIGURE 5.11
Following the subject as it moves across the field of view allows for a slower shutter speed and adds a sense of motion.

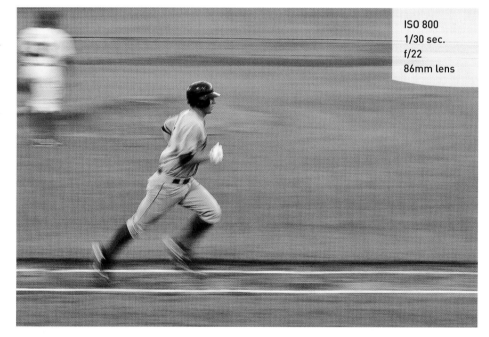

ISO 800
1/30 sec.
f/22
86mm lens

MOTION BLUR

Another way to let the viewer in on the feel of the action is to simply include some blur in the image. This isn't accidental blur from choosing the wrong shutter speed. This blur is more exaggerated, and it tells a story. In **Figure 5.12**, I was interested in capturing the movement of the merry-go-round. A fast shutter speed would have surely frozen the action, but it would not have told the story of the movement of the ride and the operator who was standing in the middle. Instead of moving with the action, I let the movement of the merry-go-round create the blur as I held the camera in a stationary position.

Just as in panning, there is no preordained shutter speed to use for this effect. It is simply a matter of trial and error until you have a look that conveys the action. I try to get some area of the subject that is frozen. The key to this technique is the correct shutter speed combined with keeping the camera still during the exposure. You are trying to capture the motion of the subject, not the photographer or the camera, so use a good shooting stance or even a tripod.

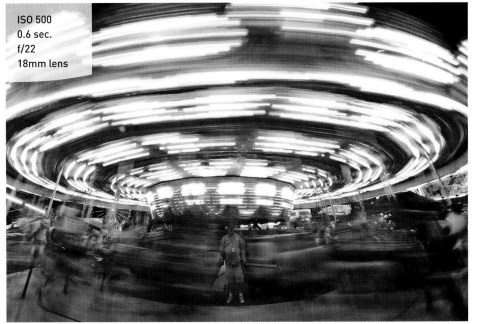

ISO 500
0.6 sec.
f/22
18mm lens

FIGURE 5.12
The movement of the ride coupled with the slow shutter speed conveys the action of the merry-go-round as it spins around the operator.

TIPS FOR SHOOTING ACTION

GIVE THEM SOMEWHERE TO GO

Whether you are shooting something as simple as your child's soccer match or as complex as the wild motion of a bucking bronco, where you place the subject in the frame is equally as important as how well you expose the image. A poorly composed shot can completely ruin a great moment by not holding the viewer's attention.

The one mistake I see many times in action photography is that the photographer doesn't use the frame properly. If you are dealing with a subject that is moving horizontally across your field of view, give the subject somewhere to go by placing them to the side of the frame, with their motion leading toward the middle of the frame (**Figure 5.13**). This offsetting of the subject will introduce a sense of direction and anticipation for the viewer. Unless you are going to completely fill the image with the action, try to avoid placing your subject in the middle of the frame.

FIGURE 5.13
Try to leave space in front of your subject to lead the action in a direction.

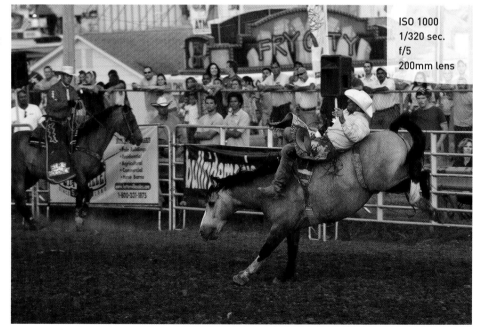

ISO 1000
1/320 sec.
f/5
200mm lens

GET IN FRONT OF THE ACTION

Here's another one. When shooting action, show the action coming toward you (**Figure 5.14**). Don't shoot the action going away from you. People want to see faces.

Faces convey the action, the drive, the sense of urgency, and the emotion of the moment. So if you are shooting action involving people, always position yourself so that the action is either coming at you or is at least perpendicular to your position.

ISO 800
1/1000 sec.
f/5.6
300mm lens

FIGURE 5.14

Shooting from the front with a telephoto gives a feeling that the action is coming right at you.

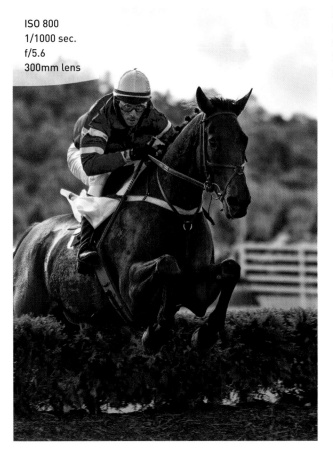

PUT YOUR CAMERA IN A DIFFERENT PLACE

Changing your vantage point is a great way of finding new angles. Shooting from a low position with a wide-angle lens might let you incorporate some foreground to give depth to the image. Shooting from farther away with a telephoto lens will compress the elements in a scene and allow you to crop in tighter on the action. Don't be afraid to experiment and try new things.

The image in **Figure 5.15** is one of my favorite action shots, and it all happened because I tried something different. As I was waiting for the race to begin, the horses started running out of their holding area and passing within a few yards of me. I had a wide-angle lens on the camera, and instead of bringing it up to eye level, I just held it down to my side and started shooting frames in Continuous mode. The AI Servo focus mode was picking up the horse and getting great focus, and I knew that my shutter speed was set very high from the last race. The wide-angle lens was capturing the horse in the foreground, the trees in the middle ground, and the great-looking sky overhead. The horse was positioned to the right of the frame, running toward the empty space on the left. It was also placed in the lower third of the frame, giving an excellent "rule of thirds" balance. (See p. 186 for more on the rule of thirds.) And this image is the result—just because I said, "What the heck?" and tried something a little outside the box.

FIGURE 5.15
Putting your camera in a different place can yield pleasing results.

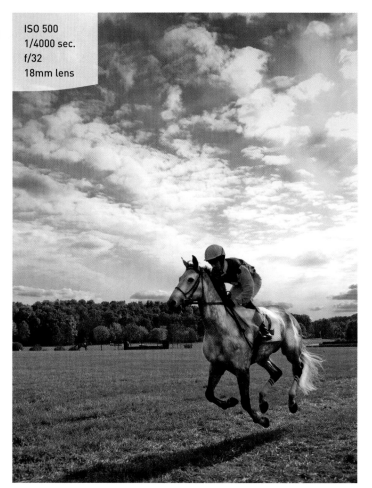

ISO 500
1/4000 sec.
f/32
18mm lens

Chapter 5 Assignments

The mechanics of motion

For this first assignment, you need to find some action. Explore the relationship between the speed of an object and its direction of travel. Use the same shutter speed to record your subject moving toward you and across your view. Try using the same shutter speed for both to compare the difference made by the direction of travel.

Wide vs. telephoto

Just as with the first assignment, photograph a subject moving in different directions, but this time, use a wide-angle lens and then a telephoto. Check out how the telephoto setting on the zoom lens will require faster shutter speeds than the lens at its wide-angle setting.

Getting a feel for focusing modes

We discussed two different ways to auto focus for action: AI Servo and AI Focus AF. Starting with AI Servo mode, find a moving subject and use the mode to get familiar with the way the mode works. Change from autofocus point selection to a single-point selection.

Now repeat the process using the AI Focus AF mode. The point of the exercise is to become familiar enough with the two modes to decide which one to use for the situation you are photographing.

Anticipating the spot using manual focus

For this assignment, you will need to find a subject that you know will cross a specific line that you can pre-focus on. A street with moderate traffic works well for this. Focus on a spot on the street that the cars will travel across (don't forget to set your lens for manual focus). To do this right, you need to set the drive mode on the camera to the continuous mode. Now, when a car approaches the spot, start shooting. Try shooting in three- or four-frame bursts.

Following the action

Panning is a great way to show motion. To begin, find a subject that will move across your path at a steady speed and practice following it in your viewfinder from side to side. Now, with the camera in Tv mode, set your shutter speed to 1/30 of a second and the focus mode to AI Servo. Now pan along with the subject and shoot as it moves across your view. Experiment with different shutter speeds and focal lengths. Panning is one of those skills that takes some time to get a feel for, so try it with different types of subjects moving at different speeds.

Feeling the movement

Instead of panning with the motion, use a stationary camera position and adjust the shutter speed until you get a blurred effect that gives the sense of motion while still being able to identify the subject. There is a big difference between a slightly blurred photo that looks like you just picked the wrong shutter speed and one that looks intentional for the purpose of showing motion. Just like panning, it will take some experimentation to find just the right shutter speed to achieve the desired effect.

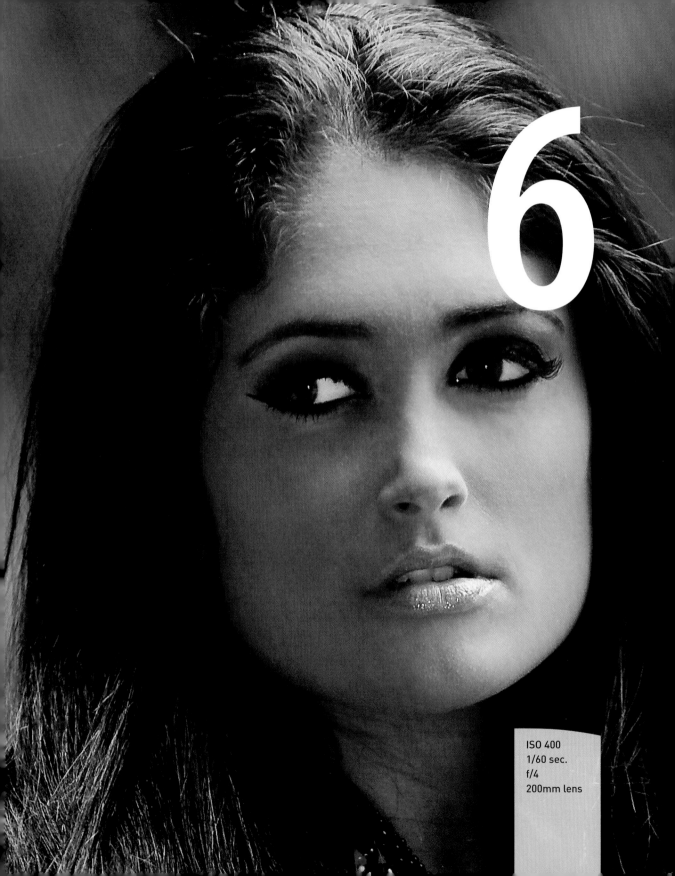

6

ISO 400
1/60 sec.
f/4
200mm lens

Say Cheese!

SETTINGS AND FEATURES TO MAKE GREAT PORTRAITS

Taking pictures of people is one of the great joys of photography. You will experience a great sense of accomplishment when you capture the spirit and personality of someone in a photograph. At the same time, you have a great responsibility because the person in front of the camera is depending on you to make them look good. You can't always change how someone looks, but you can control the way you photograph that individual. In this chapter, we will explore some camera features and techniques that can help you create great portraits.

PORING OVER THE PICTURE

While walking the streets of the French Quarter I came upon some street musicians singing the blues. They were located in a side alley and were shaded from the harsh afternoon sun. This softened all of the shadows and really made the colors look saturated.

The vivid colors worn by the musicians contrasts nicely with the plain white walls behind them.

The lower light levels
in the alley forced me
to raise my ISO.

The longer lens helped
to crop out the unwanted
space surrounding
them, making for a
more intimate image.

Several shots were taken
before getting just the right
expression on their faces.

ISO 400
1/25 sec.
f/5.6
90mm lens

PORING OVER THE PICTURE

While visiting Seattle, I was invited to a portrait shoot by a couple of friends. We were lucky to have a couple of fanstastic models so I was excited to add some great portraits to my portfolio. We shot outdoors in a shaded location that provided some wonderful, soft light that really complemented the models and reduced the need for additional lighting setups.

A large aperture helped blur the background.

Holding the camera vertically creates a more natural frame for her face.

Using a telephoto lens let me crop tightly without having to get in the model's face.

The shady location helped
soften the light and reduced
harsh shadows.

ISO 400
1/125 sec.
f/3.5
120mm lens

AUTOMATIC PORTRAIT MODE

In Chapter 3, we reviewed all of the automatic modes in the Basic zone. One of them, Portrait mode, is dedicated to shooting portraits. While this is not my preferred camera setting, it is a great jumping-off point for those who are just starting out. The key to using this mode is to understand what is going on with the camera so that when you venture further into portrait photography, you can expand on the settings and get the most from your camera and, more importantly, your subject.

Whether you are photographing an individual or a group, the emphasis should always be on the subject. Portrait mode utilizes a larger aperture setting to keep the depth of field very narrow, which means that the background will appear slightly blurred or out of focus. To take full advantage of this effect, use a medium- to telephoto-length lens. Also, keep a pretty close distance to your subject. If you shoot from too far away, the narrow depth of field will not be as effective.

USING APERTURE PRIORITY MODE

If you took a poll of portrait photographers to see which shooting mode was most often used for portraits, the answer would certainly be Aperture Priority (Av) mode. Selecting the right aperture is important for placing the most critically sharp area of the photo on your subject, while simultaneously blurring all of the distracting background clutter (**Figure 6.1**). Not only will a large aperture give the narrowest depth of field, it will also allow you to shoot in lower light levels at lower ISO settings.

This isn't to say that you have to use the largest aperture on your lens. A good place to begin is f/5.6. This will give you enough depth of field to keep the entire face in focus, while providing enough blur to eliminate distractions in the background. This isn't a hard-and-fast setting; it's just a good, all-around number to start with. Your aperture might change depending on the focal length of the lens you are using and on the amount of blur that you want for your foreground and background elements.

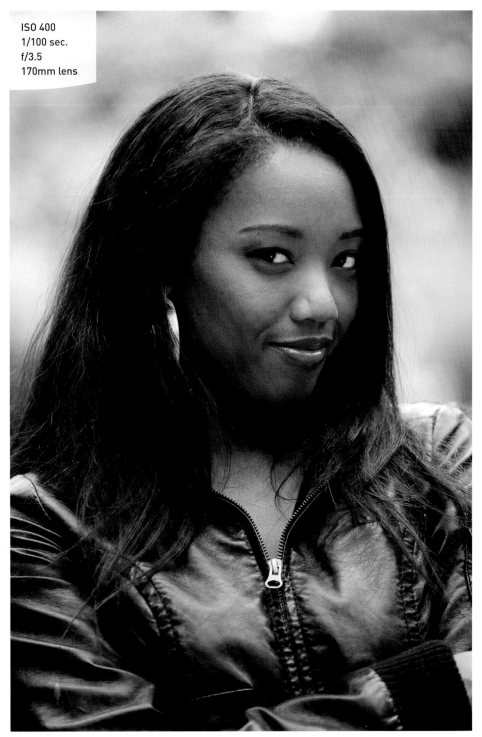

ISO 400
1/100 sec.
f/3.5
170mm lens

FIGURE 6.1
Using a wide
aperture, especially
with a longer lens,
blurs distracting
background details.

GO WIDE FOR ENVIRONMENTAL PORTRAITS

There will be times when your subject's environment is of great significance to the story you want to tell. This might mean using a smaller aperture to get more detail in the background or foreground. Once again, by using Av mode, you can set your aperture to a higher f-stop, such as f/8 or f/11, and include the important details of the scene that surrounds your subject.

Using a wider-than-normal lens can also assist in getting more depth of field as well as showing the surrounding area. A wide-angle lens requires less stopping down of the aperture to achieve an acceptable depth of field. This is due to the fact that wide-angle lenses are covering a greater area, so the depth of field appears to cover a greater percentage of the scene.

A wider lens might also be necessary to relay more information about the scenery (**Figure 6.2**). Select a lens length that is wide enough to tell the story but not so wide that you distort the subject. There's nothing quite as unflattering as giving someone a big, distorted nose (unless you are going for that sort of look). When shooting a portrait with a wide-angle lens, keep the subject away from the edge of the frame. This will reduce the distortion, especially in very wide focal lengths. As the lens length increases, distortion will be reduced. I generally don't like to go wider than about 24mm for portraits. For standard portraits, I prefer a 55mm lens setting.

FIGURE 6.2
I used a wide-angle lens, a tripod, and the self-timer to capture this self-portrait on top of the Bakheng Temple in Cambodia.

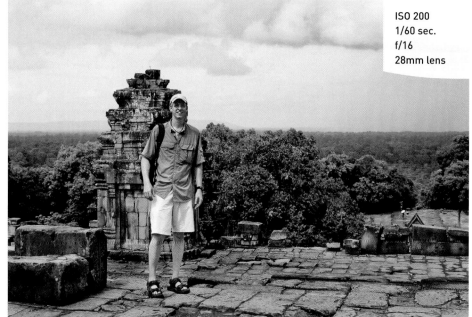

ISO 200
1/60 sec.
f/16
28mm lens

METERING BASICS

There are multiple metering modes in your camera, but the way they work is very similar. A light meter measures the amount of light being reflected off your subject and then renders a suggested exposure value based on the brightness of the subject and the ISO setting of the sensor. To establish this value, the meter averages all of the brightness values to come up with a middle tone, sometimes referred to as 18 percent gray. The exposure value is then rendered based on this middle gray value. This means that a white wall would be underexposed and a black wall would be overexposed in an effort to make each one appear gray. To assist with special lighting situations, the T1i has four metering modes: Evaluative (**Figure 6.3**), which uses the entire frame; Partial (**Figure 6.4**), which uses the middle 9 percent of the frame; Spot (**Figure 6.5**), which takes specific readings from small areas (often used with a gray card); and Center-Weighted (**Figure 6.6**), which looks at the entire frame but places most of the exposure emphasis on the center of the frame.

FIGURE 6.3
The Evaluative metering mode uses the entire frame.

FIGURE 6.4
The Partial metering mode uses the middle of the frame.

FIGURE 6.5
The Spot metering mode uses a very small area of the frame.

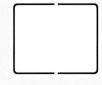

FIGURE 6.6
The Center-Weighted metering mode looks at the entire frame but emphasizes the center of it.

METERING MODES FOR PORTRAITS

For most portrait situations, the Evaluative metering mode is ideal. (For more on how metering works, see the "Metering Basics" sidebar.) This mode measures light values from all portions of the viewfinder and then establishes a proper exposure for the scene. The only problem that you might encounter when using this metering mode is when you have very light or dark backgrounds in your portrait shots.

In these instances, the meter might be fooled into using the wrong exposure information because it will be trying to lighten or darken the entire scene based on the prominence of dark or light areas (**Figure 6.7**). You can deal with this in one of two ways. You can use the Exposure Compensation feature, which we cover in Chapter 7, to dial in adjustments for over- and underexposure. Or you can change the metering mode from Evaluative to Partial metering. The Partial metering mode only uses the center area of the viewfinder (about 9 percent) to get its exposure information. This is the best way to achieve proper exposure for most portraits; metering off skin tones, averaged with hair and clothing, will often give a more accurate exposure (**Figure 6.8**). This metering mode is also great to use when the subject is strongly backlit.

FIGURE 6.7
(left) The light background color and clothing fooled the meter into choosing a slightly underexposed setting for the photo.

FIGURE 6.8
(right) When I switched to the Partial metering mode, my camera was able to ignore much of the background and add a little more time to the exposure.

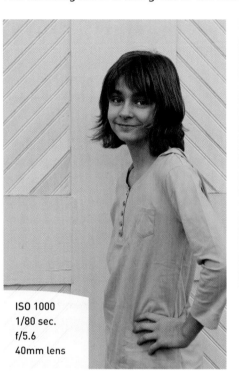

ISO 1000
1/80 sec.
f/5.6
40mm lens

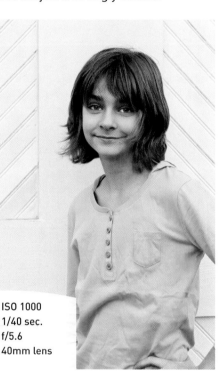

ISO 1000
1/40 sec.
f/5.6
40mm lens

SETTING YOUR METERING MODE TO PARTIAL METERING

1. Press the Set button on the back of the camera to activate the Quick Control screen.

2. Move the selection to the metering mode icon (**A**).

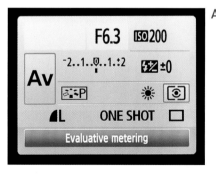

A

3. Use the Main dial to scroll through the metering modes until you find the symbol for Partial metering mode. The names of the different modes will appear near the bottom of the screen. If you press the Set button a second time, you can see all of the available metering modes (**B**).

4. Press the Set button to return to shooting mode.

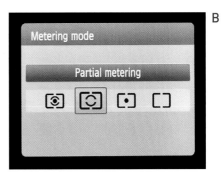

USING THE AE LOCK FEATURE

There will often be times when your subject is not in the center of the frame but you still want to use the Partial metering mode. So how can you get an accurate reading if the subject isn't in the center? Try using the AE (Auto Exposure) Lock feature to hold the exposure setting while you recompose.

AE Lock lets you use the exposure setting from any portion of the scene that you think is appropriate, and then lock that setting in regardless of how the scene looks when you recompose. An example of this would be when you're shooting a photograph of someone and a large amount of blue sky appears in the picture. Normally, the meter might be fooled by all that bright sky and try to reduce the exposure. Using AE Lock, you can establish the correct metering by zooming in on the subject (or even pointing the camera toward the ground), taking the meter reading and locking it in with AE Lock, and then recomposing and taking your photo with the locked-in exposure.

SHOOTING WITH THE AE LOCK FEATURE

1. Find the ✶ AE Lock button on the back of the camera and place your thumb on it.

2. While looking through the viewfinder, place the center focus point on your subject.

3. Press and hold the AE Lock button to get a meter reading. A star will appear in your viewfinder, letting you know that the exposure has been locked.

4. Recompose your shot, and then take the photo.

5. To take more than one photo without having to take another meter reading, just hold down the AE Lock button until you are done using the meter setting.

FOCUSING: THE EYES HAVE IT

It has been said that the eyes are the windows to the soul, and nothing could be truer when you are taking a photograph of someone (**Figure 6.9**). You could have the perfect composition and exposure, but if the eyes aren't sharp the entire image suffers. While there are many different focusing modes to choose from on your T1i, for portrait work you can't beat One Shot mode using a single focusing point. One Shot focusing will establish a single focus for the lens and then hold it until you take the photograph; the other focusing modes continue focusing until the photograph is taken. The single-point selection lets you place the focusing point right on your subject's eye and set that spot as the critical focus point. Using One Shot mode lets you get that focus and recompose all in one motion.

FIGURE 6.9
When photographing people, you should almost always place the emphasis on the eyes.

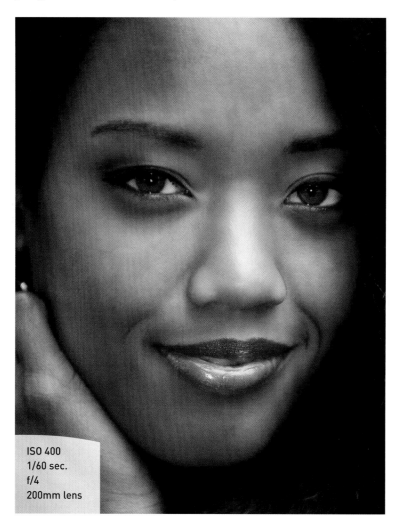

ISO 400
1/60 sec.
f/4
200mm lens

SETTING UP FOR ONE SHOT DRIVE MODE

1. Press the right Cross key, the one labeled AF, on the back of your camera.

2. Rotate the Main dial or use the left/right Cross keys to change the shooting mode to One Shot.

SETTING YOUR FOCUS TO A SINGLE POINT

1. Press the Focus Point Selection button (at the top right on the back of the camera) and then look in your viewfinder.

2. Rotate the Main dial, and watch the illuminated points change on the rear LCD (or in the viewfinder) as you move the dial. Select any single point from among the nine available points. If all of the points are lit up, that means you are in automatic point selection mode. Keep going until you have just the one point you want selected.

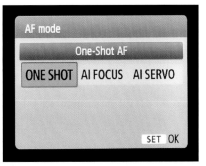

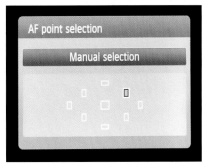

Now, to shoot using this focus point, place that point on your subject's eye, and press the shutter button halfway until the focus point flashes and you hear the chirp. While still holding the shutter button down halfway, recompose and take your shot.

I typically use the center point for focus selection. I find it easier to place that point directly on the location where my critical focus should be established and then recompose the shot. Even though the single point can be selected from any of the focus points, it typically takes longer to figure out where that point should be in relation to my subject. By using the center point, I can quickly establish focus and get on with my shooting.

CLASSIC BLACK AND WHITE PORTRAITS

There is something timeless about a black and white portrait. It eliminates the distraction of color and puts all the emphasis on the subject. To get great black and whites without having to resort to any image-processing software, set your picture style to Monochrome (**Figure 6.10**). You should know that the picture styles are automatically applied when shooting with the JPEG file format. If you are shooting in RAW, the picture that shows up on your rear LCD display will look black and white, but it will appear as a color image when you open it in your Digital Photo Professional software. You can use the software to apply the Monochrome, or any other style, to your RAW image within the image-editing software.

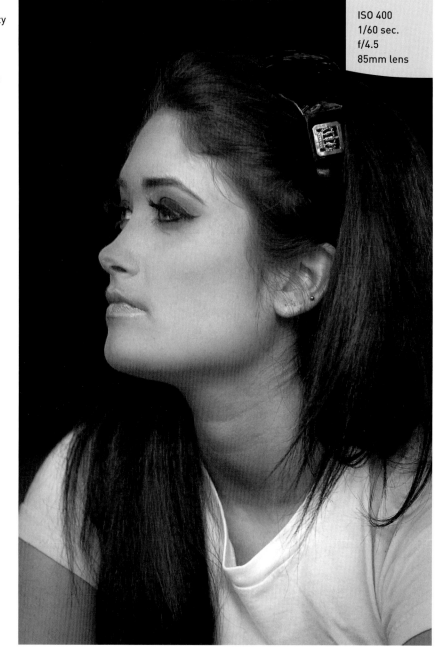

FIGURE 6.10
Getting high-quality black and white portraits is as simple as setting the picture style to Monochrome.

ISO 400
1/60 sec.
f/4.5
85mm lens

The real key to using the Monochrome picture style is to customize it for your portrait subject. The style can be changed to alter the sharpness and contrast. For women, children, puppies, and anyone else who should look somewhat soft, set the Sharpness setting to 0 or 1. For old cowboys, longshoremen, and anyone else who you want to look really detailed, try a setting of 6 or 7. I typically like to leave Contrast at a setting of around −1 or −2. This gives me a nice range of tones throughout the image.

The other adjustment that you should try is to change the picture style's Filter effect from None to one of the four available settings (Yellow, Orange, Red, and Green). Using the filters will have the effect of either lightening or darkening the skin tones. The Red and Yellow filters usually lighten skin, while the Green filter can make skin appear a bit darker. Experiment to see which one works best for your subject.

SETTING YOUR PICTURE STYLE TO MONOCHROME

1. Start by pressing the Menu button.

2. Use the Main dial to scroll to the second camera shooting menu (second from the left).

3. Using the Cross keys, highlight the Picture Style setting and press the Set button (**A**).

4. Use the down Cross key to highlight the Monochrome setting, and lock it in by pressing the Set button again (**B**).

Your camera will continue to shoot with the Monochrome picture style until you change it to another setting.

A

Expo.comp./AEB	-2..1..0..1.:2
Metering mode	
Custom WB	
WB SHIFT/BKT	0.0/±0
Color space	sRGB
Picture Style	Standard
Dust Delete Data	

B

Picture Style	
N Neutral	0 , 0 , 0 , 0
F Faithful	0 , 0 , 0 , 0
M Monochrome	3 , 0 , N , N
1 User Def. 1	Standard
2 User Def. 2	Standard
3 User Def. 3	Standard
DISP. Detail set.	SET OK

CUSTOMIZING THE PICTURE STYLE SETTINGS

1. When you're in the Picture Style section of the menu where you have Monochrome selected, press the Display (Disp.) button located to the left of your viewfinder.

2. Use the up/down Cross keys to highlight the setting you would like to change and press the Set button.

3. Now use the left/right Cross keys to move the cursor to a new position on the scale (the default setting will remain marked with a gray arrow), or to select a different filter, and press the Set button (**A, B**).

4. Perform the same process for the other options, then press the Menu button to return to the regular menu screen. You can now start shooting with your new settings.

Detail set.	Monochrome
Sharpness	0—+—+—7
Contrast	—+—0—+—
Filter effect	N:None
Toning effect	N:None
Default set.	MENU

A

Detail set.	Monochrome
	N:None
	Ye:Yellow
Filter effect	Or:Orange
	R:Red
	G:Green
Default set.	MENU

B

THE PORTRAIT PICTURE STYLE FOR BETTER SKIN TONES

As long as we are talking about picture styles for portraits, there is another style on your T1i that has been tuned specifically for this type of shooting. Oddly enough, it's called Portrait. To set this style on your camera, simply follow the same directions as earlier, except this time select the Portrait style instead of Monochrome. There are also individual options for the Portrait style that, like the Monochrome style, include sharpness and contrast. You can also change the saturation (how intense the colors will be) and color tone, which lets you change the skin tones from more reddish to more yellowish. I prefer brighter colors, so I like to boost the Saturation setting to +2 and leave everything else at the defaults. You won't be able to use the same adjustments for everyone, especially when it comes to color tone, so do some experimenting to see what works best.

DETECT FACES WITH LIVE VIEW

Face detection in digital cameras has been around for a few years, but it's still a new concept in the world of the dSLR. Your T1i has three different autofocus modes for Live View: Quick, Live, and my personal favorite, Face Detection. These modes are different from the standard modes like One Shot, AI Servo, and AI Focus. Face Detection mode is probably the slowest of the Live View focusing modes, so I use it mostly when I am working with a tripod or my subjects are going to remain fairly still. When you turn on Live View with Face Detection focusing, the camera does an amazing thing: it zeroes in on any face appearing on the LCD and places a box around it **(Figure 6.11)**. I'm not sure how it works; it just does.

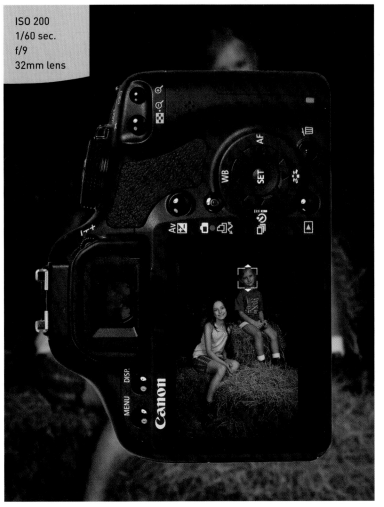

ISO 200
1/60 sec.
f/9
32mm lens

FIGURE 6.11
The Live View Face Detection mode can lock in on your subject's face for easy focusing.

If there is more than one face in the frame, the box will appear over just one of them, but it will have little arrows to the side of it. Just press the Cross key buttons from side to side to make the box jump from one face to the other until you have selected the one that you want to focus on.

Manual Callout

There is a complete chapter in your manual that is dedicated to using Live View mode. It can be found in your manual on pages 105–120.

SETTING UP AND SHOOTING WITH LIVE VIEW AND FACE DETECTION FOCUSING

1. Press the Menu button and use the Main dial to highlight the second camera setup menu screen. Then highlight the Live View function settings option and press the Set button (**A**).

2. Now highlight the Live View shoot option and enable it by pressing Set and then selecting Enable (**B**).

3. Now move down to the AF mode setting at the bottom of the menu, press Set, and select Live Face mode.

4. Press the Menu button to exit the menu mode and get ready for shooting.

5. Activate the Live View function by pressing the Live View button located to the right of the rear LCD screen.

6. Point your camera at a person and watch as the frame appears over the face in the LCD.

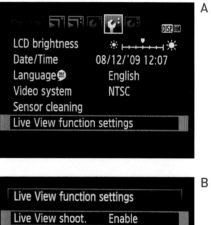

7. Press and hold the ✳ button to focus on the face and wait until you hear the confirmation chirp.

8. Press the shutter button fully to take the photograph.

If you are having difficulty getting a face to focus, you can press the Set button to activate the Live View options and make sure the AF option is highlighted. Then just turn the Main dial to switch from the Face Detection focusing mode to AF Live mode

(**Figure 6.12**). This will bring up a focus point in the center of the screen that you can toggle to a new location.

Live View only works when you are using the modes in the Creative zone, such as Av and Tv. It absolutely will not function in any of the modes in the Basic zone. Also, the Live View menu options can only be changed while working in the Creative zone.

USING LIVE VIEW'S GRID OVERLAY

There is another benefit to using Live View: the Grid overlay. This is a feature that actually places a grid over your image, dividing it into thirds, which can be of great benefit in properly composing your image.

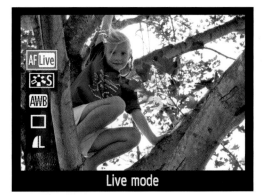

FIGURE 6.12
Change the focus mode if you can't get the camera to detect any faces.

SETTING UP LIVE VIEW'S GRID OPTION

1. Press the Menu button and then use the Main dial to get to the second camera setup screen.

2. Using the Cross keys, scroll down to Live View function settings and press the Set button (**A**).

3. Scroll down to Grid display, press Set, and then choose Grid 1 (**B**).

4. Press the Menu button to return to the main Live View settings and make sure to set the Live View shooting option to Enable (**C**).

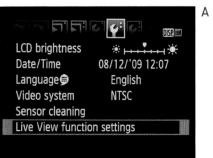

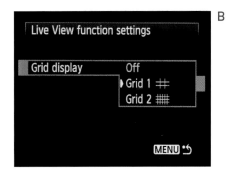

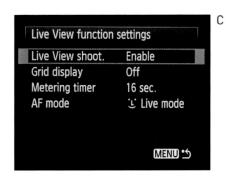

Now, when you activate Live View, you will see the one-third grid overlay superimposed on the rear display (**Figure 6.13**). This effect only shows up on the display and will not be visible in your final image.

FIGURE 6.13
Using Live View's
Grid option can help
you compose your
shots.

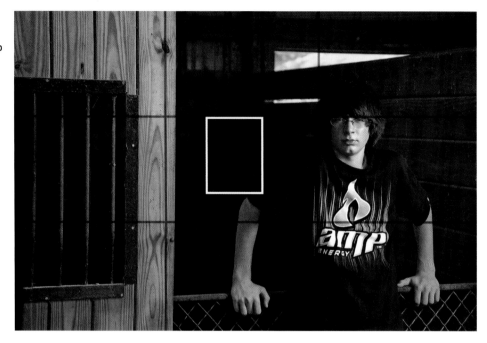

USE FILL FLASH FOR REDUCING SHADOWS

A common problem when taking pictures of people outside, especially during the midday hours, is that the overhead sun can create dark shadows under the eyes and chin. You could have your subject turn his or her face to the sun, but that is usually considered cruel and unusual punishment. So how can you have your subject's back to the sun and still get a decent exposure of the face? Try turning on your flash to fill in the shadows. This also works well when you are photographing someone with a ball cap or someone who has a bright scene behind them (**Figure 6.14**). The fill flash helps lighten the subject so they don't appear in shadow, while providing a really nice catchlight in the eyes.

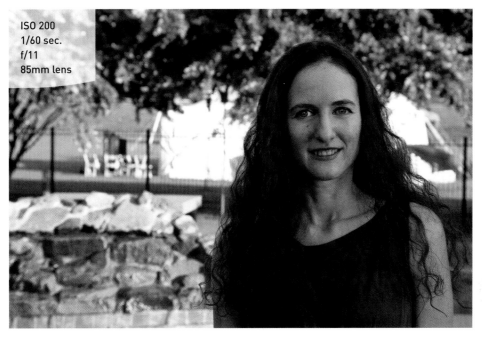

ISO 200
1/60 sec.
f/11
85mm lens

CATCHLIGHT

A *catchlight* is that little sparkle that adds life to the eyes. When you are photographing a person with a light source in front of them, you will usually get a reflection of that light in the eye, be it your flash, the sun, or something else brightly reflecting in the eye. The light is reflected off the surface of the eyes as bright highlights and serves to bring attention to the eyes.

The key to using the flash as a fill is to not use it on full power. If you do, the camera will try to balance the flash with the daylight, and you will get a very flat and featureless face.

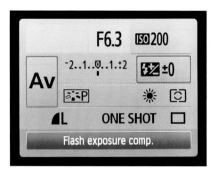

1. Press the pop-up flash button to raise your pop-up flash into the ready position.

2. Press the Set button to activate the Quick Control screen.

3. Use the Cross keys to position the cursor over the Flash Compensation option.

4. Use the Main dial to select the desired amount of flash compensation.

5. Lightly press the shutter release button to exit the Quick Control screen.

One problem that can quickly surface when using the on-camera flash is red-eye. Not to worry, though—we will talk about that in Chapter 8.

PORTRAITS ON THE MOVE

Not all portraits are shot with the subject sitting in a chair, posed and ready for the picture. Sometimes you might want to get an action shot that says something about the person, similar to an environmental portrait. Children, especially, just like to move. Why fight it? Set up an action portrait instead.

For the photo in **Figure 6.15**, I used the Portrait picture style and set my camera to Tv mode. I knew that there would be a good deal of movement involved, and I wanted to make sure that I had a fairly high shutter speed to freeze the action, so I set it to 1/320 of a second. I set the focus mode to AI Servo, the drive mode to Continuous, and just let it rip. There were quite a few throwaway shots, but I was able to capture one that conveyed the energy and action.

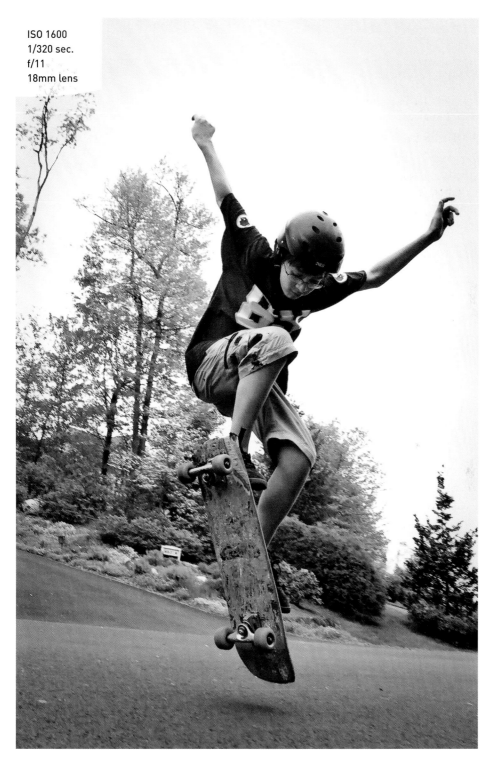

ISO 1600
1/320 sec.
f/11
18mm lens

FIGURE 6.15
A high ISO
allowed me to
use a fast shutter
speed to stop the
action, along with
a small aperture
to increase depth
of field.

TIPS FOR SHOOTING BETTER PORTRAITS

Before we get to the assignments for this chapter, I thought it might be a good idea to leave you with a few extra pointers on shooting portraits that don't necessarily have anything specific to do with your camera. There are entire books that cover things like portrait lighting, posing, and so on. But here are a few pointers that will make your people pics look a lot better.

AVOID THE CENTER OF THE FRAME

This falls under the category of composition. Place your subject to the side of the frame (**Figure 6.16**)—it just looks more interesting than plunking them smack dab in the middle (**Figure 6.17**).

CHOOSE THE RIGHT LENS

Choosing the correct lens can make a huge impact on your portraits. A wide-angle lens can distort features of your subject, which can lead to an unflattering portrait (**Figure 6.18**). Select a longer focal length if you will be close to your subject (**Figure 6.19**).

FIGURE 6.16
Try cropping in a bit, and place the subject's face off center to improve the shot.

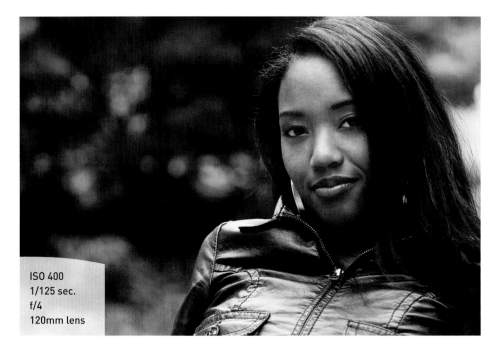

ISO 400
1/125 sec.
f/4
120mm lens

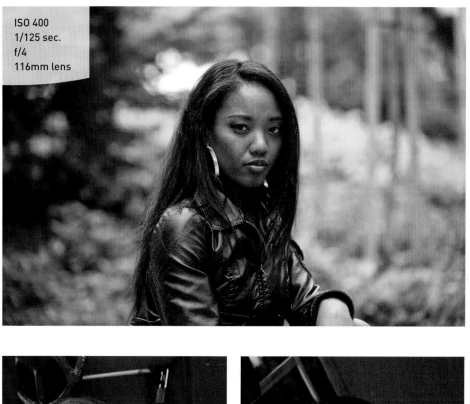

ISO 400
1/125 sec.
f/4
116mm lens

FIGURE 6.17
Having the subject in the middle of the frame with so much empty space on the sides can make for a less-than-interesting portrait.

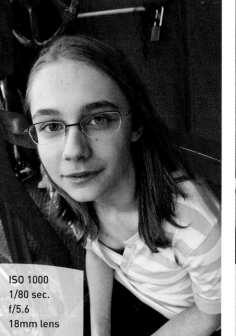

ISO 1000
1/80 sec.
f/5.6
18mm lens

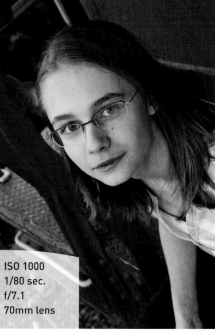

ISO 1000
1/80 sec.
f/7.1
70mm lens

FIGURE 6.18
(left) At this close distance, the 18mm lens is distorting the subject's face.

FIGURE 6.19
(right) By zooming out to 70mm, I am able to remove the distortion for a much better photo.

DON'T CUT THEM OFF AT THE KNEES

There is an old rule about photographing people: never crop the picture at a joint. This means no cropping at the ankles or the knees. If you need to crop at the legs, the proper place to crop is mid-shin or mid-thigh (**Figure 6.20**).

FIGURE 6.20
A good crop for people is when it intersects at mid-shin or mid-thigh.

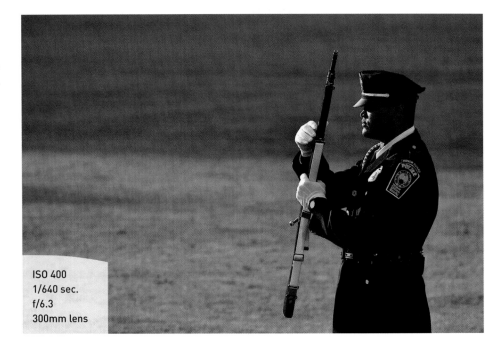

ISO 400
1/640 sec.
f/6.3
300mm lens

USE THE FRAME

Have you ever noticed that most people are taller than they are wide? Turn your camera vertically for a more pleasing composition (**Figure 6.21**).

SUNBLOCK FOR PORTRAITS

The midday sun can be harsh and can do unflattering things to people's faces. If you can, find a shady spot out of the direct sunlight. You will get softer shadows, smoother skin tones, and better detail (**Figure 6.22**). This holds true for overcast skies as well. Just be sure to adjust your white balance accordingly.

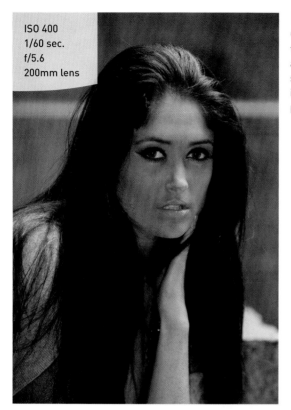

ISO 400
1/60 sec.
f/5.6
200mm lens

FIGURE 6.21
Get in the habit of turning your camera to a vertical position when shooting portraits. This is also referred to as portrait orientation.

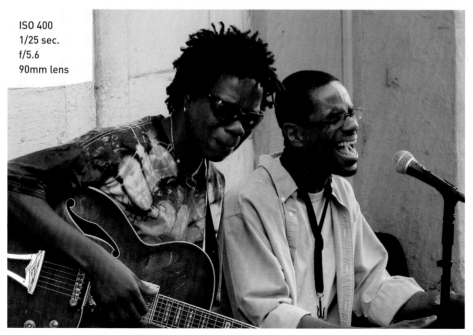

ISO 400
1/25 sec.
f/5.6
90mm lens

FIGURE 6.22
A back alley in the French Quarter provided a shady environment for photographing this pair of musicians.

GIVE THEM A HEALTHY GLOW

Nearly everyone looks better with a warm, healthy glow. Some of the best light of the day happens just a little before sundown, so shoot at that time if you can (**Figure 6.23**).

FIGURE 6.23
You just can't beat the glow of the late afternoon sun for adding warmth to your portraits.

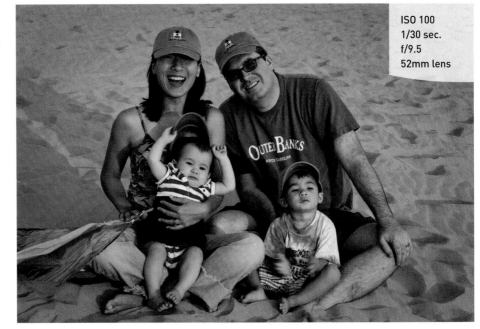

ISO 100
1/30 sec.
f/9.5
52mm lens

KEEP AN EYE ON YOUR BACKGROUND

Sometimes it's so easy to get caught up in taking a great shot that you forget about the smaller details. Try to keep an eye on what is going on behind your subject so they don't end up with things popping out of their heads (**Figures 6.24** and **6.25**).

FRAME THE SCENE

Using elements in the scene to create a frame around your subject is a great way to draw the viewer in. You don't have to use a window frame to do this. Just look for elements in the foreground that could be used to force the viewer's eye toward your subject (**Figure 6.26**).

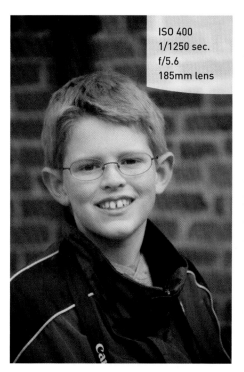

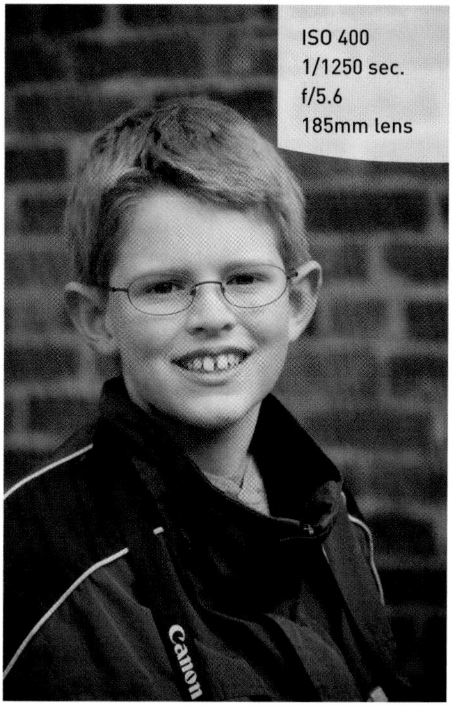

ISO 400
1/1250 sec.
f/5.6
185mm lens

ISO 400
1/1250 sec.
f/5.6
185mm lens

FIGURE 6.24
(left) A downspout in the background is going right into the subject's head.

FIGURE 6.25
(right) By moving the camera position a little to the left, I was able to remove the distracting pipe from the photo.

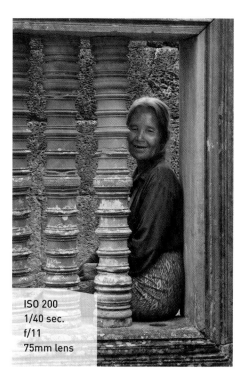

ISO 200
1/40 sec.
f/11
75mm lens

FIGURE 6.26
It wasn't hard to frame this wonderful subject, since she was already sitting in the window. Learn to use the elements of the scene to frame your subject and draw in the viewer's eyes.

GET DOWN ON THEIR LEVEL

If you want better pictures of children, don't shoot from an adult's eye level. Getting the camera down to the child's level will make your images look more personal (**Figure 6.27**).

FIGURE 6.27
Sometimes taking photographs of children means lying on the ground, but the end result is a much better image. (Photo: Suzanne Revell)

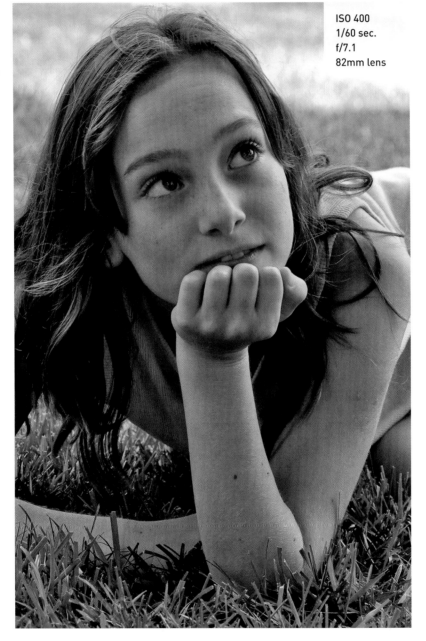

ISO 400
1/60 sec.
f/7.1
82mm lens

ELIMINATE SPACE BETWEEN YOUR SUBJECTS

One of the problems you can encounter when taking portraits of more than one person is that of personal space. What feels like a close distance to the subjects can look impersonal to the viewer. Have your subjects move close together, eliminating any open space between them (**Figure 6.28**).

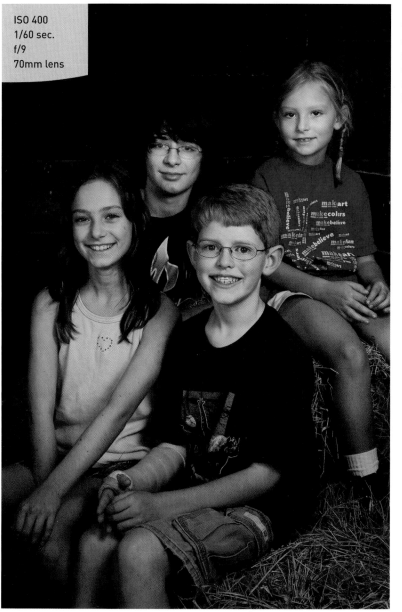

ISO 400
1/60 sec.
f/9
70mm lens

FIGURE 6.28
Getting siblings close together can sometimes be a challenge, but the results are worth the effort.

DON'T BE AFRAID TO GET CLOSE

When you are taking someone's picture, don't be afraid of getting close and filling the frame (**Figure 6.29**). This doesn't mean you have to shoot from a foot away; try zooming in and capture the details.

FIGURE 6.29
Filling the frame with the subject's face can lead to a much more intimate portrait.

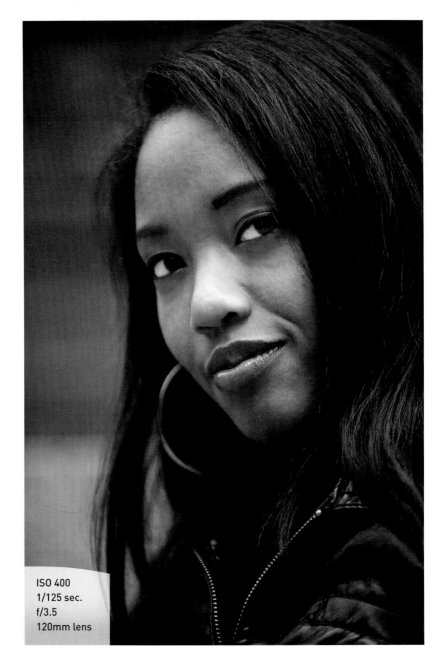

ISO 400
1/125 sec.
f/3.5
120mm lens

Chapter 6 Assignments

Depth of field in portraits

Let's start with something simple. Grab your favorite person and start experimenting with using different aperture settings. Shoot wide open (the widest your lens goes, such as f/2.8 or f/4) and then really stopped down (like f/22). Look at the difference in the depth of field and how it plays an important role in placing the attention on your subject. (Make sure you don't have your subject standing against the background. Give some distance so that there is a good blurring effect of the background at the wide f-stop setting.)

Discovering the qualities of natural light

Pick a nice sunny day and try shooting some portraits in the midday sun. If your subject is willing, have them turn so the sun is in their face. If they are still speaking to you after blinding them, have them turn their back to the sun. Try this with and without the fill flash so you can see the difference. Finally, move them into a completely shaded spot and take a few more.

Picking the right metering method

Find a very dark or light background and place your subject in front of it. Now take a couple of shots, giving a lot of space around your subject for the background to show. Now switch metering modes and use the AE Lock feature to get a more accurate reading of your subject. Notice the differences in exposure between the metering methods.

Picture styles for portraits

Have some fun playing with the different picture styles. Try the Portrait style as compared to the Standard style. Then try out Monochrome and play with the different color filter options to see how they affect skin tones.

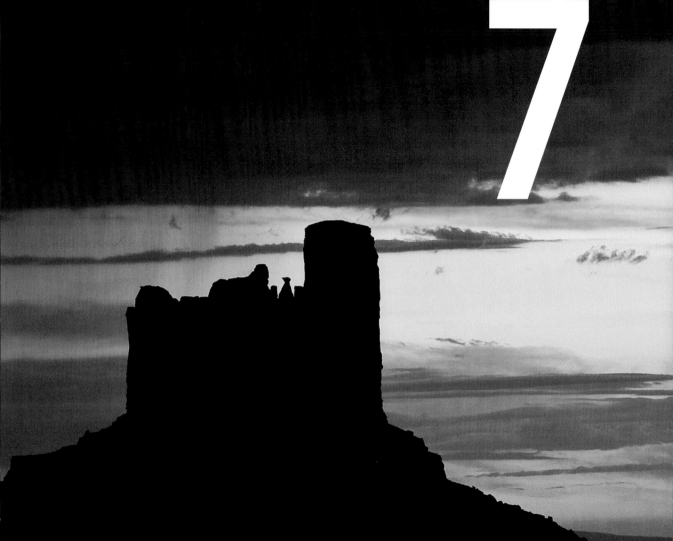

Landscape Photography

TIPS, TOOLS, AND TECHNIQUES TO GET THE MOST OUT OF YOUR LANDSCAPE PHOTOGRAPHY

There has always been something about shooting landscapes that has brought a sense of joy to my photography. It might have something to do with being outdoors and working at the mercy of Mother Nature. Maybe it's the way it challenges me to visualize the landscape and try to capture it with my camera. It truly is a celebration of light, composition, and the world we live in.

In this chapter, we will explore some of the features of the T1i that not only improve the look of your landscape photography, but also make it easier to take great shots. We will also explore some typical scenarios and discuss methods to bring out the best in your landscape work.

PORING OVER THE PICTURE

Sometimes it's necessary to break from the pack and venture down the less-traveled path to find a great shot. This was the case as I drove through Red Rock Canyon with all the other tourists. It's a nice drive, but I was looking for something a little more interesting to shoot. I parked at a trailhead and hiked for about 45 minutes into Ice Box Canyon where I found this great location.

Using the Shade white balance setting corrected for the bluish color cast in the shadow areas.

For maximum sharpness I used a tripod and a very small aperture setting.

A wide-angle lens was needed to capture all of the elements in the scene.

Due to all of the changing light levels, I bracketed my exposures until I found one that balanced the bright areas in the background with the darker foreground elements.

ISO 100
1.3 sec.
f/22
12mm lens

PORING OVER THE PICTURE

While my buddies Scott and Jeff soared overhead in a hot air balloon over the Dubai landscape, I hung out with the ground support team. We made several stops as we tracked the balloon overhead. At one particular stop I noticed these great looking trees with a small town and the mountains in the background. It was early morning and the sun was painting the scene with a great warm light that I just couldn't resist.

The composition of the elements in the scene gives a feeling of depth.

Although most landscape images aren't shot with a telephoto lens, it was the right tool for capturing all of the elements in this image.

ISO 400
1/250 sec.
f/6.3
200mm lens

The Landscape picture style added warmth and contrast to the scene.

The tree in the foreground was my source for focus in the image.

SHARP AND IN FOCUS: USING TRIPODS

Throughout the previous chapters we have concentrated on using the camera to create great images. We will continue that trend through this chapter, but there is one additional piece of equipment that is crucial in the world of landscape shooting: the tripod. Tripods are critical to your landscape work for a couple of reasons. The first relates to the time of day that you will be working. For reasons that will be explained later, the best light for most landscape work happens at sunrise and just before sunset. While this is the best time to shoot, it's also kind of dark. That means you'll be working with slow shutter speeds. Slow shutter speeds mean camera shake. Camera shake equals bad photos.

The second reason is also related to the amount of light that you're gathering with your camera. When taking landscape photos, you will usually want to be working with very small apertures, as they give you lots of depth of field (DOF). This also means that, once again, you will be working with slower-than-normal shutter speeds.

Slow shutter = camera shake = bad photos.

Do you see the pattern here? The one tool in your arsenal to truly defeat the camera shake issue and ensure tack-sharp photos is a good tripod (**Figure 7.1**).

FIGURE 7.1
A sturdy tripod is the key to sharp landscape photos. (Photo: Scott Kelby)

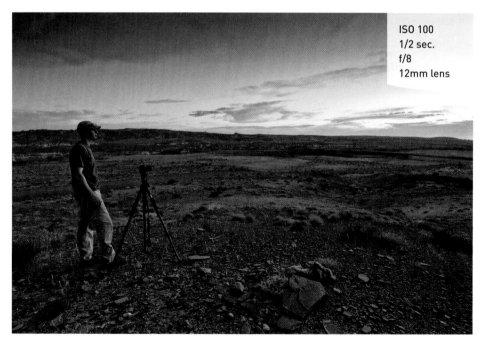

ISO 100
1/2 sec.
f/8
12mm lens

So what should you look for in a tripod? Well, first make sure it is sturdy enough to support your camera and any lens that you might want to use. Next, check the height of the tripod. Your day will end much better if you haven't been bent over all day to look through your viewfinder. Finally, think about getting a tripod that utilizes a quick-release head. This usually employs a plate that screws into the bottom of the camera and then quickly snaps into place on the tripod. This will be especially handy if you are going to move between shooting by hand and using the tripod. You can find more info on tripods in the bonus chapter.

TRIPOD STABILITY

Most tripods have a center column that allows the user to extend the height of the camera above the point where the tripod legs join together. This might seem like a great idea, but the reality is that the further you raise that column, the less stable your tripod becomes. Think of a tall building that sways near the top. To get the most solid base for your camera, always try to use it with the center column at its lowest point so that your camera is right at the apex of the tripod legs.

IS LENSES AND TRIPODS DON'T MIX

If you are using image stabilization (IS) lenses on your camera, remember to turn this feature off when you use a tripod (**Figure 7.2**). This is because the image stabilization can, while trying to minimize camera movement, actually *create* movement when the camera is already stable. To turn off the IS feature, just slide the Stabilizer selector switch on the side of the lens to the Off position.

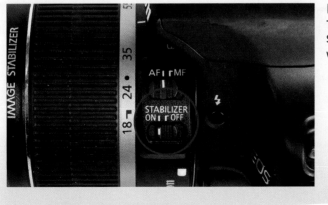

FIGURE 7.2
Turn off the Image Stabilization feature when using a tripod.

USING A-DEP TO MAXIMIZE DEPTH OF FIELD

 As discussed in Chapter 4, A-DEP is what I would refer to as an advanced automatic mode. The camera evaluates the distance of objects in the viewfinder and then determines the proper aperture setting to render everything in focus. It is automatic because it requires no input from the camera operator, but it is advanced because it is not just trying to select the maximum aperture as with the Landscape mode in the Basic zone.

Take a look at **Figure 7.3** and let's see what A-DEP is thinking.

There were two main subjects in the image of Monument Valley. The large mesa on the left could be considered the main subject, but the buttes in the distance are of equal importance to me. There was quite a bit of distance between these two subjects, so quite a bit of depth of field was necessary to give sharp focus to each of them.

Using the A-DEP mode, the camera would utilize the autofocus information to evaluate the distance of the rock formations in the foreground as well as the buttes in the background. While checking the subjects' distances, it would also be gathering information on the available light levels. Based on all of this data, it would determine that an exposure of f/8 at 1/60 of a second with an ISO of 100 is the proper setting to make all of the subjects appear in focus. The aperture setting is dependent upon the lens you are using.

FIGURE 7.3
A-DEP looks at objects in the foreground and background and selects an aperture to give enough depth of field to keep the scene looking sharp and in focus.

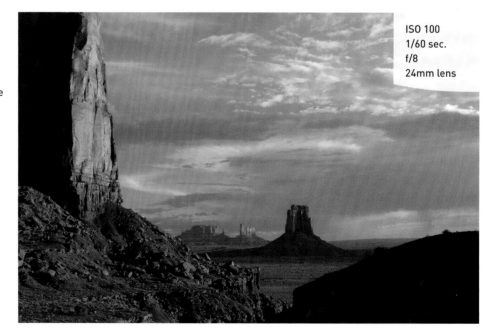

ISO 100
1/60 sec.
f/8
24mm lens

The problem with A-DEP is the control factor: you really have none. If the mode calls for an exposure of more than 30 seconds, you have no choice except to raise your ISO. If the shutter speed should be greater than 1/4000 of a second, then you have to lower the ISO. Considering the limitations of this mode, it might best be used as an evaluation of the scene and exposure. Think of it as asking the camera for its opinion.

SELECTING THE PROPER ISO

One of the downfalls of A-DEP mode is the use of ISO to change exposure settings. When shooting most landscape scenes, the ISO is the one factor that should only be changed as a last resort. While it is easy to select a higher ISO to get a smaller aperture, the noise that it can introduce into your images can be quite harmful (**Figures 7.4** and **7.5**). The noise is not only visible as large grainy artifacts, it can also be multicolored, which further degrades the image quality. Take a look at the image in Figure 7.4, which was taken with an ISO of 1600. The purpose was to shorten the shutter speed and still use a small aperture setting of f/22. The problem is that the noise level is so high that, in addition to being distracting, it is obscuring fine details in the canyon wall.

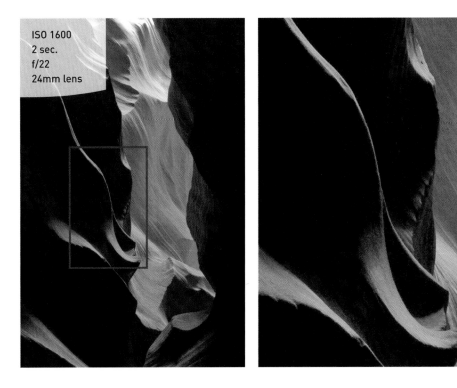

ISO 1600
2 sec.
f/22
24mm lens

FIGURE 7.4
(left) A high ISO setting created a lot of digital noise in the shadows.

FIGURE 7.5
(right) When the image is enlarged, the noise is even more apparent.

Now check out another image that was taken in the same canyon light but with a much lower ISO setting (**Figures 7.6** and **7.7**). As you can see, the noise levels are much lower, which means that my blacks look black, and the fine details are beautifully captured.

FIGURE 7.6
By lowering the ISO to 100, I was able to avoid the noise and capture a clean image.

FIGURE 7.7
Zooming in shows that the noise levels for this image are almost nonexistent.

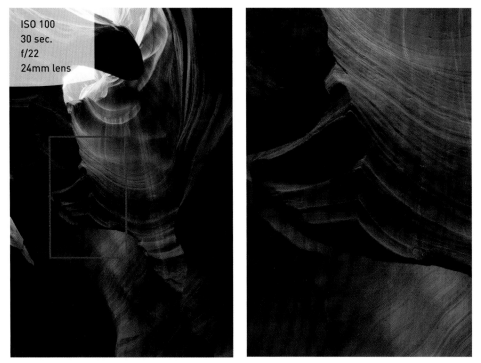

ISO 100
30 sec.
f/22
24mm lens

When shooting landscapes, set your ISO to the lowest possible setting at all times. Between the use of image stabilization lenses (if you are shooting handheld) and a good tripod, there should be few circumstances where you would need to shoot landscapes with anything above an ISO of 400.

USING NOISE REDUCTION

Both canyon images were taken with a tripod, but the image set to an ISO of 100 required four times the shutter speed duration (30 seconds at ISO 100) of the high ISO image (2 seconds at ISO 1600). The temptation to use higher ISOs should always be avoided, as the end result will be more image noise and less detail.

There can be an issue when using a low ISO setting: the sometimes-lengthy shutter speeds can also introduce noise. This noise is a result of the heating of the camera sensor as it is being exposed to light. This effect is not visible in short exposures, but as you start shooting with shutter speeds that exceed one second, the level of image noise can increase. Your camera has a couple of features that you can turn on to combat noise from long exposures and high ISOs.

SETTING UP NOISE REDUCTION

1. Press the Menu button, then use the Main dial to get to the Custom Functions menu (**A**).

2. Using the Cross keys, select C. Fn II: Image 5, and then press the Set button (**B**). The default setting is Standard but you may require the Strong setting for really high ISO settings.

3. Press the Menu button to return to the Custom Functions menu and then select screen 4, Long exp. noise reduction. Press the Set button to change the options. The default setting is Auto, which will handle most scenarios. If you know you are going to be making extremely long exposures you should probably go ahead and set it to On (**C**).

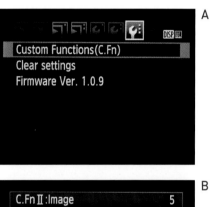

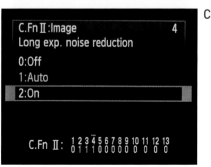

SELECTING A WHITE BALANCE

This probably seems like a no-brainer. If it's sunny, select Daylight. If it's overcast, choose the Shade or Cloudy setting. Those choices wouldn't be wrong for those circumstances, but why limit yourself? Sometimes you can change the mood of the photo by selecting a white balance that doesn't quite fit the light for the scene that you are shooting. **Figure 7.8** is an example of a correct white balance. It was late afternoon and the sun was starting to move low in the sky, giving everything that warm afternoon glow. The white balance for this image was set to Daylight. But what if I want to make the scene look like it was shot in the early morning hours? Simple; I just change the white balance to Fluorescent, which is a much cooler setting (**Figure 7.9**).

You can select the most appropriate white balance for your shooting conditions in a couple of ways. The first is to just take a shot, review it on the LCD, and keep the one you like. Of course, you would need to take one for each white balance setting, which means that you will have to take about seven different shots to see which is most pleasing. The second method, and my personal favorite, doesn't require taking a single shot. Instead, it uses Live View to get perfectly selected white balances. Live View gives instant feedback as you scroll through all of the white balance settings and displays them for you right on the LCD. Even better, you can choose a custom setting that will let you dial in exactly the right look for your image. To use Live View, you must first activate it in the menu system (as described in Chapter 6).

FIGURE 7.8
Using the "proper" white balance yields predictable results.

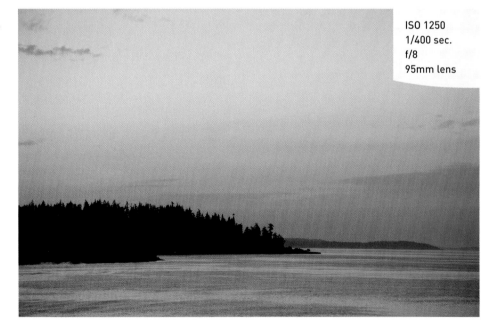

ISO 1250
1/400 sec.
f/8
95mm lens

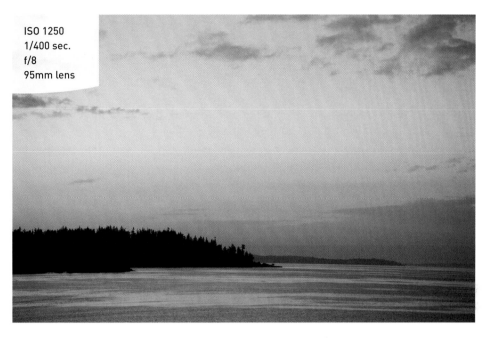

ISO 1250
1/400 sec.
f/8
95mm lens

FIGURE 7.9
Changing the white
balance to Fluo-
rescent gives the
impression that the
picture was taken
at a different time
of day than it really
was.

USING LIVE VIEW TO PREVIEW DIFFERENT WHITE BALANCE SETTINGS

1. Press the Live View button located to the right of the rear LCD screen.

2. With Live View activated, press the Set button, which will bring up the Live View options on the left side of the screen.

3. Use the up/down Cross keys to high-light the White Balance icon and then rotate the Main dial to change the white balance.

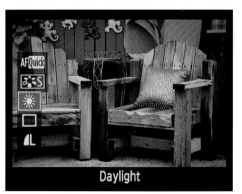

4. Select the white balance setting that looks most appropriate for your scene, then press the Set button to lock in your change and resume shooting.

5. Press the Live View button once again to exit Live View mode.

USING THE LANDSCAPE PICTURE STYLE

When shooting landscapes, I always look for great color and contrast. This is one of the reasons that so many landscape shots are taken in the early morning or during sunset. The light is much more vibrant and colorful at these times of day and adds a sense of drama to an image. You can help boost this effect, especially in the less-than-golden hours of the day, by using the Landscape picture style (**Figure 7.10**). Just as in the Landscape mode found in the Basic zone, you can set up your landscape shooting so that you capture images with increased sharpness and a slight boost in blues and greens. This style will add some pop to your landscapes without the need for additional processing in any software.

FIGURE 7.10
Using the Landscape picture style can add sharpness and more vivid color to skies and vegetation.

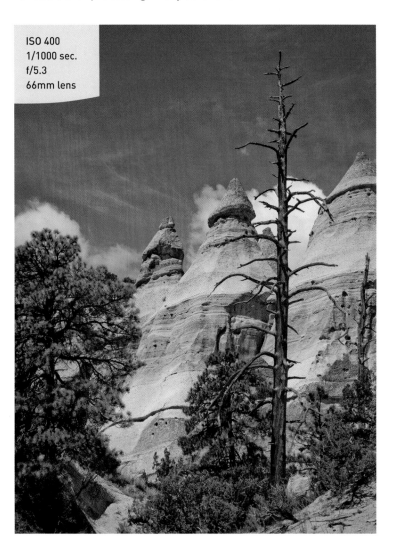

ISO 400
1/1000 sec.
f/5.3
66mm lens

SETTING UP THE LANDSCAPE PICTURE STYLE

1. Press your Menu button, and then rotate the Main dial to the second shooting menu.

2. Use the Cross keys to navigate down the menu list until you get to Picture Style, then press the Set button (**A**).

3. Use the down Cross key to highlight the Landscape setting and then press the Set button to lock in your change (**B**).

TAMING BRIGHT SKIES WITH EXPOSURE COMPENSATION

Balancing exposure in scenes that have a wide contrast in tonal ranges can be extremely challenging. The one thing you should try not to do is overexpose your skies to the point of blowing out your highlights (unless, of course, that is the look you are going for). It's one thing to have white clouds, but it's a completely different and bad thing to have no detail at all in those clouds. This usually happens when the camera is trying to gain exposure in the darker areas of the image (**Figure 7.11**).

The one way to tell if you have blown out your highlights is to check the Highlight Alert, or "blinkies," feature on your camera (see the "How I Shoot" section in Chapter 4). When you take a shot where the highlights are exposed beyond the point of having any detail, that area will blink in your LCD display. It is up to you to determine if that particular area is important enough to regain detail by altering your exposure. If the answer is yes, then the easiest way to go about it is to use some exposure compensation.

With this feature, you can force your camera to choose an exposure that ranges, in 1/3-stop increments, from two stops over to two stops under the metered exposure (**Figure 7.12**).

FIGURE 7.11
The trees in the foreground are well exposed, but the hoodoos in the sun have no detail whatsoever.

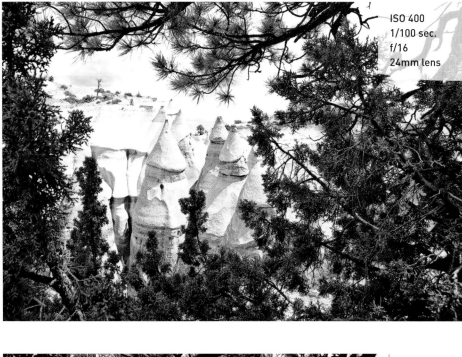

ISO 400
1/100 sec.
f/16
24mm lens

FIGURE 7.12
A compensation of 1 1/3 stops of underexposure brought back the detail in the highlights.

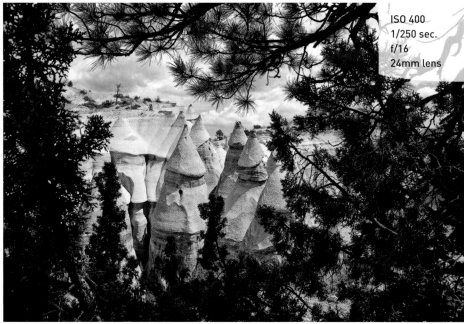

ISO 400
1/250 sec.
f/16
24mm lens

USING EXPOSURE COMPENSATION TO REGAIN DETAIL IN HIGHLIGHTS

1. Activate the camera meter by lightly pressing the shutter release button.

2. Press the Set button to activate the Quick Control screen.

3. Use the Cross keys to highlight the Exposure Compensation setting.

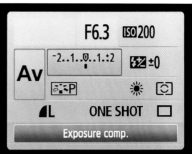

4. Rotate the Main dial to reduce your exposure by 1/3-stop increments and then take another photo.

5. If the blinkies are gone, you are good to go. If not, keep subtracting from your exposure by 1/3 of a stop until you have a good exposure in the highlights.

I generally keep my camera set to −1/3 stop for most of my landscape work unless I am working with a location that is very dark or low key.

HIGH-KEY AND LOW-KEY IMAGES

When you hear someone refer to a subject as being *high-key*, it usually means that the entire image is composed of a very bright subject with very few shadow areas—think snow or beach. It makes sense, then, that a *low-key* subject has very few highlight areas and a predominance of shadow areas. Think of a cityscape at night as an example of a low-key photo.

SHOOTING BEAUTIFUL BLACK AND WHITE LANDSCAPES

There is nothing as timeless as a beautiful black and white landscape photo. For many, it is the purest form of photography. The genre conjures up thoughts of Ansel Adams out in Yosemite Valley, capturing stunning monoliths with his 8x10 view camera. Well, just because you are shooting with a digital camera doesn't mean you can't create your own stunning photos using the power of the Monochrome picture style. (See the "Classic Black and White Portraits" section of Chapter 6 for instructions on setting up this feature.) Not only can you shoot in black and white, you can also apply built-in filters to lighten or darken different elements within your scene, as well as add contrast and definition.

The four filter colors are red, yellow, green, and orange. The most typically used filters in black and white photography are red and yellow. This is because the color of the filter will darken opposite colors and lighten similar colors. So if you want to darken a blue sky, you would use a yellow filter because blue is the opposite of yellow. To darken green foliage, you would use a red filter. Check out the series of shots in **Figure 7.13** with different filters applied.

You can see that there is no real difference in contrast between the color and the black and white image with no filter. The green filter has the effect of darkening the skies slightly and giving a significantly lighter look to the vegetation. Using the Orange filter makes the vegetation lighter but darkens the sky. For this particular shot, I much prefer the look of the darkened skies.

Other options in the Monochrome picture style enable you to adjust the sharpness, contrast, and even add some color toning to the final image. This information is also in the "Classic Black and White Portraits" section of Chapter 6. I like to have Sharpness set to 5 and Contrast set to 1 for my landscape images. This gives an overall look to the black and white image that is reminiscent of the classic black and white films. Experiment with the various settings to find the combination that is most pleasing to you.

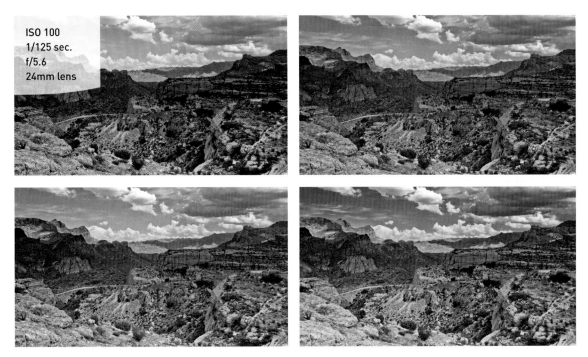

ISO 100
1/125 sec.
f/5.6
24mm lens

FIGURE 7.13

Adding color filter settings to the Monochrome picture style allows you to brighten or darken elements in your scene. The top right image has no filter applied to it. The bottom left has a green filter, and the bottom right has an orange filter.

THE GOLDEN LIGHT

If you ask any professional landscape photographer what their favorite time of day to shoot is, chances are they will tell you it's the hours surrounding daybreak and sunset (**Figures 7.14** and **7.15**). The reason for this is that the light is coming from a very low angle to the landscape, which creates shadows and gives depth and character. There is also a quality to the light that seems cleaner and is more colorful than the light you get when shooting at midday. One thing that can dramatically improve any morning or evening shot is the presence of clouds. The sun will fill the underside of the clouds with a palette of colors and add drama to your skies.

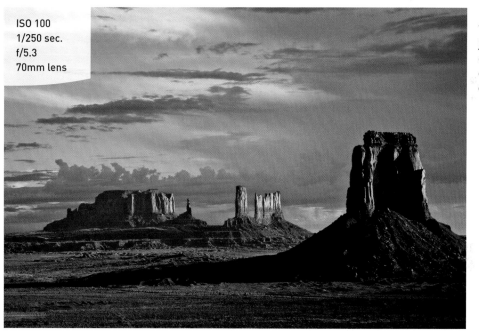

ISO 100
1/250 sec.
f/5.3
70mm lens

FIGURE 7.14
The few minutes just prior to sunrise can add great colors to a partly cloudy sky.

WARM AND COOL COLOR TEMPERATURES

These two terms are used to describe the overall colorcast of an image. Reds and yellows are said to be *warm*, which is usually the look that you get from the late afternoon sun. Blue is usually the predominant color when talking about a *cool* cast.

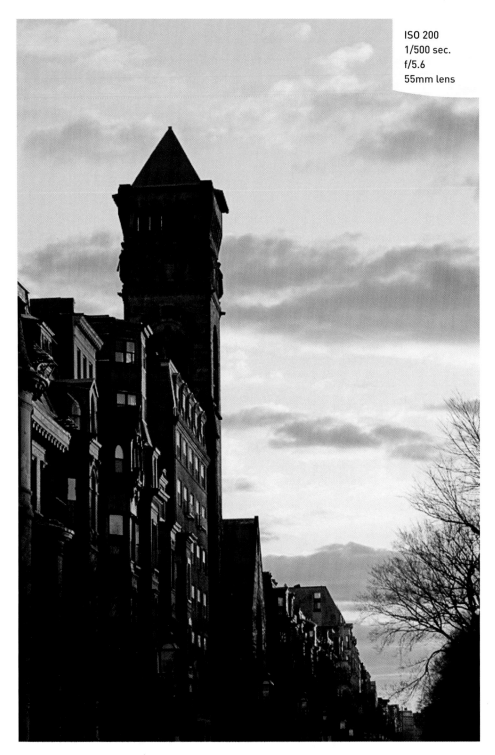

FIGURE 7.15
Late afternoon sun is usually warmer and adds drama and warmth to the clouds.

ISO 200
1/500 sec.
f/5.6
55mm lens

WHERE TO FOCUS

Large landscape scenes are great fun to photograph, but they can present a problem: where exactly do you focus when you want everything to be sharp? Since our goal is to create a great landscape photo, we will need to concentrate on how to best create an image that is tack sharp, with a depth of field that renders great focus throughout the scene.

I have already stressed the importance of a good tripod when shooting landscapes. The tripod lets you concentrate on the aperture portion of the exposure without worrying how long your shutter will be open. This is because the tripod provides the stability to handle any shutter speed you might need when shooting at small apertures. I find that for most of my landscape work I set my camera to Aperture Priority mode and the ISO to 100 (for a clean, noise-free image).

However, shooting with the smallest aperture on your lens doesn't necessarily mean that you will get the proper sharpness throughout your image. The real key is knowing where in the scene to focus your lens to maximize the depth of field for your chosen aperture. To do this, you must utilize something called the "hyper focal distance" of your lens.

Hyper focal distance, also referred to as HFD, is the point of focus that will give you the greatest acceptable sharpness from a point near your camera all the way out to infinity. If you combine good HFD practice in combination with a small aperture, you will get images that are sharp to infinity.

There are a couple of ways to do this, and the one that is probably the easiest, as you might guess, is the one that is most widely used by working pros. When you have your shot all set up and composed, focus on an object that is about one-third of the distance into your frame (**Figure 7.16**). It is usually pretty close to the proper distance

TACK SHARP

Here's one of those terms that photographers like to throw around. *Tack sharp* refers not only to the focus of an image but also the overall sharpness of the image. This usually means that there is excellent depth of field in terms of sharp focus for all elements in the image. It also means that there is no sign of camera shake, which can give soft edges to subjects that should look nice and crisp. To get your images tack sharp, use a small depth of field, don't forget your tripod, use the self-timer to activate the shutter if no cable release is handy, and practice achieving good hyper focal distance (HFD) when picking your point of focus.

and will render favorable results. When you have the focus set, use your Depth of Field preview button to check the sharpness of all the objects in your scene. The button is located just under the lens release button and is activated once you have depressed the shutter button partway (**Figure 7.17**).

FIGURE 7.16
To get maximum focus from near to far, the focus was set one-third of the way down the bridge. I then recomposed before taking the picture. Using this point of focus with an aperture of f/14 gave me a sharply focused image all the way back to the distant building. This is another excellent place to use the One Shot focus mode as well.

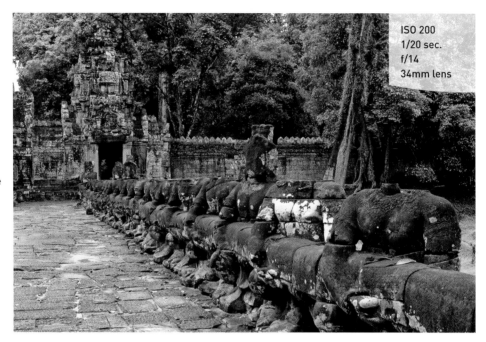

ISO 200
1/20 sec.
f/14
34mm lens

FIGURE 7.17
Using the Depth of Field preview button can help you ensure that the image is sharp.

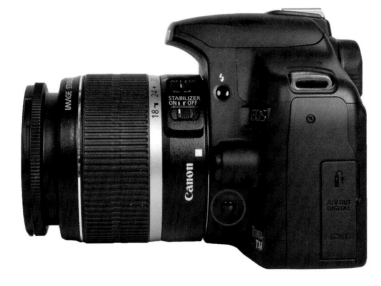

When the Depth of Field preview button is depressed, it will cause the lens to stop down to the selected aperture and let you preview the depth of field directly through your viewfinder. You can also use this feature during Live View mode to see the depth of field directly on your LCD display.

One thing to remember is that as your lens gets wider in focal length, your HFD will be closer to the camera position. This is because the wider the lens, the greater depth of field you can achieve. This is yet another reason why a good wide angle lens is indispensable to the landscape shooter.

EASIER FOCUSING

There's no denying that the automatic focus features on the T1i are great, but sometimes it just pays to turn them off and go manual. This is especially true if you are shooting on a tripod: once you have your shot composed in the viewfinder and you are ready to focus, chances are that the area you want to focus on is not going to be in the area of one of the focus points. Often this is the case when you have a foreground element that is fairly low in the frame. You could use a single focus point set low in your viewfinder and then pan the camera down until it rests on your subject. But then you would have to press the shutter button halfway to focus the camera and then try to recompose and lock down the tripod. It's no easy task.

But you can have the best of both worlds by having the camera focus for you, then switching to manual focus to comfortably recompose your shot (**Figure 7.18**).

GETTING FOCUSED WHILE USING A TRIPOD

1. Set up your shot and find the area that you want to focus on.
2. Pan your tripod head so that your active focus point is on that spot.
3. Press the shutter button halfway to focus the camera and then remove your finger from the button.
4. Switch the camera to manual focus by sliding the switch on the lens barrel from AF to MF.
5. Recompose the composition on the tripod and then take the shot.

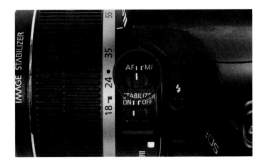

The camera will fire without trying to refocus the lens. This works especially well for wide-angle lenses, which can be difficult to focus in manual mode.

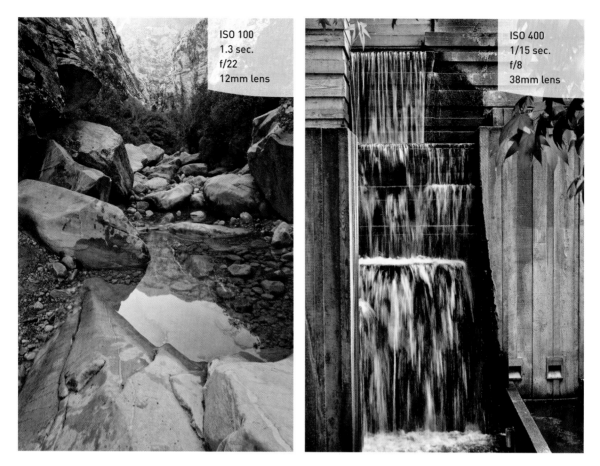

ISO 100
1.3 sec.
f/22
12mm lens

ISO 400
1/15 sec.
f/8
38mm lens

FIGURE 7.18
Using the DOF one-third rule, I focused on the rock bed in front of the boulder, then switched the lens to manual focus before recomposing for the final shot.

FIGURE 7.19
I actually handheld this shot thanks to the Image Stabilization feature of the lens. If the exposure were any longer I would have definitely needed a tripod.

MAKING WATER FLUID

There's nothing quite as satisfying for the landscape shooter as capturing a silky water-fall shot. Creating the smooth-flowing effect is as simple as adjusting your shutter speed to allow the water to be in motion while the shutter is open. The key is to have your camera on a stable platform (such as a tripod) so that you can use a shutter speed that's long enough to work (**Figure 7.19**). To achieve a great effect, use a shutter speed that is at least 1/15 of a second or longer.

SETTING UP FOR A WATERFALL SHOT

1. Attach the camera to your tripod, then compose and focus your shot.

2. Make sure the ISO is set to 100.

3. Using Av mode, set your aperture to the smallest opening (such as f/22 or f/36).

4. Press the shutter button halfway so the camera takes a meter reading.

5. Check to see if the shutter speed is 1/15 or slower.

6. Take a photo and then check the image on the LCD.

If the water is blinking on the LCD, indicating a loss of detail in the highlights, then use the Exposure Compensation feature (as discussed earlier in this chapter) to bring details back into the waterfall. You will need to have the Highlight Alert feature turned on to check for overexposure (see "How I Shoot" in Chapter 4).

There is a possibility that you will not be able to have a shutter speed that is long enough to capture a smooth, silky effect, especially if you are shooting in bright day-light conditions. To overcome this obstacle, you need a filter for your lens—either a polarizing filter or a neutral density filter. The polarizing filter redirects wavelengths of light to create more vibrant colors, reduce reflections, and darken blue skies. It is a handy filter for landscape work (**Figure 7.20**). The neutral density filter is typically just a dark piece of glass that serves to darken the scene by one, two, or three stops. This allows you to use slower shutter speeds during bright conditions. Think of it as sunglasses for your camera lens. You will find more discussion on filters in the bonus chapter.

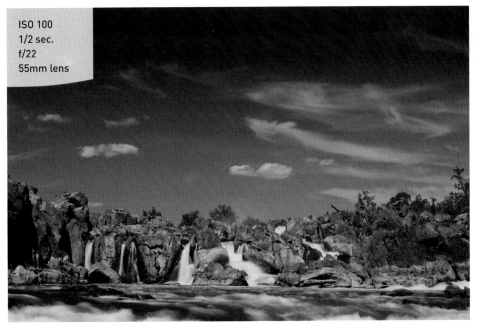

ISO 100
1/2 sec.
f/22
55mm lens

FIGURE 7.20
I used a polarizing filter to add two stops of exposure, thus allowing for a longer exposure time under the midday sun. I got the added benefit of darkening the blue sky.

DIRECTING THE VIEWER: A WORD ABOUT COMPOSITION

As a photographer, it's your job to lead the viewer through your image. You accomplish this by utilizing the principles of composition, which is the arrangement of elements in the scene that draws the viewer's eye through your image and holds their attention. As the director of this viewing, you need to understand how people see, and then use that information to focus their attention on the most important elements in your image.

There is a general order at which we look at elements in a photograph. The first is brightness. The eye wants to travel to the brightest object within a scene. So if you have a bright sky, it's probably the first place the eye will travel to. The second order of attention is sharpness. Sharp, detailed elements will get more attention than soft, blurry areas. Finally, the eye will move to vivid colors while leaving the dull, flat colors for last. It is important to know these essentials in order to grab—and keep—the viewer's attention and then direct them through the frame.

In **Figure 7.21**, the eye is drawn to the bright white cloud in the middle of the frame. From there, it is pulled toward the sharpness and color of the large boulder that is anchoring the lower-left portion of the image. The eye moves around the curved section of stone at the bottom of the frame, where it is then lifted back up to the sky and clouds, right back to the beginning. The elements within the image all help to keep the eye moving but never leave the frame.

RULE OF THIRDS

There are, in fact, quite a few philosophies concerning composition. The easiest one to begin with is known as the "rule of thirds." Using this principle, you simply divide your viewfinder into thirds by imagining two horizontal and two vertical lines that divide the frame equally.

The key to using this method of composition is to have your main subject located at or near one of the intersecting points (**Figure 7.22**).

By placing your subject near these intersecting lines, you are giving the viewer space to move within the frame. The one thing you don't want to do is place your subject smack dab in the middle of the frame. This is sometimes referred to as "bull's eye" composition, and it requires the right subject matter for it to work. It's not always wrong, but it will usually be less appealing and may not hold the viewer's focus.

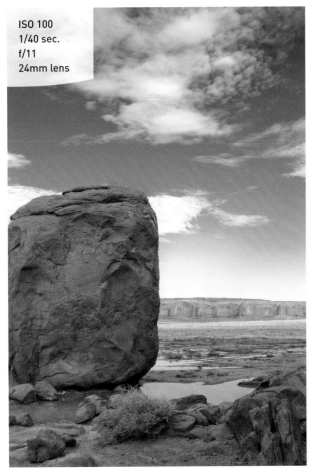

ISO 100
1/40 sec.
f/11
24mm lens

FIGURE 7.21
The composition of the elements pulls the viewer's eyes around the image, leading from one element to the next in a circular pattern.

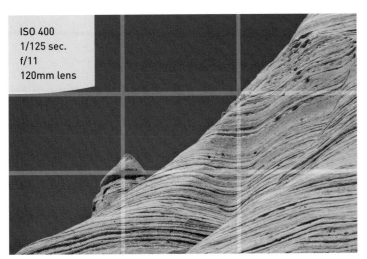

ISO 400
1/125 sec.
f/11
120mm lens

FIGURE 7.22
Placing the small hoodoo in the lower-left portion of the image creates a much more interesting com-position than having it dead center in the frame.

Speaking of the middle of the frame: the other general rule of thirds deals with horizon lines. Generally speaking, you should position the horizon one third of the way up or down in the frame. Splitting the frame in half by placing your horizon in the middle of the picture is akin to placing the subject in the middle of the frame; it doesn't lend a sense of importance to either the sky or the ground.

In **Figure 7.23**, I incorporated the rule of thirds by aligning my horizon in the bottom third of the frame and the mountains near the top third. I have also placed the large tree in the foreground at one of the intersecting lines and the peak of one of the mountains in another. I achieved this by choosing the right focal length (in this case, it was 200mm) and by moving my camera position until I had all of the key elements in the right place.

FIGURE 7.23
Placing the horizon of this image at the bottom third of the frame places emphasis on the subjects above it— the large tree and the mountains.

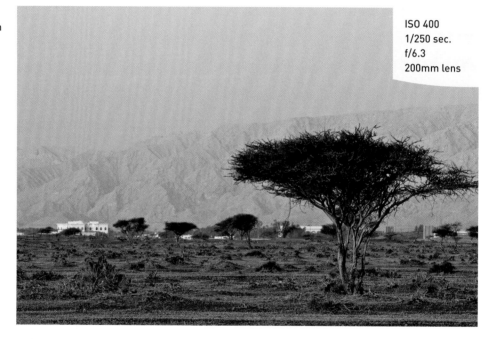

ISO 400
1/250 sec.
f/6.3
200mm lens

CREATING DEPTH

Because a photograph is a flat, two-dimensional space, you need to create a sense of depth by using the elements in the scene to create a three-dimensional feel. This is accomplished by including different and distinct spaces for the eye to travel: a foreground, middle ground, and background. By using these three spaces, you draw the viewer in and render depth to your image.

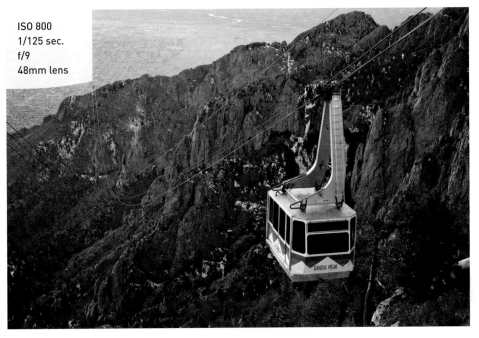

ISO 800
1/125 sec.
f/9
48mm lens

FIGURE 7.24
The tramway car,
mountainside, and
valley floor all add
to the feeling of
depth in the image.

The view from the top of Sandia Peak in Albuquerque, New Mexico, shown in
Figure 7.24, illustrates this well. The tramway car strongly defines the foreground
area. The darker area of the mountainside is strongly defining the middle ground,
and the valley in the top left is adding greater depth.

ADVANCED TECHNIQUES TO EXPLORE

This section comes with a warning attached. All of the techniques and topics up to
this point have been centered on your camera. The following two sections, covering
panoramas and high dynamic range (HDR) images, require you to use image-processing software to complete the photograph. They are, however, important enough that
you should know how to correctly shoot for success, should you choose to explore
these two popular techniques.

SHOOTING PANORAMAS

If you have ever visited the Grand Canyon, you know just how large and wide open it truly is—so much so that it would be difficult to capture its splendor in just one frame. The same can be said for a mountain range, or a cityscape, or any extremely wide vista. There are two methods that you can use to capture the feeling of this type of scene.

THE "FAKE" PANORAMA

The first method is to shoot as wide as you can, and then crop out the top and bottom portion of the frame. Panoramic images are generally two or three times wider than a normal image.

CREATING A FAKE PANORAMA

1. To create the look of the panorama, find your widest lens focal length. In my case, it would be the 18mm setting on the 18–55mm kit lens.

2. Using the guidelines discussed earlier in the chapter, compose and focus your scene, and select the smallest aperture possible.

3. Shoot your image. That's all there is to it, from a photography standpoint.

4. Then, open the image in your favorite image-processing software and crop the extraneous foreground and sky from the image, leaving you with a wide panorama of the scene.

Figure 7.25 shows an example using a photo taken in Harpers Ferry, West Virginia.

As you can see, the image was shot with a very wide perspective, using an 18mm lens. It's not a terrible photo, but it lacks impact and suffers from poor composition. This isn't a problem, though, because it was shot for the purpose of creating a "fake" panorama. Now look at the same image, cropped for panoramic view (**Figure 7.26**). As you can see, it makes a huge difference in the image and gives much higher visual impact by reducing the uninteresting foreground and background, drawing your eyes across the length of the image.

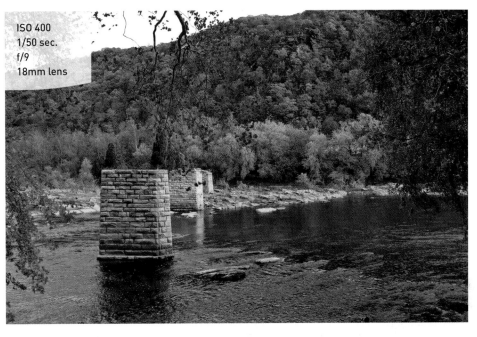

ISO 400
1/50 sec.
f/9
18mm lens

FIGURE 7.25
This is an okay image, but it lacks visual impact.

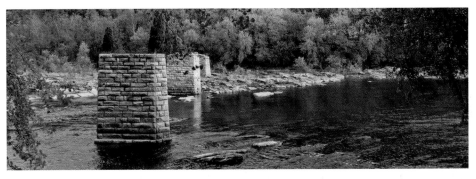

FIGURE 7.26
Cropping adds more visual impact and makes for a more appealing image.

THE MULTIPLE-IMAGE PANORAMA

The reason the previous method is sometimes referred to as a "fake" panorama is because it is made with a standard-size frame and then cropped down to a narrow perspective. To shoot a true panorama, you need to use either a special panorama camera that shoots a very wide frame, or the following method, which requires the combining of multiple frames.

The multiple-image pano has gained in popularity in the past few years; this is principally due to advances in image-processing software. Many software options are available now that will take multiple images, align them, and then "stitch" them into a single panoramic image. The real key to shooting a multiple-image pano is to overlap your shots by about 30 percent from one frame to the next (**Figures 7.27** and **7.28**).

FIGURE 7.27
Here you see the makings of a panorama, with four shots overlapping by about 30 percent from frame to frame.

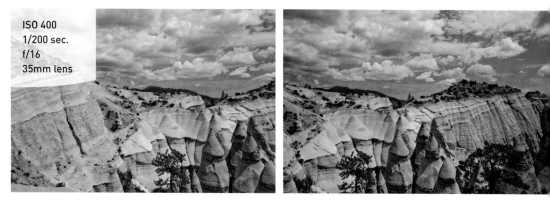

ISO 400
1/200 sec.
f/16
35mm lens

FIGURE 7.28
I used Adobe Photoshop to combine all of the exposures into one large panoramic image.

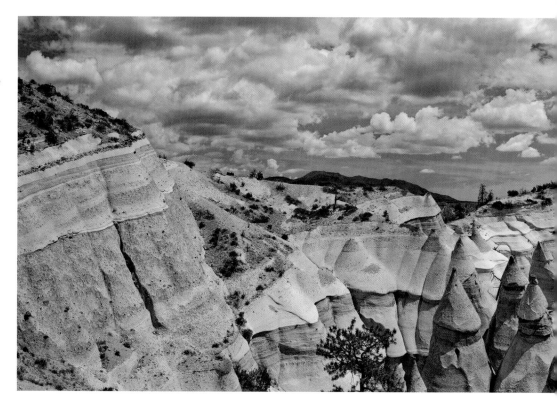

It is possible to handhold the camera while capturing your images, but the best method for capturing great panoramic images is to use a tripod.

Now that you have your series of overlapping images, you can import them into your image-processing software to stitch them together and create a single panoramic image.

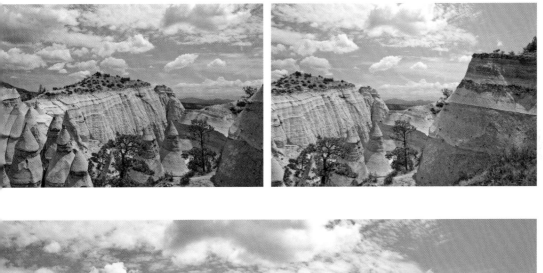

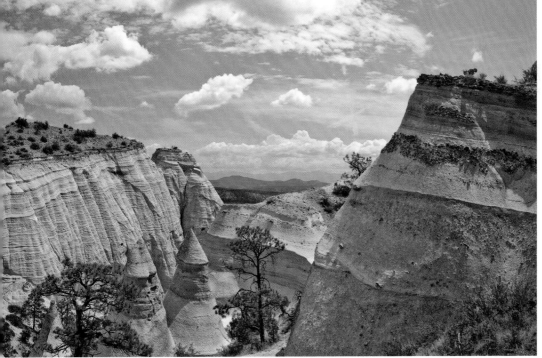

1. Mount your camera on your tripod and make sure it is level.

2. Choose a focal length for your lens that is somewhere between 35mm and 50mm (a wide angle lens can distort the edges, making it harder to stitch together).

3. In Av mode, use a very small aperture for the greatest depth of field. Take a meter reading of a bright part of the scene, and make note of it.

4. Now change your camera to Manual mode (M), and dial in the aperture and shutter speed that you obtained in the previous step.

5. Set your lens to manual focus, and then focus your lens for the area of interest using the HFD method of finding a point one-third of the way into the scene. (If you use the autofocus, you risk getting different points of focus from image to image, which will make the image stitching more difficult for the software.) If you want to use the autofocus, just remember to set the lens to MF before shooting your images.

6. While carefully panning your camera, shoot your images to cover the entire area of the scene from one end to the other, leaving a 30 percent overlap from one frame to the next.

SHOOTING HIGH DYNAMIC RANGE (HDR) IMAGES

One of the more recent trends in digital photography is the use of high dynamic range (HDR) to capture the full range of tonal values in your final image. Typically, when you photograph a scene that has a wide range of tones from shadows to highlights, you have to make a decision regarding which tonal values you are going to emphasize, and then adjust your exposure accordingly. This is because your camera has a limited dynamic range, at least as compared to the human eye. HDR photography allows you to capture multiple exposures for the highlights, shadows, and midtones, and then combine them into a single image using software (**Figures 7.29–7.32**). A number of software applications allow you to combine the images and then perform a process called "tonemapping," whereby the complete range of exposures is represented in a single image. I will not be covering the software applications, but I will explore the process of shooting a scene to help you render properly captured images for the HDR process. Note that using a tripod is absolutely necessary for this technique, since you need to have perfect alignment of each image when they are combined.

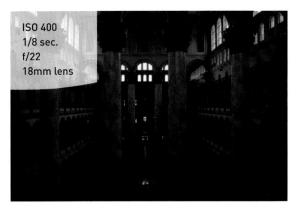

FIGURE 7.29
Underexposing two stops will render more detail in the highlight areas of the fountain.

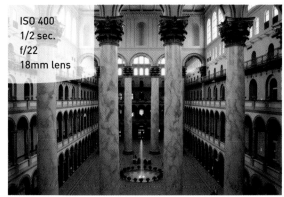

FIGURE 7.30
This is the normal exposure as dictated by the camera meter.

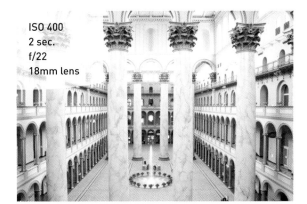

FIGURE 7.31
Overexposing by two stops ensures that the darker areas are exposed to get detail in the shadows.

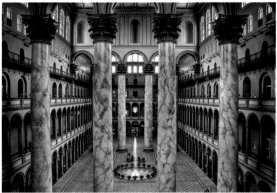

FIGURE 7.32
This is the final HDR image that was rendered from the three other exposures you see here.

SORTING YOUR SHOTS FOR THE MULTI-IMAGE PANORAMA

If you shoot more than one series of shots for your panoramas, it can sometimes be difficult to know when one series of images ends and the other begins. Here is a quick tip for separating your images.

Set up your camera using the steps listed here. Now, before you take your first good exposure in the series, hold up one finger in front of the camera and take a shot. Now move your hand away and begin taking your overlapping images. When you have taken your last shot, hold two fingers in front of the camera and take another shot.

Now, when you go to review your images, use the series of shots that falls between the frames with one and two fingers in them. Then just repeat the process for your next panorama series.

SETTING UP FOR SHOOTING AN HDR IMAGE

1. Set your ISO to 100 to ensure clean, noise-free images.

2. Set your program mode to Av. During the shooting process, you will be taking three shots of the same scene, creating an overexposed image, an underexposed image, and a normal exposure. Since the camera is going to be adjusting the exposure, you want it to make changes to the shutter speed, not the aperture, so that your depth of field is consistent.

3. Set your camera file format to RAW. This is extremely important because the RAW format contains a much larger range of exposure values than a JPEG file, and the HDR software will need this information.

4. Change your shooting mode to Continuous. This will allow you to capture your exposures quickly. Even though you will be using a tripod, there is always a chance that something within your scene will be moving (like clouds or leaves). Shooting in the Continuous mode minimizes any subject movement between frames.

5. Adjust the auto exposure bracket (AEB) mode to shoot three exposures in two-stop increments. To do this, press the Menu button and navigate to the second shooting screen (**A**).

6. Use the Cross keys to highlight the Expo.comp./AEB setting and press the Set button.

7. Now turn the Main dial to the right until the AEB indicators move all the way out to –2 and +2 (**B**). Press the Set button to lock in your changes.

8. Focus the camera using the manual focus method discussed earlier in the chapter, compose your shot, secure the tripod, and hold down the shutter button until the camera has fired three consecutive times.

A

B

A software program, such as Adobe Photoshop or Photomatix Pro, can now process your exposure-bracketed images into a single HDR file. You can find more information on HDR photography and creating HDR images in the Tutorials section at www.photowalkpro.com.

BRACKETING YOUR EXPOSURES

In HDR, *bracketing* is the process of capturing a series of exposures at different stop intervals. You can bracket your exposures even if you aren't going to be using HDR. Sometimes this is helpful when you have a tricky lighting situation and you want to ensure that you have just the right exposure to capture the look you're after. You can bracket in increments as small as a third of a stop. This means that you can capture several images with very subtle exposure variances and then decide later which one is best.

Chapter 7 Assignments

We've covered a lot of ground in this chapter, so it's definitely time to put this knowledge to work in order to get familiar with these new camera settings and techniques.

Comparing depth of field: Wide-angle vs. telephoto

You should practice using the hyper focal distance of your lens to maximize the depth of field. You can do this by picking a focal length to work with on your lens. If you have a zoom lens, try using the longest length. Compose your image and find an object to focus on. Set your aperture to f/22 and take a photo.

Now do the same thing with the zoom lens at its widest focal length. Use the same aperture and focus point.

Review the images and compare the depth of field when using wide angle as opposed to a tele-photo lens. Try this again with a large aperture as well.

Applying hyper focal distance to your landscapes

Pick a scene that once again has objects that are near the camera position and something that is clearly defined in the background. Try using a wide to medium-wide focal length for this (18–35mm). Use a small aperture and focus on the object in the foreground; then recompose and take a shot. Without moving the camera position, use the object in the background as your point of focus and take another shot. Finally, find a point that is one-third of the way into the frame from near to far and use that as the focus point. Compare all of the images to see which method delivered the greatest range of depth of field.

Using Live View and the rule of thirds

Using the Live View grid, practice shooting while placing your main subject in one of the intersecting line locations. Take some comparison shots with the subject at one of the intersecting locations and then shoot the same subject in the middle of the frame.

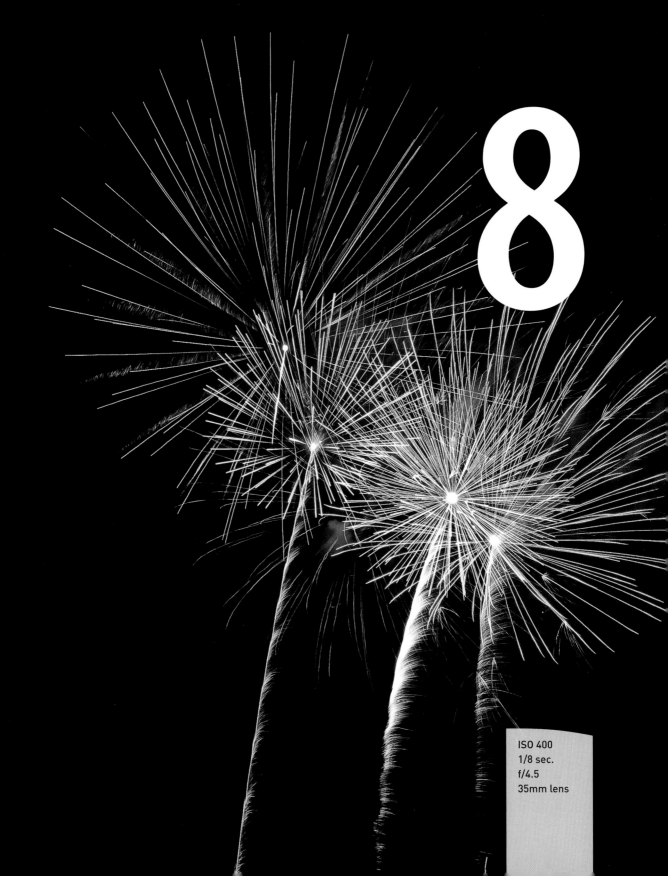

8

ISO 400
1/8 sec.
f/4.5
35mm lens

Mood Lighting

SHOOTING WHEN THE LIGHTS GET LOW

There is no reason to put your camera away when the sun goes down.
Your T1i has some great features that let you work with available light as
well as the built-in flash. In this chapter, we will explore ways to push your
camera's technology to the limit in order to capture great photos in difficult lighting situations. We will also explore the use of flash and how best
to utilize your built-in flash features to improve your photography. But
let's first look at working with low-level available light.

PORING OVER THE PICTURE

I had the pleasure of driving around the Bay Area with some photo buddies to shoot the sites. We were just about done for the evening when we decided to make a run up to this scenic overlook for one last look at the bridge. The haze from the afternoon had cleared and we were left with a great view of this iconic bridge.

A Tungsten white balance setting corrected the color for the lights on the bridge and made the sky more blue.

Long Exposure Noise Reduction was used to reduce the noise that can occur from an exposure of this length.

ISO 100
10 sec.
f/8
90mm lens

The sky was metered to make it a little darker and give the colors more saturation.

A tripod and shutter release cable were used to keep the image sharp.

PORING OVER THE PICTURE

To help get a sharp image, I braced myself against a column and made sure the Image Stabilization was turned on.

Although there was light coming in from above, it was not sufficient for me to use a lower ISO and still be able to handhold the camera.

A slightly longer shutter speed was selected to give a silky look to the fountain.

EXIT

Architecture of Auth

Photographs by R

Information

You might recognize this interior from the HDR section in Chapter 7. This is a shot from ground level in the amazing National Building Museum in Washington, D.C. This was my first time visiting the museum, and I was really taken with the grand size of the columns and the wonderful light coming in from the skylights.

A wide angle lens was selected to capture the side columns and the fountain in one shot.

ISO 800
1/10 sec.
f/8
36mm lens

RAISING THE ISO: THE SIMPLE SOLUTION

Let's begin with the obvious way to keep shooting when the lights get low: raising the ISO (**Figure 8.1**). By now you know how to change the ISO: just press the ISO button on the top of the camera and turn the Main dial to adjust. In typical shooting situations, you should keep the ISO in the 100–800 range. This will keep your pictures nice and clean by keeping the digital noise to a minimum. But as the available light gets low, you might find yourself working in the higher ranges of the ISO scale, which could lead to more noise in your image.

FIGURE 8.1
To get a good exposure inside a museum, you will often be forced to raise your ISO. I also braced myself against a column to help steady the shot.

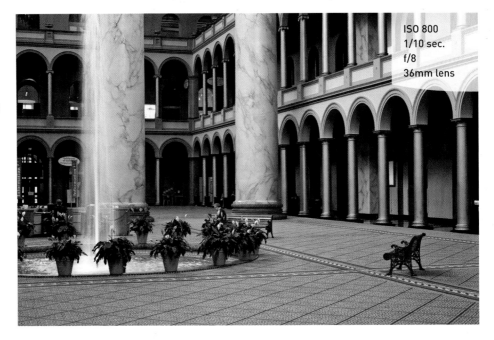

ISO 800
1/10 sec.
f/8
36mm lens

You could use the flash, but that has a limited range (15–20 feet) that might not work for you. Also, you could be in a situation where flash is prohibited, or at least frowned upon, like at a wedding or in a museum.

And what about a tripod in combination with a long shutter speed? That is also an option, and we'll cover it a little further into the chapter. The problem with using a tripod and a slow shutter speed in low-light photography, though, is that it performs best when subjects aren't moving. Besides, try to set up a tripod in a museum and see how quickly you grab the attention of the security guards.

So if the only choice to get the shot is to raise the ISO to 800 or higher, make sure that you turn on the High ISO Speed Noise Reduction feature. This custom menu function is set to Standard by default, but as you start using higher ISO values you should consider changing it to the Strong setting. (See Chapter 7 for setting the noise reduction features.)

To see the effect of High ISO Speed Noise Reduction, you need to zoom in and take a closer look (**Figures 8.2** and **8.3**).

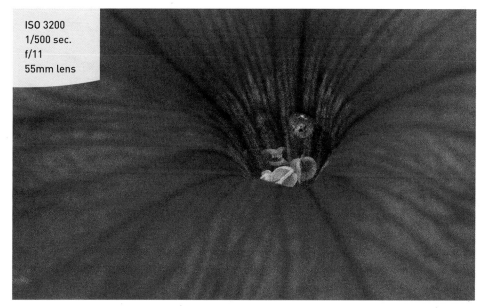

ISO 3200
1/500 sec.
f/11
55mm lens

FIGURE 8.2
Here is an enlargement of a flower shot without any ISO noise reduction.

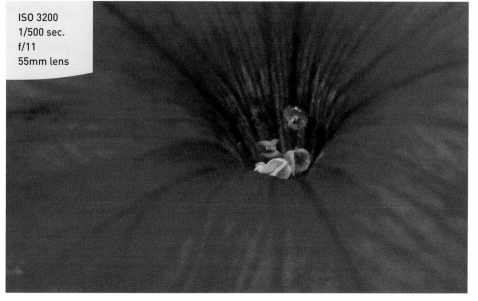

ISO 3200
1/500 sec.
f/11
55mm lens

FIGURE 8.3
Here is the same flower with noise reduction set to Strong.

Raising the noise reduction to the Strong setting slightly increases the processing time for your images, so if you are shooting in the Continuous drive mode you might see a little reduction in the speed of your frames per second.

NOISE REDUCTION SAVES SPACE

When shooting at very high ISO settings, running High ISO Speed Noise Reduction at the Standard or Strong setting can save you space on your memory card. If you are saving your photos as JPEGs, the camera will compress the information in the image to take up less space. When you have excessive noise, you can literally add megabytes to the file size. This is because the camera has to deal with more information: it views the noise in the image as photo information and, therefore, tries not to lose that information during the compression process. That means more noise equals bigger files. So not only will turning on the High ISO Speed Noise Reduction feature improve the look of your image, it will also save you some space so you can take a few more shots.

USING VERY HIGH ISOS

Is ISO 3200 just not enough for you? Well, in that case, you will need to turn on the ISO Expansion setting. This setting opens up two more stops of ISO, raising the new limit to an incredible 12800. The highest setting will not appear in your ISO scale as a number, but as H for 12800.

SETTING UP THE ISO EXPANSION FEATURE

1. Press the Menu button and locate the Custom Functions screen (**A**).

2. The ISO Expansion setting is located in the C. Fn I: Exposure section. Highlight it and press Set.

3. Locate the ISO Expansion menu and change the setting from Off to On (**B**).

4. Press the Menu button twice to exit, then press the ISO button to find the additional ISO settings of 6400 and H (12800).

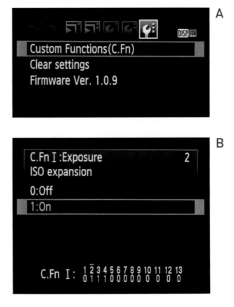

A word of warning about the expanded ISO settings: although it is great to have these high ISO settings available during low-light shooting, they should always be your last resort. Even with the High ISO Speed Noise Reduction turned on, the amount of visible noise will be extremely high. I can't think of a situation where I ever need to use the 12800 (H) setting, but you might find yourself at a nighttime sporting event under the lights, which would require ISOs of 3200 or 6400 to improve your shutter speeds and capture the action (**Figure 8.4**).

Manual Callout

For a complete table listing of all the programmable custom functions, including the ISO Expansion feature, turn to page 183 in your owner's manual.

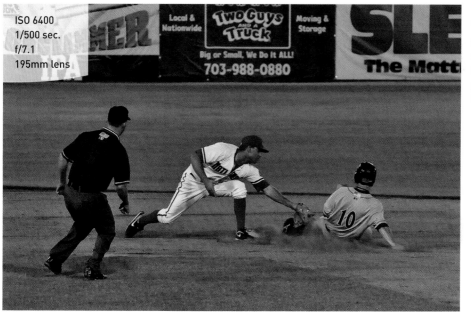

ISO 6400
1/500 sec.
f/7.1
195mm lens

FIGURE 8.4
The only way to get a fast-enough shutter speed during this night game was to raise the ISO to 6400.

STABILIZING THE SITUATION

If you purchased your camera with one of the new image stabilization (IS) lenses, you already own a great tool to squeeze two stops of exposure out of your camera when shooting without a tripod (**Figure 8.5**). Typically, the average person can handhold their camera down to about 1/60 of a second before blurriness results due to hand shake. As the length of the lens is increased (or zoomed), the ability to handhold at slow shutter speeds (1/60 and slower) and still get sharp images is further reduced.

FIGURE 8.5
Set the Stabilizer to the On position when using longer shutter speeds while handholding your camera.

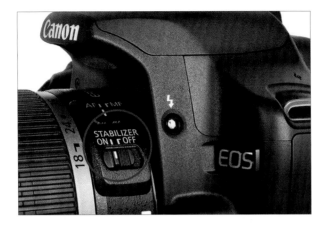

The Canon IS lenses contain small gyro sensors and servo-actuated optical elements, which correct for camera shake and stabilize the image. The IS function is so good that it is possible to improve your handheld photography by two or three stops, meaning that if you are pretty solid at a shutter speed of 1/60, the IS feature lets you shoot at 1/15, and possibly even 1/8 of a second (**Figures 8.6** and **8.7**).

FIGURE 8.6
This image was handheld without the IS turned on.

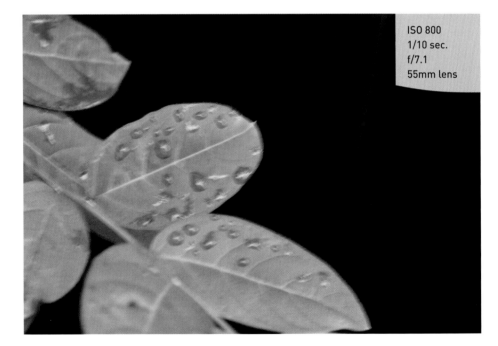

ISO 800
1/10 sec.
f/7.1
55mm lens

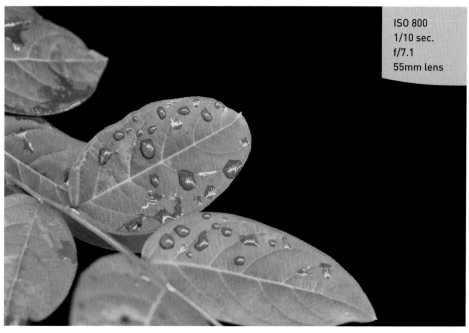

ISO 800
1/10 sec.
f/7.1
55mm lens

FIGURE 8.7
Here is the same
subject shot with
the same settings
but this time with IS
turned on.

SELF-TIMER

Whether you are shooting with a tripod or even resting your camera on a wall, you can increase the sharpness of your pictures by taking your hands out of the equation. Whenever you use your finger to depress the shutter release button, you are increasing the chance that there will be a little bit of shake in your image. To eliminate this possibility, try setting your camera up to use the self-timer. To turn on the self-timer, just press the Set button to activate the Quick Control screen, highlight the drive mode icon, and then turn the Main dial until the self-timer icon appears. There are two self-timer modes to choose from: two seconds and ten seconds. I generally use the two-second mode to cut down on time between exposures.

FIGURE 8.8
Focusing on the
night sky is best
done in manual
focus mode.

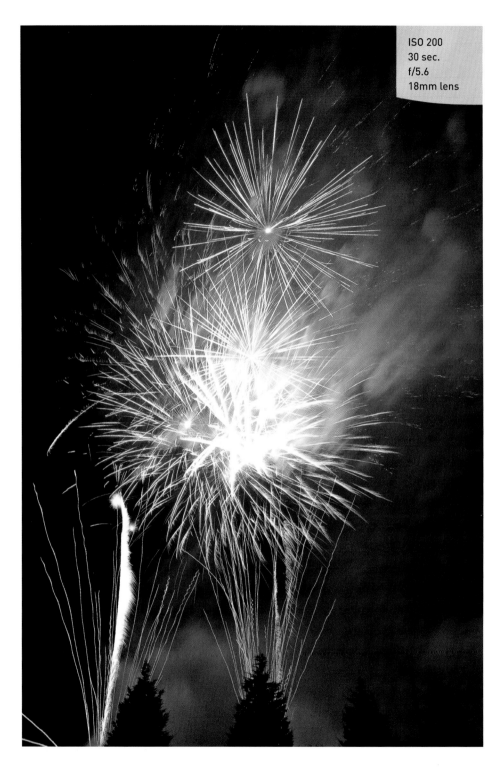

ISO 200
30 sec.
f/5.6
18mm lens

FOCUSING IN LOW LIGHT

The T1i has a great focusing system, but occasionally the light levels might be too low for the camera to achieve an accurate focus. There are a few things that you can do to overcome this obstacle.

First, you should know that the camera utilizes contrast in the viewfinder to establish a point of focus. This is why your camera will not be able to focus when you point it at a white wall or a cloudless sky. It simply can't find any contrast in the scene to work with. Knowing this, you might be able to use a single focus point in One Shot mode to find an area of contrast that is of the same distance as your subject. You can then hold that focus by holding down the shutter button halfway and recomposing your image.

Then there are those times when there just isn't anything there for you to focus on. A perfect example of this would be a fireworks display. If you point your lens to the night sky in any automatic focus (AF) mode, it will just keep searching for—and not finding—a focus point. On these occasions, you can simply turn off the autofocus feature and manually focus the lens (**Figure 8.8**). Look for the AF/MF switch on the side of the lens and slide it to the MF position.

Don't forget to put it back in AF mode at the end of your shoot.

FOCUS ASSIST

Another way to ensure good focus is to enable the T1i's Focus Assist mode. Focus Assist uses a short burst from your pop-up flash to shine some light on the scene, which assists the autofocus system in locating more detail. This feature is automatically activated when shooting in the Basic zone (except in Landscape, Sports, and Flash Off modes for the following reasons: in Landscape mode, the subject is usually too far away; in Sports mode, the subject is probably moving; and in Flash Off mode, you've disabled the flash entirely). The Focus Assist should be enabled by default, but you can check the menu just to make sure.

TURNING ON THE FOCUS ASSIST FEATURE

1. Press the Menu button and then use the Main dial to get to the Custom Functions menu tab, highlight Custom Functions, and press the Set button.

2. Use the left/right Cross keys to get to the C. Fn. III: Autofocus/Drive AF-assist beam firing feature and press the Set button (**A**).

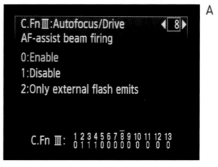

3. If it is not enabled, highlight Enable and press the Set button (**B**).

4. To use it when working in the Creative zone, simply press the flash button to raise the pop-up flash.

5. With the flash in the "up" position, press the shutter button to focus and Focus Assist will activate if necessary.

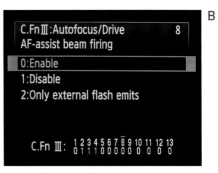

If you don't want the flash to fire during the actual exposure, you must first disable the flash.

DISABLING THE FLASH

1. Press the Menu button and then scroll the Main dial to highlight the first shooting menu (far left).

2. Scroll down to Flash control and press the Set button (**C**).

3. Select Flash firing and press the Set button (**D**).

4. Set the Flash firing option to Disable (**E**).

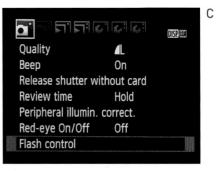

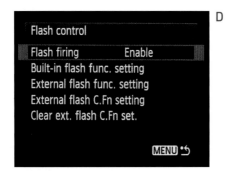

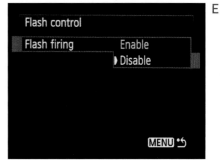

SHOOTING LONG EXPOSURES

We have covered some of the techniques for shooting in low light, so let's go through the process of capturing a night or low-light scene for maximum image quality (**Figure 8.9**). The first thing to consider is that in order to shoot in low light with a low ISO, you will need to use shutter speeds that are longer than you could possibly handhold (longer than 1/15 of a second). This will require the use of a tripod or stable surface for you to place your camera on. For maximum quality, the ISO should be low—somewhere below 400. The long exposure noise reduction should be turned on to minimize the effects of exposing for longer durations. (To set this up, see Chapter 7.)

Once you have the noise reduction turned on, set your camera to Aperture Priority (Av) mode. This way, you can concentrate on the aperture that you believe is most appropriate and let the camera determine the best shutter speed. If it is too dark for the autofocus to function properly, try manually focusing. Finally, consider using a cable release (see the bonus chapter) to activate the shutter. If you don't have one, check out the sidebar on using the self-timer (page 209). Once you shoot the image, you may notice some lag time before it is displayed on the rear LCD. This is due to the noise reduction process, which can take anywhere from a fraction of a second up to 30 seconds, depending on the length of the exposure.

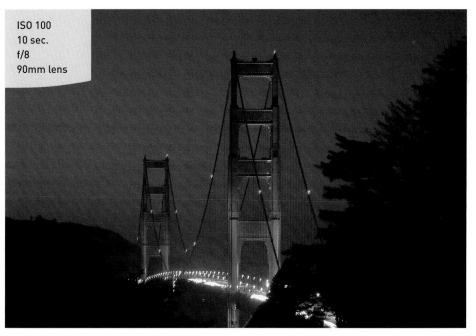

ISO 100
10 sec.
f/8
90mm lens

FIGURE 8.9
A fairly long exposure and a tripod were necessary to catch this nighttime view of the Golden Gate bridge.

FLASH SYNC

The basic idea behind the term *flash synchronization* (*flash sync* for short) is that when you take a photograph using the flash, the camera needs to ensure that the shutter is fully open at the time that the flash goes off. This is not an issue if you are using a long shutter speed such as 1/15 of a second but does become more critical for fast shutter speeds. To ensure that the flash and shutter are synchronized so that the flash is going off while the shutter is open, the T1i implements a top sync speed of 1/200 of a second. This means that when you are using the flash, you will not be able to have your shutter speed set any faster than 1/200. If you did use a faster shutter speed, the shutter would actually start closing before the flash fired, which would cause a black area to appear in the frame where the light from the flash was blocked.

USING THE BUILT-IN FLASH

There are going to be times when you have to turn to your camera's built-in flash to get the shot. The pop-up flash on the T1i is not extremely powerful, but with the camera's advanced metering system it does a pretty good job of lighting up the night…or just filling in the shadows.

If you are working in the Creative zone, you will have to turn the flash on for yourself. To do this, just press the pop-up flash button located on the front of the camera (**Figure 8.10**). Once the flash is up, it is ready to go (**Figure 8.11**). It's that simple.

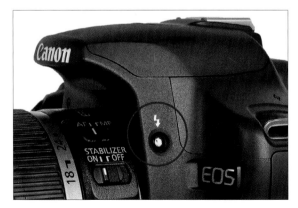

FIGURE 8.10
A quick press of the pop-up flash button will release the built-in flash to its ready position.

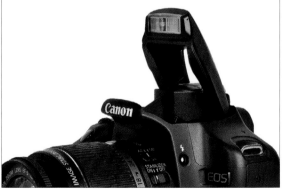

FIGURE 8.11
The pop-up flash in its ready position.

SHUTTER SPEEDS

The standard flash synchronization speed for your camera is between 1/60 and 1/200 of a second. When you are working with the built-in flash in the Basic zone, the camera will typically use a shutter speed of 1/60 of a second. The exception to this is when you use the Night Portrait mode, which will fire the flash with a slower shutter speed so that some of the ambient light has time to record in the image.

The real key to using the flash to get great pictures is to control the shutter speed. The goal is to balance the light from the flash with the existing light so that everything in the picture has an even illumination. Let's take a look at the shutter speeds for the modes in the Creative zone.

 Program (P): The shutter speed stays at 1/60 of a second. You can make changes to the aperture by pressing in the Av button on the back of the camera while turning the Main dial, but you risk over- or underexposing your image.

 Shutter Priority (Tv): You can adjust the shutter speed to as fast as 1/200 of a second all the way down to 30 seconds. The lens aperture will adjust accordingly, but typically at long exposures the lens will be set to its smallest aperture.

 Aperture Priority (Av): This mode has three custom settings for adjusting the shutter speed when using the flash, depending on your needs. The whole point of this setting is to allow you to use the aperture of your choice while still getting good flash exposures.

The default value is Auto, which adjusts from 1/200 all the way down to 30 seconds, depending on the available light. As the aperture gets smaller, the shutter speeds will get longer. There are also two speed-limiting settings to choose from. The first is "1/200 to 1/60 sec. auto." This limits the shutter speed to a maximum duration of 1/60 of a second. If you have the aperture open to an f-stop that has a very small opening for a proper exposure, the shutter speed indicator will flash, letting you know that you are risking underexposure. For all other exposures, the camera will moderate the shutter speed to a selection that is within the 1/60–1/200 range. The other setting is "1/200 sec. (fixed)." This setting maintains a shutter speed of 1/200 of a second no matter what the f-stop is set to. Your flash will try and vary its power output to meet the needs of the setting that you have selected.

SETTING THE SYNC SPEED WHEN USING FLASH IN AV MODE

1. Press the Menu button and use the Main dial to get to the Custom Functions menu tab and then press the Set button.

2. Select C. Fn I: Exposure / Flash sync. speed in Av mode using the Cross keys and press the Set button (**A**).

3. Select the Av sync speed that you desire using the Cross keys and press Set once more (**B**).

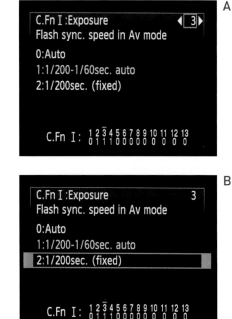

Manual (M): Manual mode works the same as Tv mode, with a range of 1/200 down to 30 seconds. The difference, of course, is that you must manually set the f-stop.

A-DEP: The shutter speed for this mode stays at 1/60 of a second.

Generally speaking, I like to have my Mode dial set to the Shutter Priority (Tv) mode when shooting pictures with flash. This enables me to balance out the existing light with the flash, which sometimes requires longer shutter speeds.

METERING MODES

The built-in flash uses a technology called E-TTL II (Evaluative Through The Lens) metering to determine the appropriate amount of flash power to output for a good exposure. When you depress the shutter button, the camera quickly adjusts focus while gathering information from the entire scene to measure the amount of ambient light. As you press the shutter button down completely, a pre-flash occurs to meter the light off the subject from the flash, and a determination is made as to how much power is needed to balance the subject with the ambient light. This applies to all of the modes in the Creative zone, with the exception of Manual mode.

The default setting for the flash meter mode is Evaluative. The meter can be set to Average mode but should probably be avoided. Your best results will come from the E-TTL mode.

FLASH RANGE

Because the pop-up flash is fairly small, it does not have enough power to illuminate a large space (**Figure 8.12**). The effective distance varies depending on the ISO setting. At ISO 100, the range is about 12 feet. This range can be extended to as far as 138 feet when the camera is set to an ISO of 12800. For the best image quality, your ISO setting should not go above 800. Anything higher will begin to introduce excessive noise into your photos.

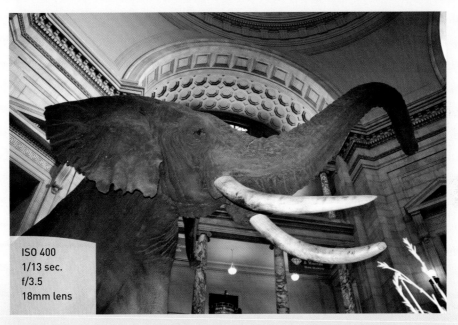

ISO 400
1/13 sec.
f/3.5
18mm lens

FIGURE 8.12
The pop-up flash was used to fill in shadows on the elephant while the long exposure time allowed the ambient light to illuminate the rest of the scene.

But if you have special metering needs, such as a background that is very light or dark, you might consider using the Flash Exposure (FE) Lock to meter off your subject and then recompose your image in the viewfinder.

This feature works much like the Automatic Exposure (AE) Lock function that was discussed in Chapter 6.

USING THE FE LOCK FEATURE

1. Point the camera at the area that you want to base the flash exposure on. This is normally your subject.

2. Press the ✱ AE/FE Lock button (near the top right on the back of the camera) button to obtain the exposure setting. The flash will fire a small burst to evaluate the exposure and you will see FEL (Flash Exposure Lock) in the viewfinder. The AE/FE Lock symbol (the asterisk) will also appear in the viewfinder.

3. Recompose the scene as you like, and press the shutter button completely.

The FE Lock will cancel after each exposure, so you have to repeat these steps each time you need to lock the flash exposure.

Using the Average metering mode might also require that you tweak the flash output by using Flash Exposure Compensation. This is because the camera will be metering the entire scene to set the exposure, so you might have to add or subtract flash power to balance out the scene.

COMPENSATING FOR THE FLASH EXPOSURE

The E-TTL system will usually do an excellent job of balancing the flash and ambient light for your exposure, but it does have the limitation of not knowing what effect you want in your image. You may want more or less flash in a particular shot. You can achieve this by using the Flash Exposure Compensation feature.

Just as with exposure compensation, flash compensation allows you to dial in a change in the flash output in increments of 1/3 of a stop. You will probably use this most often to tone down the effects of your flash, especially when you are using the flash as a subtle fill light (**Figures 8.13** and **8.14**).

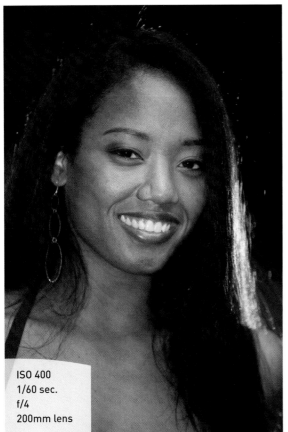

ISO 400
1/60 sec.
f/4
200mm lens

FIGURE 8.13
This shot was taken with the pop-up flash at normal power. As you can see, it was trying too hard to illuminate my subject.

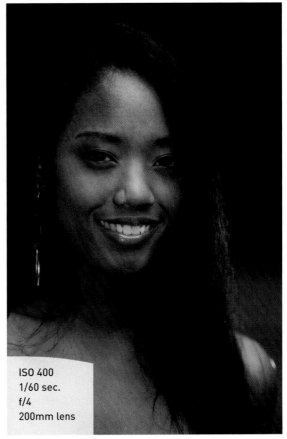

ISO 400
1/60 sec.
f/4
200mm lens

FIGURE 8.14
This image was taken with the same exposure settings. The difference is in the –1 1/3 stops of compensation set for the flash.

USING THE FLASH EXPOSURE COMPENSATION FEATURE TO CHANGE THE FLASH OUTPUT

1. Press the Set button to activate the Quick Control screen on the LCD.

2. Use the Cross keys to move the cursor to the Flash Exposure Compensation icon.

3. Rotate the Main dial to adjust the flash compensation in 1/3-stop increments (left to subtract and right to add).

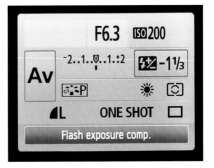

4. Press the shutter button halfway to return to shooting mode, and then take the picture.

5. Review your image to see if more or less flash compensation is required, and repeat these steps as necessary.

The Flash Exposure Compensation feature does not reset itself when the camera is turned off, so whatever compensation you have set will remain in effect until you change it. Your only clue to knowing that the flash output is changed will be the presence of the Flash Exposure Compensation symbol on the rear LCD so make sure you check it. It will disappear when there is zero compensation set.

REDUCING RED-EYE

We've all seen the result of using on-camera flashes when shooting people: the dreaded red-eye! This demonic effect is the result of the light from the flash entering the pupil and then reflecting back as an eerie red glow. The closer the flash is to the lens, the greater the chance that you will get red-eye. This is especially true when it is dark and the subject's eyes are dilated. There are two ways to combat this problem. The first is to get the flash away from the lens. That's not really an option, though, if you are using the pop-up flash. Therefore, you will need to turn to the Red-Eye Reduction feature.

This is a simple feature that shines a light from the camera at the subject, causing their pupils to shrink, thus eliminating or reducing the effects of red-eye (**Figure 8.15**).

The feature is set to Off by default and needs to be turned on in the shooting menu.

TURN ON THE LIGHTS!

When shooting indoors, another way to reduce red-eye, or just shorten the length of time that the reduction lamp needs to be shining into your subject's eyes, is to turn on a lot of lights. The brighter the ambient light levels, the smaller the subject's pupils will be. This will reduce the time necessary for the red-eye reduction lamp to shine. It will also allow you to take more candid pictures because your subjects won't be required to stare at the red-eye lamp while waiting for their pupils to reduce.

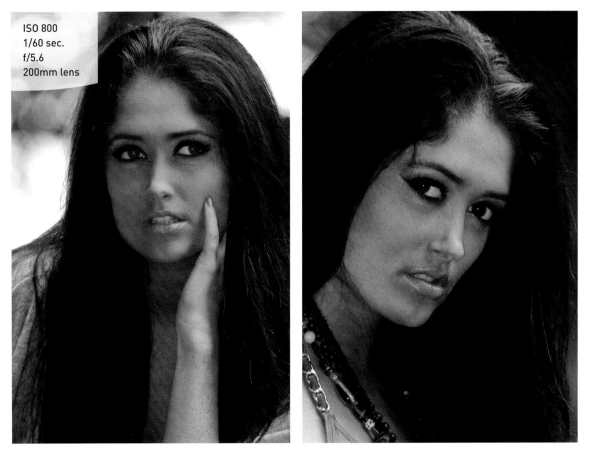

ISO 800
1/60 sec.
f/5.6
200mm lens

FIGURE 8.15
Notice that the pupils on the image without red-eye are smaller as a result.

TURNING ON THE RED-EYE REDUCTION FEATURE

1. Press the Menu button and then turn the Main dial to get to the first shooting menu.

2. Use the Cross keys to scroll down to Red-eye On/Off.

3. Press the Set button and then, using the Cross keys, select On and press the Set button.

4. Press the Menu button twice or the shutter release button to return to shooting mode.

Quality	⊿L
Beep	On
Release shutter without card	
Review time	Hold
Peripheral illumin. correct.	
Red-eye On/Off	Off
Flash control	

To get the full benefit from the Red-Eye Reduction feature, you should hold down the shutter button halfway, which causes the reduction light to shine into your subject's eyes. A small scale will appear in the viewfinder that shows how long to hold the shutter button before pressing completely. Once the countdown scale has reduced down to nothing, press the shutter button completely to take the picture.

Truth be told, I rarely shoot with red-eye reduction turned on because of the time it takes before being able to take a picture. If I am after candid shots and have to use the flash, I will take my chances on red-eye and try to fix the problem in my image-processing software. The Canon Image Browser software that comes with your T1i has a red-eye reduction feature that works really well.

2ND CURTAIN SYNC

There are two flash synchronization modes in the T1i. There's first curtain and second curtain. You may be asking, "What in the world does synchronization do, and what are these 'curtains'?" Good question.

When your camera fires, there are two curtains that open and close to make up the shutter. The first curtain moves out of the way, exposing the camera sensor to the light. At the end of the exposure, the second curtain moves in front of the sensor, ending that picture cycle. In flash photography, timing is extremely important because the flash fires in milliseconds and the shutter is usually opening in tenths or hundredths of a second. To make sure these two functions happen in order, the camera usually fires the flash just as the first curtain moves out of the way (see the sidebar earlier in the chapter about flash sync).

In 2nd Curtain Sync mode, the flash will not fire until just before the second shutter curtain ends the exposure. So, why have this mode at all? Well, there might be times when you want to have a longer exposure to balance out the light from the background to go with the subject needing the flash. Imagine taking a photograph of a friend standing in Times Square at night with all the traffic moving about and the bright lights of the streets overhead. If the flash fires at the beginning of the exposure, and then the objects around the subject move, those objects will often blur the subject a bit. If the camera is set to 2nd Curtain Sync, though, all of the movement is recorded by the existing light first, and then the subject is "frozen" by the flash at the end by the exposure.

There is no right or wrong to it. It's just a decision on what type of effect it is that you would like to create. Many times, 2nd Curtain Sync is used for artistic purposes or to record movement in the scene without it overlapping the flash-exposed subject

(**Figure 8.16**). To make sure that the main subject is always getting the final pop of the flash, I leave my camera set to 2nd Camera Sync.

Using 1st Curtain Sync mode will give a similar effect, but the flash will fire at the beginning of the sequence (**Figure 8.17**). If you do intend to use a long exposure with first curtain synchronization, you need to have your subject remain fairly still so that any movement that occurs after the flash goes off will be minimized in the image.

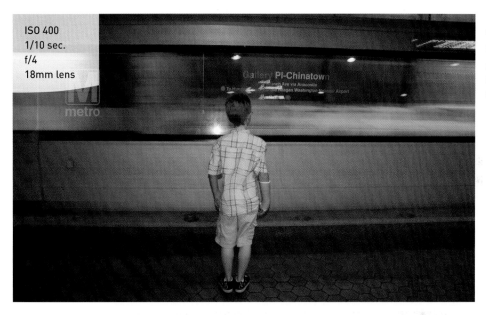

ISO 400
1/10 sec.
f/4
18mm lens

FIGURE 8.16
The use of 2nd Curtain Sync is most evident during long flash exposures.

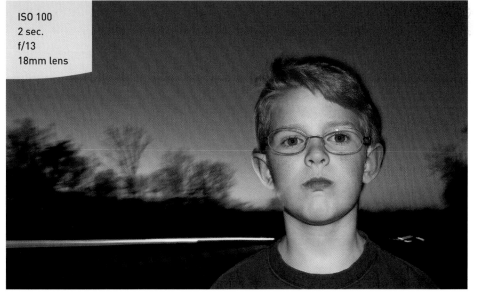

ISO 100
2 sec.
f/13
18mm lens

FIGURE 8.17
1st Curtain Sync is the default setting for flash photography and can be used for longer exposures as long as the subject remains still.

SETTING YOUR FLASH SYNC MODE

1. Press the Menu button and navigate to first shooting menu, select Flash control, and press Set (**A**).

2. Use the Cross keys to select Built-in flash func. setting, and then press the Set button (**B**).

3. Use the Cross keys once again to select the Shutter sync option, and then select either the 1st or 2nd curtain option for the type of flash sync that you desire (**C**).

A

Quality	▲L
Beep	On
Release shutter without card	
Review time	Hold
Peripheral illumin. correct.	
Red-eye On/Off	Off
Flash control	

B

Flash control

Flash firing   Enable
Built-in flash func. setting
External flash func. setting
External flash C.Fn setting
Clear ext. flash C.Fn set.

MENU ↰

C

Built-in flash func. setting

Flash mode   E-TTL II
Shutter sync.   1st curtain
Flash exp. comp   ¯2..1..0..1..⁺2
E-TTL II   Evaluative

MENU ↰

FLASH AND GLASS

If you find yourself in a situation where you want to use your flash to shoot through a window or display case, try placing your lens right against the glass so that the reflection of the flash won't be visible in your image (**Figures 8.18** and **8.19**). This is extremely useful in museums and aquariums.

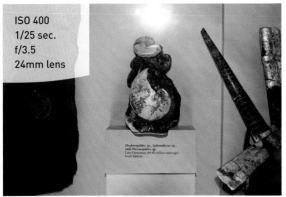

ISO 400
1/25 sec.
f/3.5
24mm lens

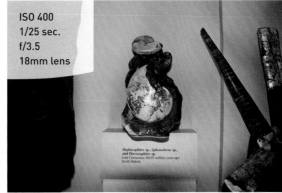

ISO 400
1/25 sec.
f/3.5
18mm lens

FIGURE 8.18
The bright spot at the top of the frame is a result of the flash reflecting off the display case.

FIGURE 8.19
To eliminate the reflection, place the lens against the glass or as close to it as possible. This might also require zooming the lens out a little.

A FEW WORDS ABOUT EXTERNAL FLASH

We have discussed several ways to get control over the built-in pop-up flash on the T1i. The reality is that, as flashes go, it will only render fairly average results. For people photography, it is probably one of the most unflattering light sources that you could ever use. This isn't because the flash isn't good—it's actually very sophisticated for its size. The problem is that light should come from any direction besides the camera to best flatter a human subject. When the light emanates from directly above the lens, it gives the effect of becoming a photocopier. Imagine putting your face down on a scanner: the result would be a flatly lit, featureless photo.

To really make your flash photography come alive with possibilities, you should consider buying an external flash such as the Canon Speedlite 430EX II. The 430EX has a swiveling flash head, more power, and communicates with the camera and the E-TTL system to deliver balanced flash exposures. For more information about the Canon Speedlite system, be sure to check out the bonus chapter.

Manual Callout

The external Speedlite menu settings are covered in your owner's manual on pages 139 and 196.

Chapter 8 Assignments

Now that we have looked at the possibilities of shooting after dark, it's time to put it all to the test. These assignments cover the full range of shooting possibilities, both with flash and without. Let's get started.

How steady are your hands?

It's important to know just what your limits are in terms of handholding your camera and still getting sharp pictures. This will change depending on the focal length of the lens you are working with. Wider angle lenses are more forgiving than telephoto lenses, so check this out for your longest and shortest lenses. Using an 18–200mm zoom as an example, set your lens to 200mm and then, with the camera set to ISO 100 and the mode set to Tv, start taking pictures with lower and lower shutter speeds. Review each image on the LCD at a zoomed-in magnification to take note of when you start seeing visible camera shake in your images. It will probably be around 1/125 of a second for a 200mm lens.

Now do the same for the wide-angle setting on the lens. My limit is about 1/30 of a second. These shutter speeds are with the Image Stabilization feature turned off. If you have an IS lens, try it with and without the IS feature enabled to see just how slow you can set your shutter while getting sharp results.

Pushing your ISO to the extreme

Turn on the Extended ISO feature. Now find a place to shoot where the ambient light level is low. This could be at night or indoors in a darkened room. Using the mode of your choice, start increasing the ISO from 100 until you get to 12800. Make sure you evaluate the level of noise in your image, especially in the shadow areas. Only you can decide how much noise is acceptable in your pictures. I can tell you from personal experience that I never like to stray above that ISO 800 mark.

Getting rid of the noise

Turn on the High ISO Speed Noise Reduction and repeat the previous assignment. Find your acceptable limits with the noise reduction turned on. Also pay attention to how much detail is lost in your shadows with this function enabled.

Long exposures in the dark

If you don't have a tripod, find a stable place to set your camera outside and try some long exposures. Set your camera to Av mode and then use the self-timer to activate the camera (this will keep you from shaking the camera while pressing the shutter button).

Shoot in an area that has some level of ambient light, be it a streetlight or traffic lights, or even a full moon. The idea is to get some late-night low-light exposures.

Reducing the noise in your long exposures

Now repeat the last assignment with the Long Exposure Noise Reduction set to On. Now look at the difference in the images that were taken before and after the noise reduction was enabled. For best results, perform this assignment and the previous assignment in the same shooting session using the same subject.

Testing the limits of the pop-up flash

Wait for the lights to get low and then press that pop-up flash button to start using the built-in flash. Try using the different shooting modes to see how they affect your exposures. Use the Flash Exposure Compensation feature to take a series of pictures while adjusting from –2 stops all the way to +2 stops so that you become familiar with how much latitude you will get from this feature.

Getting the red out

Find a friend with some patience and a tolerance for bright lights. Have them sit in a darkened room or outside at night and then take their picture with the flash. Now turn on the Red-Eye Reduction to see if you get better results. Don't forget to wait for the red-eye timer to completely extinguish before taking the picture.

Getting creative with 2nd Curtain Sync

Now it's time for a little creative fun. Set your camera up for 2nd Curtain Sync and start shooting. Moving targets are best. Experiment with Tv and Av modes to lower the shutter speeds and exaggerate the effect. Try using a low ISO so the camera is forced to use longer shutter speeds. Be creative and have some fun!

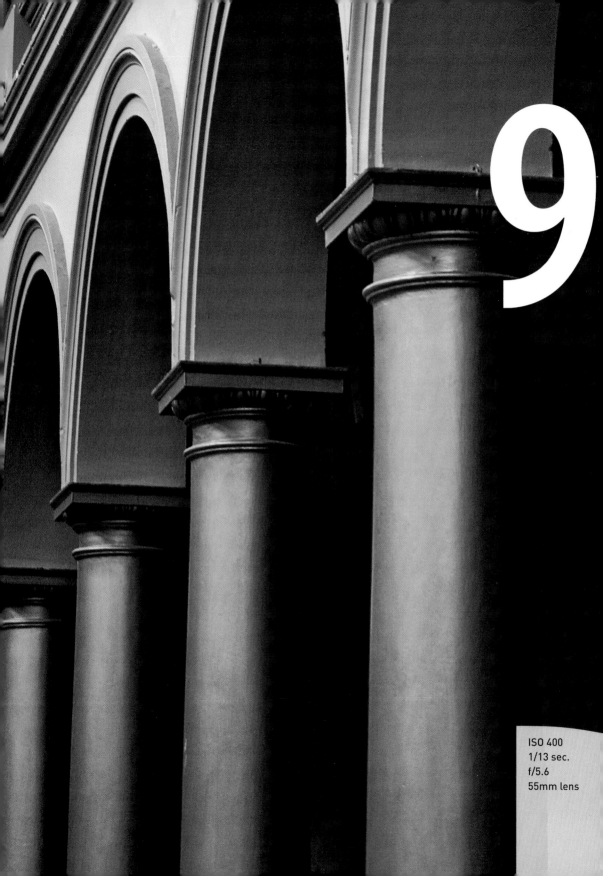

9

ISO 400
1/13 sec.
f/5.6
55mm lens

Creative
Compositions

IMPROVE YOUR PICTURES WITH SOUND COMPOSITIONAL ELEMENTS

Creating a great photograph takes more than just the right settings on your camera. To take your photography to the next level, you need to gain an understanding of how the elements within the frame come together to create a compositionally pleasing image. Composition is the culmination of light, shape, and, to borrow a word from the iconic photographer Jay Maisel, gesture. Composition is a way for you to pull your viewing audience into your image and guide them through the scene. Let's examine a few methods you can use to add interest to your photos by utilizing some common compositional elements.

PORING OVER THE PICTURE

When looking for the right location to shoot this waterfall, I had to pre-visualize the look I was trying to achieve. I knew that I wanted to photograph the falls, but I also wanted to incorporate the flow of the stream leading from the higher rocks. I decided to walk downstream a bit until I found a location that would let me frame the waterfall near the top of the image as the water flowed to the bottom of the frame.

A tripod was necessary to get the long shutter speed necessary for the silky look of the waterfall.

To get maximum depth of field, a very small aperture setting was used.

The S-curve of the stream acts as a guide to lead the eye to the falls.

A vertical frame orientation was used to accentuate the flow of the stream.

ISO 100
3 sec.
f/22
55mm lens

While driving through Saguaro National Park in Arizona, I saw some dark storm clouds gathering over the mountains. The late afternoon sun had already begun to blanket the landscape with a warm glow. As I stood, waiting with my camera on my tripod, the clouds started breaking a bit and let the sunlight spill into the valley in front of the mountain. I wasted no time in capturing a few frames.

I composed the shot so that several large Saguaro cacti were on the left side of the frame, adding interest to the foreground.

The frame is divided into three parts, with the dark blue storm clouds on top, the light part of the valley in the middle, and the darker foreground at the bottom.

The contrasts in color and shadow add depth to the image.

The warm tones of the late afternoon sun contrast nicely with the dark blue of the cloudy sky.

ISO 200
1/125 sec.
f/5.6
70mm lens

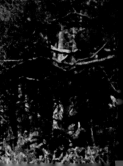

DEPTH OF FIELD

Long focal lengths and large apertures will allow you to isolate your subject from the chaos that surrounds it. I utilize the Av mode for the majority of my shooting. I also like to use a longer focal length lens to shrink the depth of field to a very narrow area (**Figure 9.1**).

The blurred background and foreground force the viewer's eye toward the sharper, in-focus areas, which gives greater emphasis to the subject.

Occasionally a greater depth of field is required to maintain a sharp focus across a greater distance. This might be due to the sheer depth of your subject, where you have objects that are near the camera but sharpness is desired at a greater distance as well (**Figure 9.2**).

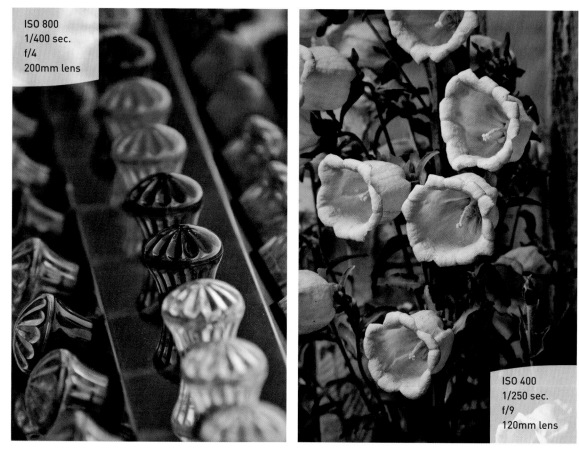

ISO 800
1/400 sec.
f/4
200mm lens

ISO 400
1/250 sec.
f/9
120mm lens

FIGURE 9.1
The combination of a telephoto lens and a large aperture can create a shallow depth of field to isolate the subject.

FIGURE 9.2
The closer you are to your subject, the smaller the aperture you will need to achieve a large depth of field.

Or perhaps you are photographing a reflection in a puddle. With a narrow depth of field, you could only get the reflected object or the puddle in focus. By making the aperture smaller, you will be able to maintain acceptable sharpness in both areas (**Figure 9.3**).

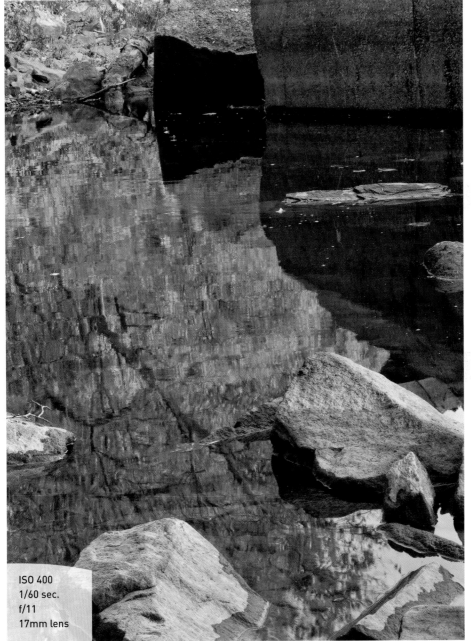

ISO 400
1/60 sec.
f/11
17mm lens

FIGURE 9.3
Getting a distant subject in focus in a reflection, along with the reflective surface, requires a small aperture.

PHOTOGRAPHING REFLECTIONS

A mirror is a two-dimensional surface, so why do I have to focus at a different distance for the image in the mirror? This was one of those questions that drove me crazy when I began to learn about photography. The answer is pretty simple, and it has to do with light. When you focus your lens, you are focusing the light being reflected off a surface onto your camera sensor. So if you wanted to focus on the mirror itself, it would be at one distance, but if you wanted to focus on the subject being reflected, you would have to take into account the distance that the object is from the mirror and then to you. Remember that the light from the subject has to travel all the way to the mirror and then to your lens. This is why a smaller aperture can be required when shooting reflected subjects. Sit in your car and take a few shots of objects in the side view mirrors to see what I mean.

ANGLES

Having strong angular lines in your image can add to the composition, especially when they are juxtaposed to each other (**Figure 9.4**). This can create a tension that is different from the standard horizontal and vertical lines that we are so accustomed to seeing in photos.

FIGURE 9.4
The strong angular lines of the building create a dynamic composition.

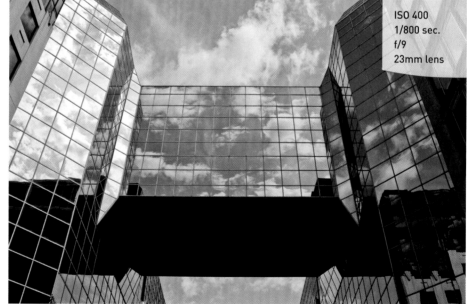

ISO 400
1/800 sec.
f/9
23mm lens

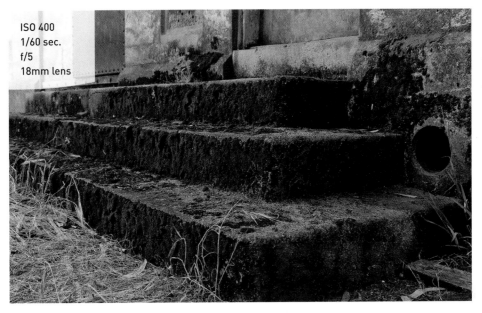

ISO 400
1/60 sec.
f/5
18mm lens

FIGURE 9.5
Put your camera in
a position
that presents an
unfamiliar view of
your subject.

POINT OF VIEW

Sometimes the easiest way to influence your photographs is to simply change your perspective. Instead of always shooting from a standing position, try moving your camera to a place where you normally would not see your subject. Try getting down on your knees or even lying on the ground. This low angle can completely change how you view your subject and create a new interest in common subjects (**Figure 9.5**).

PATTERNS

Rhythm and balance can be added to your images by finding the patterns in everyday life and concentrating on the elements that rely on geometric influences. Try to find the balance and patterns that often go unnoticed (**Figure 9.6**).

COLOR

Color works well as a tool for composition when you have very saturated colors to work with. Some of the best colors are those within the primary palette. Reds, greens, and blues, along with their complementary colors (cyan, magenta, and yellow), can all be used to create visual tension (**Figure 9.7**). This tension between bright colors will add visual excitement, drama, and complexity to your images when combined with other compositional elements.

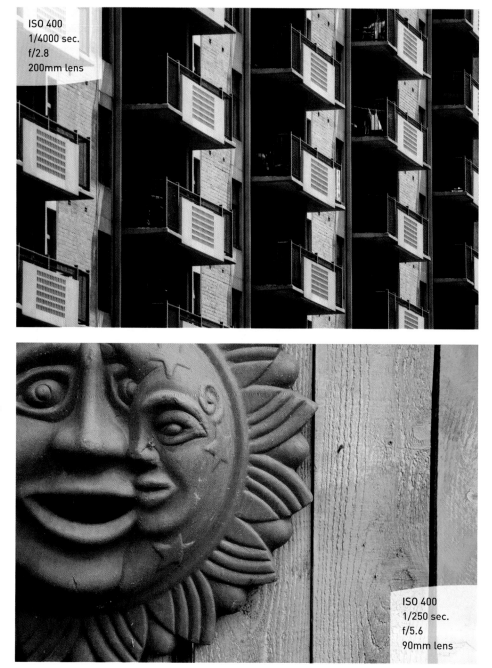

FIGURE 9.6
The patterns of these balconies, along with a shallow depth of field, create an almost three-dimensional effect.

ISO 400
1/4000 sec.
f/2.8
200mm lens

FIGURE 9.7
I was drawn to this shot by the combination of the great orange of the sun figure with the faded blue paint on the fence.

ISO 400
1/250 sec.
f/5.6
90mm lens

You can also use a color as a theme for your photography. One of the shots that I am known for is something that I call "The Blue Sky Shot." If I am out shooting when the skies are blue, I can almost guarantee that I will try to use the sky as part of a background for some element of my image (**Figure 9.8**). The blue sky can act as a color contrast to my subject, giving a pleasing contrast, visual interest, and isolation to my subject.

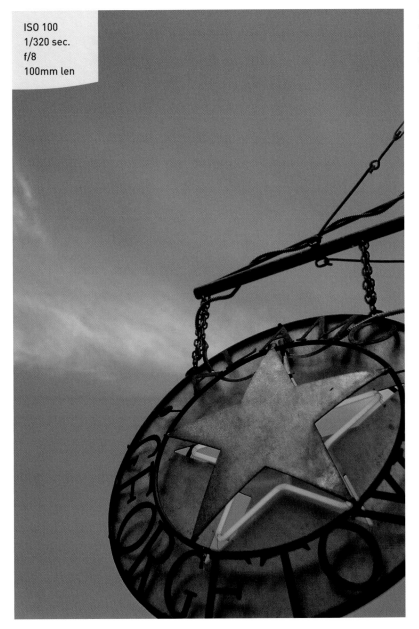

ISO 100
1/320 sec.
f/8
100mm len

FIGURE 9.8
The deep blue sky
greatly contrasts
against the sign.

CONTRAST

We just saw that you can use color as a strong compositional tool. One of the most effective uses of color is to combine two contrasting colors that make the eye move back and forth across the image (**Figure 9.9**). There is no exact combination that will work best, but consider using dark and light colors, like red and yellow, or blue and yellow, to provide the strongest contrasts.

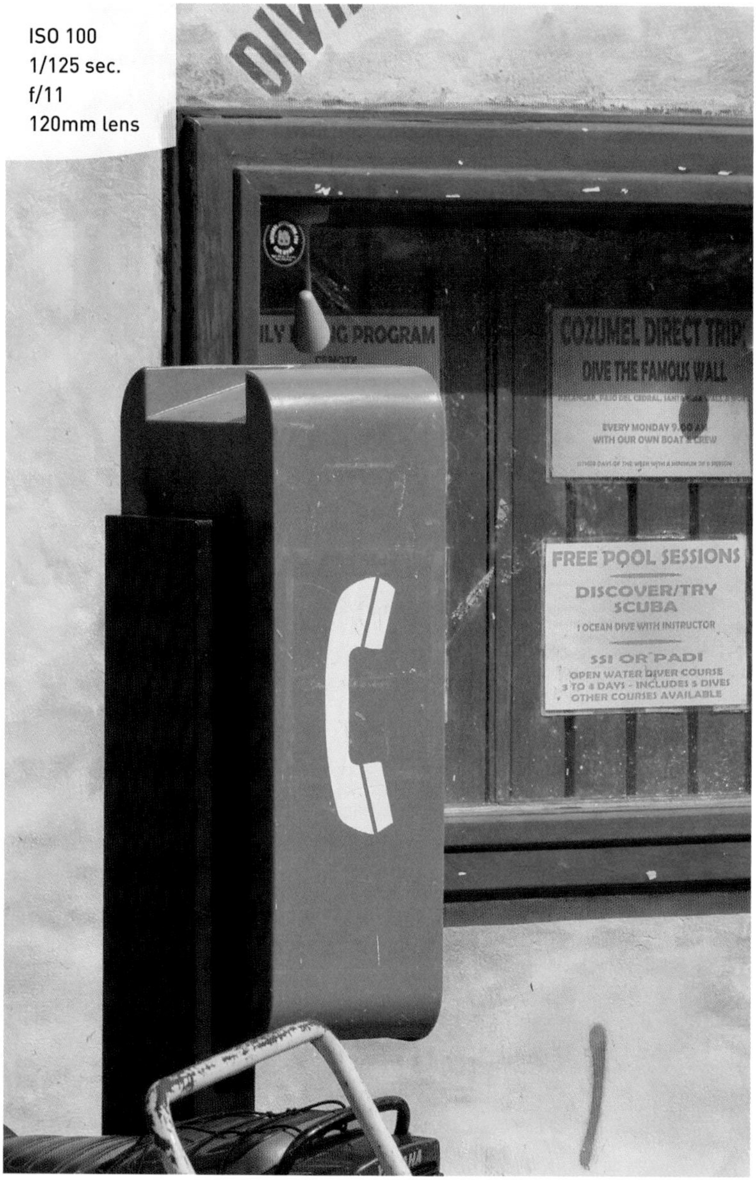

FIGURE 9.9
The contrasting colors complement each other and add balance to the scene.

ISO 100
1/125 sec.
f/11
120mm lens

You can also introduce contrast through different geometric shapes that battle (in a good way) for the attention of the viewer. You can combine circles and triangles, ovals and rectangles, curvy and straight, hard and soft, dark and light, and so many more (**Figure 9.10**). You aren't limited to just one contrasting element either. Combining more than one element of contrast will add even more interest. Look for these contrasting combinations whenever you are out shooting, and then use them to shake up your compositions.

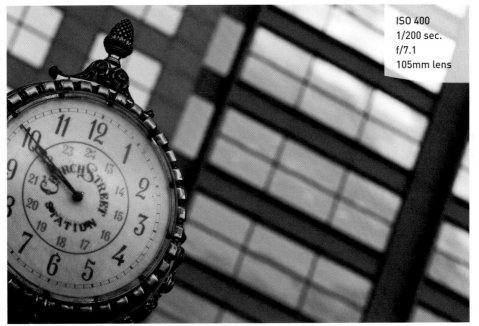

ISO 400
1/200 sec.
f/7.1
105mm lens

FIGURE 9.10
The angular lines of the building play nicely against the round clock face.

LEADING LINES

One way to pull a viewer into your image is to incorporate leading lines. These are elements that come from the edge of the frame and then lead into the image toward the main subject (**Figure 9.11**). This can be the result of vanishing perspective lines, an element such as a river, or some other feature used to move from the outer edge in to the heart of the image.

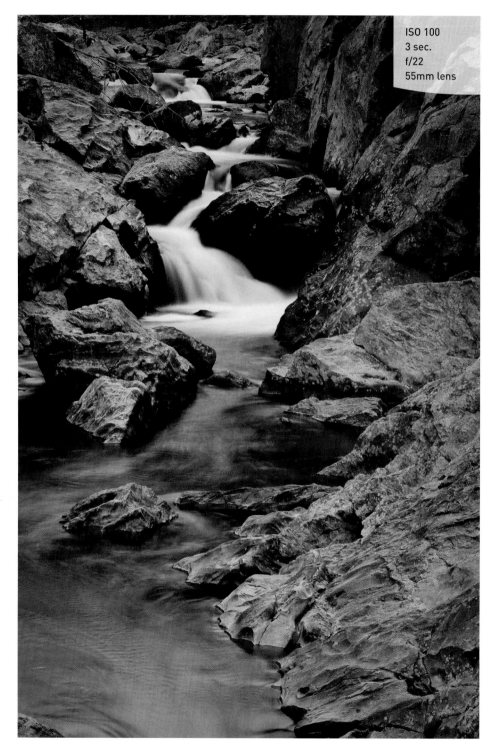

FIGURE 9.11
The curving line of the stream leads the eye directly to the waterfall.

ISO 100
3 sec.
f/22
55mm lens

SPLITTING THE FRAME

Generally speaking, splitting the frame right down the middle is not necessarily your best option. While it may seem more balanced, it can actually be pretty boring. You should utilize the rule of thirds when deciding how to divide your frame (**Figure 9.12**).

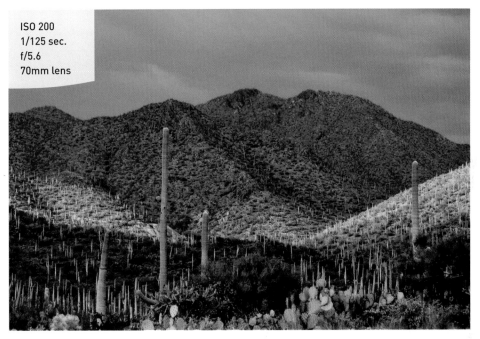

ISO 200
1/125 sec.
f/5.6
70mm lens

FIGURE 9.12
This image is a classic example of dividing the frame into thirds.

With horizons, a low horizon will give a sense of stability to the image. Typically, this is done when the sky is more appealing than the landscape below. When the emphasis is to be placed on the landscape, the horizon line should be moved upward in the frame, leaving the bottom two thirds to the subject below (**Figure 9.13**).

FRAMES WITHIN FRAMES

The outer edge of your photograph acts as a frame to hold all of the visual elements of the photograph. One way to add emphasis to your subject is through the use of internal frames (**Figure 9.14**). Depending on how the frame is used, it can create the illusion of a third dimension to your image, giving it a feeling of depth.

FIGURE 9.13
The warm glow of the Smithsonian Castle dominates the bottom two thirds of the frame, leaving no doubt as to what the main subject is.

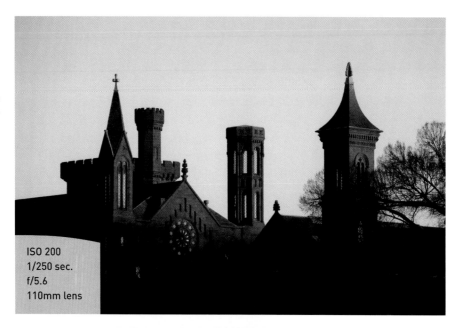

ISO 200
1/250 sec.
f/5.6
110mm lens

FIGURE 9.14
I used this doorway to create a frame for the carved face on the temple.

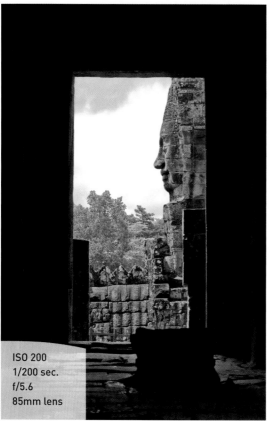

ISO 200
1/200 sec.
f/5.6
85mm lens

Chapter 9 Assignments

Apply the shooting techniques and tools that you have learned in the previous chapters to these assignments, and you'll improve your ability to incorporate good composition into your photos. Make sure you experiment with all the different elements of composition and see how you can combine them to add interest to your images.

Learning to see lines and patterns

Take your camera for a walk around your neighborhood and look for patterns and angles. Don't worry so much about getting great shots as much as developing an eye for details.

The ABCs of composition

Here's a great exercise that was given to me by my friend Vincent Versace: shoot the alphabet. This will be a little more difficult but with practice you will start to see beyond the obvious. Don't just find letters in street signs and the like. Instead, find objects that aren't really letters but have the shape of the letters.

Finding the square peg and the round hole

Circles, squares, and triangles. Spend a few sessions concentrating on shooting simple geometric shapes.

Using the aperture to focus attention

Depth of field plays an important role in defining your images and establishing depth and dimension. Practice shooting wide open, using your largest aperture for the narrowest depth of field. Then find a scene that would benefit from extended depth of field, using very small apertures to give sharpness throughout the scene.

Leading them into a frame

Look for scenes where you can use elements as leading lines and then look for framing elements that you can use to isolate your subject and add both depth and dimension to your images.

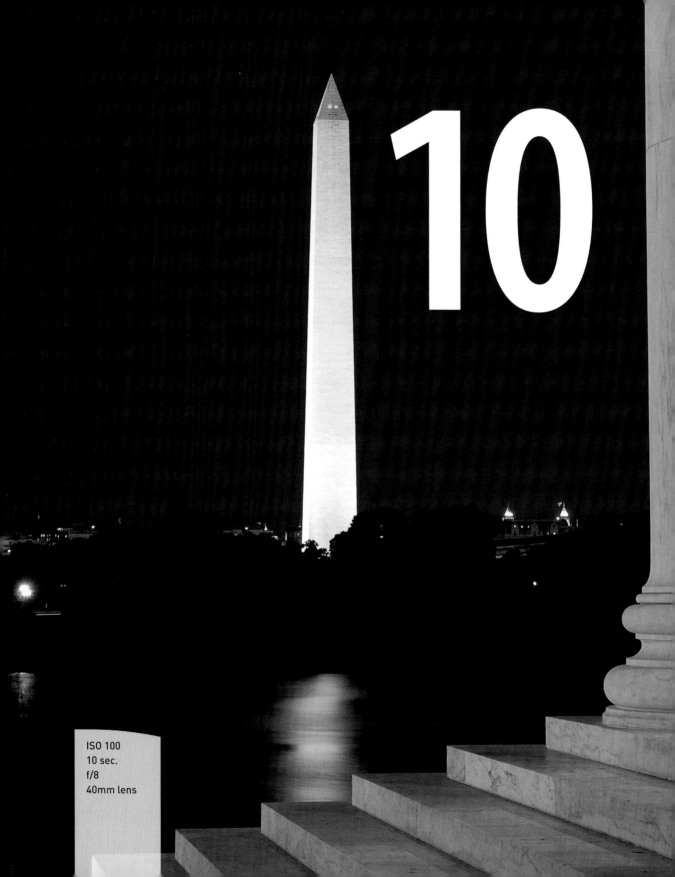

10

ISO 100
10 sec.
f/8
40mm lens

Advanced
Techniques

IMPRESS YOUR FAMILY AND FRIENDS

We've covered a lot of ground in the previous chapters, especially on the
general photographic concepts that apply to most, if not all, shooting
situations. There are, however, some specific tools and techniques that will
give you an added advantage in obtaining a great shot. Additionally, we
will look at how to customize certain controls on your camera to reflect
your personal shooting preferences and always have them at the ready.

Shortly after a storm had passed over my house, I got the idea to head out to my backyard in search of some raindrops to shoot. I knew I would be taking macro photos, so I grabbed my tripod and close-up filter. I searched until I found just the right raindrop clinging to a pine needle in a location where I could set up my tripod without making the drop fall. It took me several attempts to get just the right angle and composition but persistence was rewarded with a great shot.

The colors in the image were enhanced by the use of the Landscape picture style.

The overcast sky provided a nice soft light that added saturation to the colors.

To isolate the raindrop from the background, I used the largest aperture I had.

A tripod was used so that I could get perfect focus on the raindrop.

ISO 100
1/250 sec.
f/3.5
55mm lens

PORING OVER THE PICTURE

When I told some friends that I was going to Seattle, they all said the same thing: "You have to take a ferry ride at sunset to get the best shots of the city." So, that's exactly what I did. I rode out to Bainbridge Island for dinner and then caught the ferry back at a time when I knew there should be decent light hitting the buildings of the waterfront. There wasn't a lot of great light that night, but as we made our way closer to the dock, the clouds parted a bit in the west and allowed some great light to illuminate the city.

The exposure was a little tricky because of the all the glass, so I bracketed my exposures and selected the shot taken at −1 stop as my favorite.

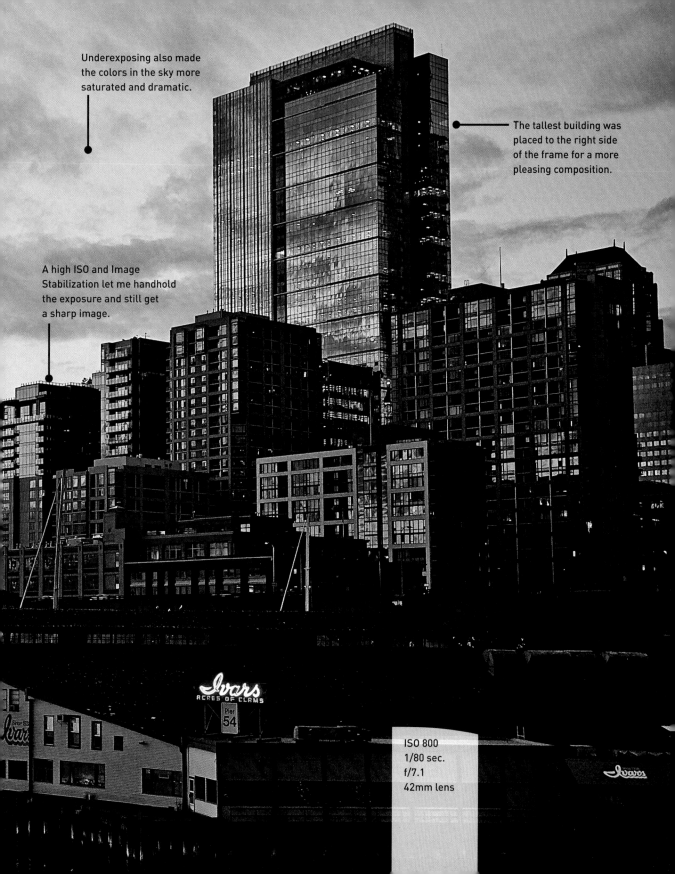

Underexposing also made the colors in the sky more saturated and dramatic.

The tallest building was placed to the right side of the frame for a more pleasing composition.

A high ISO and Image Stabilization let me handhold the exposure and still get a sharp image.

ISO 800
1/80 sec.
f/7.1
42mm lens

SPOT METER FOR MORE EXPOSURE CONTROL

Generally speaking, Evaluative metering mode provides accurate metering information for the majority of your photography. It does an excellent job of evaluating the scene and then relaying the proper exposure information to you. The only problem with this mode is that, like any metering mode on the camera, it doesn't know what it is looking at. There will be specific circumstances where you want to get an accurate reading from just a portion of a scene and discount all of the remaining area in the viewfinder. To give you greater control of the metering operation, you can switch the camera to Spot metering mode. This allows you to take a meter reading from a very small circle in the center of the viewfinder, while ignoring the rest of the viewfinder area.

So when would you need to use this? Think of a person standing in front of a very dark wall. In Evaluative metering mode, the camera would see the entire scene and try to adjust the exposure information so that the dark background is exposed to render a lighter wall in your image. This means that the scene would actually be overexposed and your subject would then appear too light. To correct this, you can place the camera in Spot metering mode and take a meter reading right off of—and *only* off of—your subject, ignoring the dark wall altogether.

Other situations that would benefit from Spot metering include:

- Snow or beach environments where the overall brightness level of the scene could fool the meter
- Strongly backlit subjects that are leaving the subject underexposed (**Figures 10.1** and **10.2**)
- Cases where the overall feel of a photo is too light or too dark

SETTING UP AND SHOOTING IN SPOT METERING MODE

1. Press the Set button to bring up the Quick Control screen on the back of the camera, and then use the Cross keys to move the icon to the Metering mode.

2. Rotate the Main dial until the Spot meter icon appears, and then press the shutter release button halfway to return to shooting mode.

3. Point the center focus point at the subject that you wish to use for the reading.

4. Press the ✱ button to enable the AE Lock, which will hold the exposure value while you recompose and then take the photo.

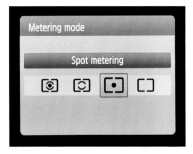

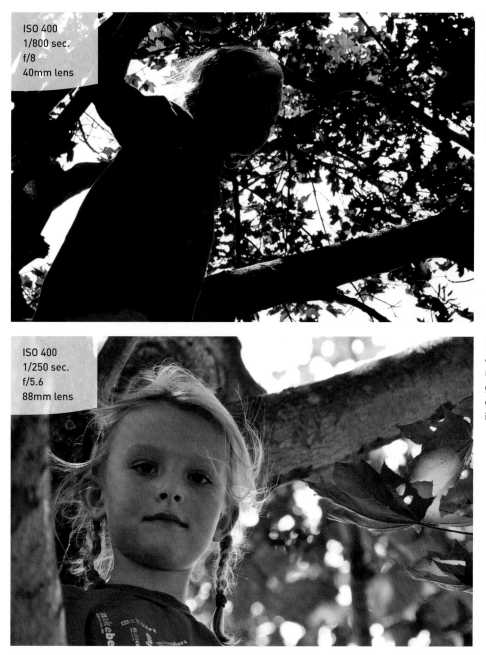

ISO 400
1/800 sec.
f/8
40mm lens

FIGURE 10.1
The very strong
sunlight coming
through the trees
is causing the
meter to be fooled
into underexposing
the image. (Photo:
Suzanne Revell)

ISO 400
1/250 sec.
f/5.6
88mm lens

FIGURE 10.2
A spot meter
reading on the face
gives the correct
exposure for this
image.

When using Spot metering mode, remember that the meter believes it is looking at a
medium gray value, so you might need to incorporate some exposure compensation
of your own to the reading that you are getting from your subject. This will come
from experience as you use the meter.

METERING FOR SUNRISE OR SUNSET

Capturing a beautiful sunrise or sunset is all about the sky. If there is too much fore-ground in the viewfinder, the camera's meter will deliver an exposure setting that is accurate for the darker foreground areas but leaves the sky looking overexposed, undersaturated, and generally just not very interesting. To gain more emphasis on the colorful sky, point your camera at the brightest part of it and take your meter reading there. Use the AE Lock and then recompose. The result will be an exposure setting that underexposes the foreground but provides a darker, more dramatic sky (**Figure 10.3**).

FIGURE 10.3
Metering for the brightest part of the sky will give you better sunset pictures.

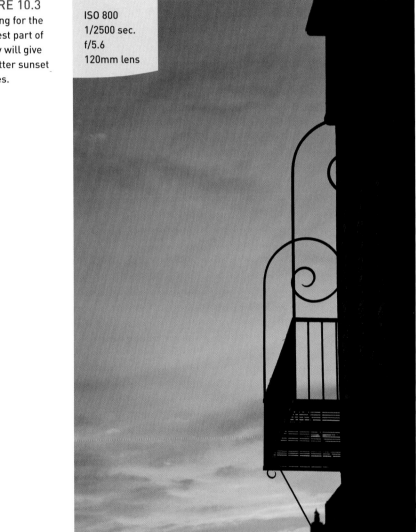

ISO 800
1/2500 sec.
f/5.6
120mm lens

MIRROR LOCKUP

If you examined the Washington Monument shot in the chapter opener, you probably noticed that I used a fairly long shutter speed. Without the use of a tripod, the likelihood of getting some degree of handshake in the image is guaranteed. A tripod at these exposure times is one way to ensure that the images are extremely sharp. Another factor that can affect the sharpness of the image comes from the mirror in the camera, which moves as it gets out of the way of the shutter.

For the absolute sharpest images, you can set the camera to raise the mirror prior to exposing the photo. Unlike the regular process of exposure—where the mirror moves at the same time that the picture is taken—the mirror is locked into the raised position until the shutter is activated, thus further reducing the possibility of camera shake.

SETTING THE MIRROR LOCKUP FEATURE

1. Press the Menu button and navigate to the third setup tab, highlight Custom Functions, and press the Set button.

2. Use the Cross keys to highlight C. Fn III: Autofocus/Drive Mirror Lockup and press the Set button (**A**).

3. Highlight Enable and press the Set button to lock in the change (**B**).

4. Exit the menu and set up your shot.

5. Press the shutter release button completely to raise the mirror.

6. Press it a second time to activate the shutter and take the picture.

To further reduce the possibility of camera shake, use a shutter release cable or set the self-timer to two seconds. In self-timer mode, the mirror will lift when you press the shutter release button but the camera will fire automatically after two seconds, so you don't have to touch the camera again. Also remember that the Mirror Lockup feature will remain active (even after turning the camera on and off) until you disable it in the menu.

MANUAL MODE

Probably one of the most advanced and yet most basic skills to master is shooting in Manual mode. With the power and utility of most of the automatic modes, Manual mode almost never sees the light of day. I have to admit that I don't select it for use very often, but there are times when no other mode will do. One of the situations that works well with Manual is studio work with external flashes. I know that when I work with studio lights, my exposure will not change, so I use Manual to eliminate any automatic changes that might happen from shooting in P, Tv, or Av mode.

Since you probably aren't too concerned with studio strobes at this point, I will concentrate on one of the ways in which you will want to use Manual mode for your photography: long nighttime exposures.

BULB PHOTOGRAPHY

If you want to work with long shutter speeds that don't quite fit into one of the selectable shutter speeds, you can select Bulb. This setting is only available in Manual mode, and its sole purpose is to open the shutter at your command and then close it again when you decide. I can think of two scenarios where this would come in handy: shooting fireworks and shooting lightning.

If you are photographing fireworks, you could certainly use one of the longer shutter speeds available in Tv mode, since they are available for exposure times up to 30 seconds. That is fine, but sometimes you don't need 30 seconds' worth of exposure and sometimes you need more.

If you open the shutter and then see a great burst of fireworks, you might decide that that is all you want for that particular frame, so you click the button to end the exposure (**Figure 10.4**). Set the camera to 30 seconds and you might get too many bursts, but if you shorten it to 10 seconds you might not get the one you want.

BULB

If you are new to the world of photography, you might be wondering where in the world the *bulb* shutter function got its name. After all, wouldn't it make more sense to call it the Manual Shutter setting? It probably would, but this is one of those terms that harkens back to the origins of photography. Way back when, the shutter was actually opened through the use of a bulb-shaped device that forced air through a tube, which, in turn, pushed a plunger down, activating the camera shutter. When the bulb was released, it pulled the plunger back, letting the shutter close, and ending the exposure.

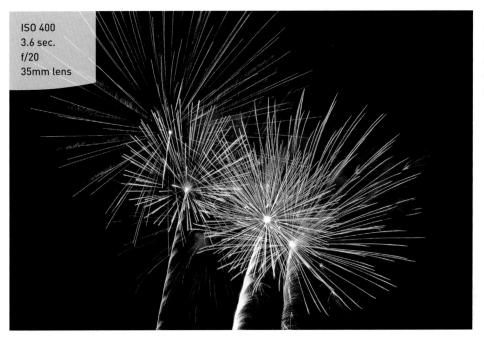

ISO 400
3.6 sec.
f/20
35mm lens

FIGURE 10.4
The Bulb setting
and a cable release
were used to
capture this series
of bursts.

The same can be said for photographing a lightning storm. I have a friend who loves electrical storms, and he has some amazing shots that he captured using the Bulb setting. Lightning can be very tricky to capture, and using the Bulb setting to open and then close the shutter at will allows for more creativity, as well as more opportunity to get the shot.

To select the Bulb setting, simply place your camera in Manual mode and then rotate the Main dial until the shutter speed displays Bulb.

If you want to make a change to the aperture, hold in the AV button on the back of the camera while turning the Main dial.

When you're using the Bulb setting, the shutter will only stay open for the duration that you are holding down the shutter button. You will also see a counter on the lower-right portion of the LCD screen that will count off the seconds that the shutter is open. You can use this counter to either add or subtract time for your next shot. You should also be using a sturdy tripod or shooting surface to eliminate any self-induced vibration. The Bulb setting can be used in conjunction with the Mirror Lockup feature for improved image sharpness.

I want to point out that using your finger on the shutter button for a bulb exposure will definitely increase the chances of getting some camera shake in your images. To get the most benefit from the bulb setting, I suggest using a remote cord such as the

Canon RS-60E3 Remote Switch or the RC-1 wireless remote (see the bonus chapter for more details). You'll also want to turn on the Long Exposure Noise Reduction, as covered in Chapter 8.

SHOOTING LIGHTNING

If you are going to photograph lightning strikes in a thunderstorm, please exercise extreme caution. Standing in the open with a tripod is like standing over a lightning rod. Work from indoors if at all possible.

AVOIDING LENS FLARE

Lens flare is one of the problems you will encounter when shooting in the bright sun. Lens flare will show itself as bright circles on the image (**Figure 10.5**). Often you will see multiple circles in a line leading from a very bright light source such as the sun. The flare is a result of the sun bouncing off the multiple pieces of optical glass in the lens and then being reflected back onto the sensor. You can avoid the problem in one of these ways:

- Try to shoot with the sun coming from over your shoulder, not in front of you or in your scene.

- Use a lens shade to block the unwanted light from striking the lens. You don't have to have the sun in your viewfinder for lens flare to be an issue. All it has to do is strike the front glass of the lens to make it happen.

- If you don't have a lens shade, just try using your hand or some other element to block the light.

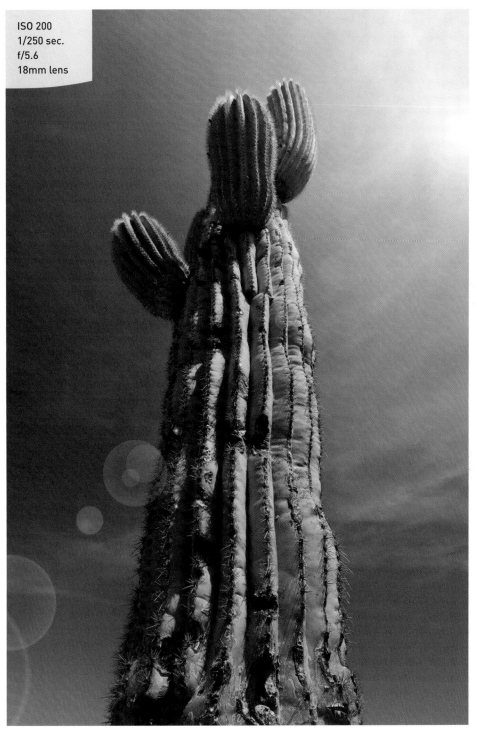

ISO 200
1/250 sec.
f/5.6
18mm lens

FIGURE 10.5
The bright sun in the upper-right corner has created flare spots that are visible as colored circles radiating down to the bottom-left corner of the image.

BRACKETING EXPOSURES

So what if you are doing everything right in terms of metering and mode selection, yet your images still sometimes come out too light or too dark? There is a technique called "bracketing" that you can use, which will help you find the best exposure value for your scene by taking a normal exposure as well as one that is over- and underexposed. Having these differing exposure values will most often present you with one frame that just looks better than the others. I use the Bracketing function all of the time.

Once you have entered the Auto-Exposure Bracket screen, you must use the Main dial to decide how much variation you want between bracketed exposures. You can choose from two-thirds of a stop all the way to two stops per bracketed exposure. You can also dial in the amount of exposure compensation that you might need. You can adjust the compensation as much as four stops in either direction, depending on the range of your bracketed exposures. Either way, bracketing will help you zero in on that perfect exposure, and you can just delete the ones that didn't make the grade (**Figures 10.6–10.8**).

FIGURE 10.6
One stop of
exposure below
normal.

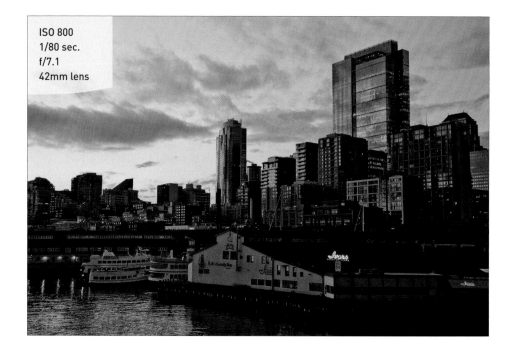

ISO 800
1/80 sec.
f/7.1
42mm lens

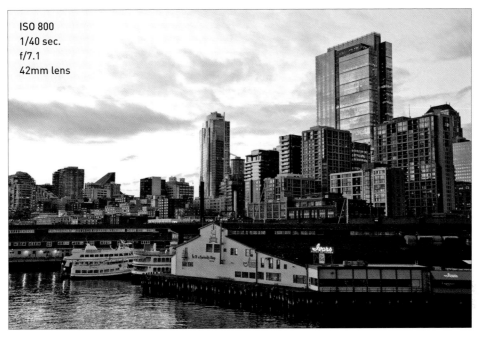

ISO 800
1/40 sec.
f/7.1
42mm lens

FIGURE 10.7
The normal
exposure as
indicated by the
camera meter.

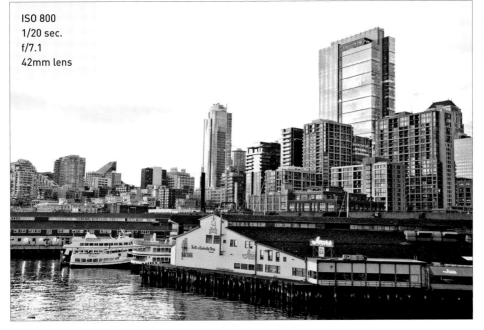

ISO 800
1/20 sec.
f/7.1
42mm lens

FIGURE 10.8
One stop of
exposure above
normal.

You can adjust the Exposure Compensation/AEB setting through the camera menu or by my favorite method, the Quick Control screen.

SETTING AUTO-EXPOSURE BRACKETING

1. Press the Set button and then move the cursor to the Exposure Compensation icon (**A**).

2. Press Set again to enter the compensation/bracketing screen (**B**).

3. Use the Main dial to set the amount of over- and underexposure that you desire (**C**).

4. If you want the "normal" exposure to be a little over- or underexposed you can adjust that with your left/right Cross keys.

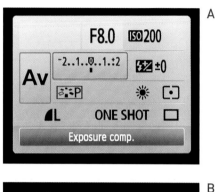

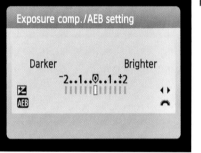

The camera will take the underexposed image first, then the normal image, then the overexposed image. Don't forget to take all three.

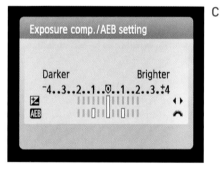

When I am out shooting, I typically shoot with my camera set to an exposure compensation of –1/3 stop to protect my highlights. If I am dealing with a subject that has a lot of different tonal ranges from bright to dark, I will often bracket by one stop over and under my already compensated exposure. That means I will have exposures of –1 1/3, –1/3, and +2/3.

MACRO PHOTOGRAPHY

Put simply, macro photography is close-up photography. Depending on the lens or lenses that you got with your camera, you may have the perfect tool for macro work. Some lenses are made to shoot in a macro mode, but you don't have to feel left out if you don't have one of those. Check the spec sheet that came with your lens to see what the minimum focusing distance is for your lens.

If you have a zoom, you should work with the lens at its longest focal length. Also, work with a tripod, because handholding will make focusing difficult. The easiest way to make sure that your focus is precisely where you want it to be is to use manual focus mode.

Since I am recommending a tripod for your macro work, I will also recommend using Av mode so that you can achieve differing levels of depth of field. Long lenses at close range can make for some very shallow depth of field, so you will need to work with apertures that are probably much smaller than you might normally use. If you are shooting outside, try shading the subject from direct sunlight by using some sort of diffusion material, such as a white sheet or a diffusion panel (see the bonus chapter). By diffusing the light, you will see much greater detail because you will have a lower contrast ratio (softer shadows), and detail is often what macro photography is all about (**Figures 10.9** and **10.10**).

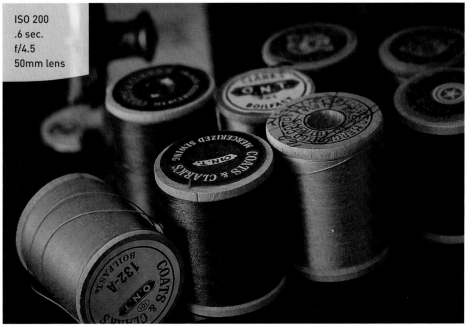

ISO 200
.6 sec.
f/4.5
50mm lens

FIGURE 10.9
The detail of this still life is enhanced by soft, natural light.

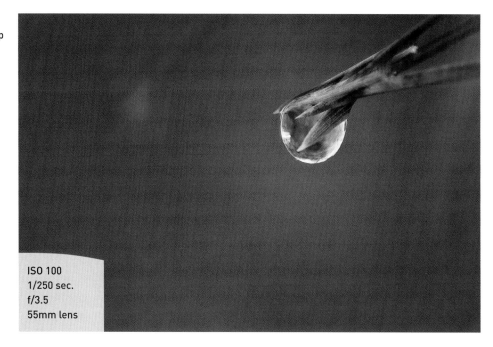

FIGURE 10.10
By using a close-up lens, I was able to get extreme detail in this raindrop clinging to a pine needle.

ISO 100
1/250 sec.
f/3.5
55mm lens

AUTO LIGHTING OPTIMIZER

Your camera provides a function that can automatically make your pictures look better: Auto Lighting Optimizer. It works this way: the camera evaluates the tones in your image and then lightens any areas that it believes are too dark or lacking in contrast (**Figures 10.11** and **10.12**). This optimization is applied automatically in the shooting modes of the Basic zone.

You can choose from four levels: Standard, Low, Strong, and Disable. You will need to evaluate the strength of the effect on your images and change it accordingly. I typically leave it set to Standard so that I have brighter, more detailed shadow areas in my photographs. You should know that the Auto Lighting Optimizer does not work with your camera set to Manual mode. Also, disable it if you are using flash exposure compensation since it will try to work against you when you alter the flash strength.

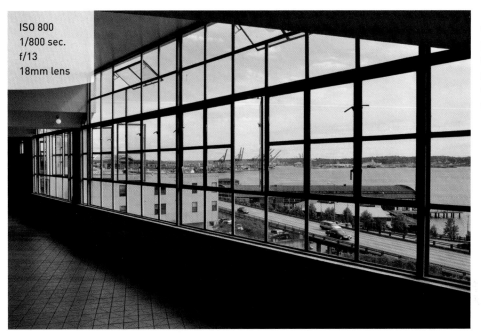

ISO 800
1/800 sec.
f/13
18mm lens

FIGURE 10.11
Without the Auto Lighting Optimizer, the shadows underneath the window are dark and contrasty.

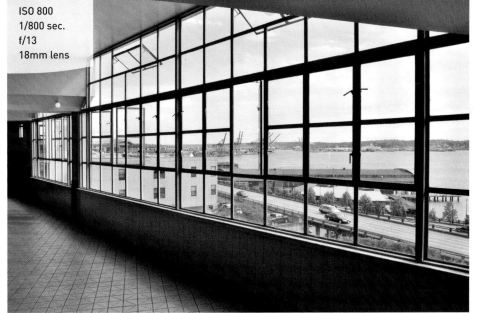

ISO 800
1/800 sec.
f/13
18mm lens

FIGURE 10.12
Although the exposure hasn't changed, the shadows are brighter after changing the Optimizer to the Strong setting.

SETTING UP THE AUTO LIGHTING OPTIMIZER

1. Press the Menu button and use the Main dial to get to the third setup tab, then highlight Custom Functions and press the Set button.

2. Using the Cross keys, select the C. Fn II: Image Auto Lighting Optimizer and press the Set button (**A**).

3. Use the Cross keys once again to select the level of optimization that you prefer and press the Set button to lock in the change (**B**).

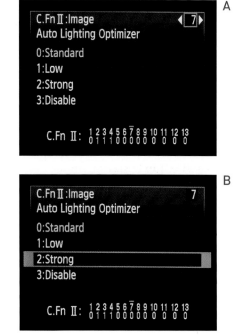

THE MY MENU SETTING

There are a lot of items in the menu that you can change, but some are used and changed more frequently than others. The My Menu function allows you to place six of your most used menu items in one place so that you can quickly get to them, make your changes, and get on with shooting. You can see what I have in my My Menu in **Figure 10.13**.

FIGURE 10.13
Here are the six functions I have stored in the My Menu function.

CUSTOMIZING YOUR MY MENU SETTING

1. Press the Menu button and select the tab with the star using the Cross keys.

2. Select My Menu settings and press Set (**A**).

3. Highlight Register and press Set (**B**).

4. Scroll through the available menu items, and when you highlight one that you want to add, press the Set button (**C**).

5. When asked if you want to register the item, highlight OK and press Set (**D**).

6. Continue adding the items that you want in the list until you have selected your favorites (up to six of them).

7. You can sort your menu items as you see fit or, if you change your mind, you can delete them individually or all at once. It's all up to you.

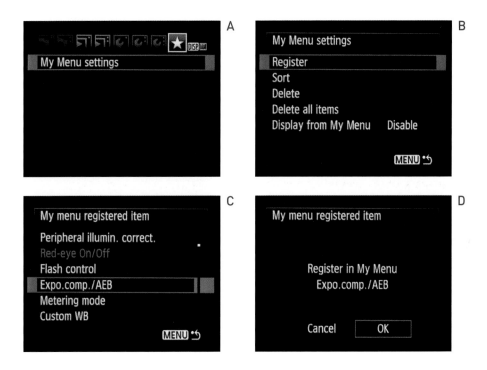

CONCLUSION

As you'll see, the online bonus chapter covers a lot of gadgets, filters, and accessories that will make your photography better. It can become an obsession to always have the latest thing out there. But here's the deal. You already have almost everything you need to take great pictures: an awesome camera and the knowledge necessary to use it. Everything else is just icing on the cake. So, while I introduce a few items in the bonus chapter that I do think will make your photographic life easier and even improve your images, don't get caught up in the technology and gadgetry.

Use your knowledge of basic photography to explore everything your camera has to offer. Explore the limits of your camera. Don't be afraid to take bad pictures. Don't be too quick to delete them off your memory card, either. Take some time to really look at them and see where things went wrong. Look at your camera settings and see if perhaps there was a change you could have made to make things better. Be your toughest critic and learn from your mistakes. With practice and reflection, you will soon find your photography getting better and better. Not only that, but your instincts will improve to the point that you will come upon a scene and know exactly how you want to shoot it before you even take your camera out of the bag.

Chapter 10 Assignments

Many of the techniques covered in this chapter are specific to certain shooting situations that may not come about very often. This is even more reason to practice them so that when the situation does present itself you will be ready.

Adding some drama to the end of the day

Most sunset photos don't reflect what the photographer saw because they didn't meter correctly for them. The next time you see a colorful sunset, pull out your camera and take a meter reading from the sky and then one without and see what a difference it makes.

Making your exposure spot on

Using the Spot meter mode can give accurate results but only when pointed at something that has a middle tone. Try adding something gray to the scene and taking a reading off it. Now switch back to your regular meter mode and see if the exposure isn't slightly different.

Using the Bulb setting to capture the moment

This is definitely one of those settings that you won't use often, but it's pretty handy when you need it. If you have the opportunity to shoot a fireworks display or a distant storm, try setting the camera to Bulb and then play with some long exposures to capture just the moments that you want.

Bracketing your way to better exposures

Why settle for just one variation of an image when you can bracket to get the best exposure choice? Set your camera up for a 1/3-bracket series and then expand it to a one-stop series. Review the results to see if the normal setting was the best, or perhaps maybe one of the bracketed exposures is even better.

Moving in for a close-up

Macro photography is best practiced on stationary subjects, which is why I like flowers. If you have a zoom lens, check the minimum focusing distance and then try to get right to that spot to squeeze the most from your subject. Try using a diffuse light source as well to minimize shadows.

INDEX

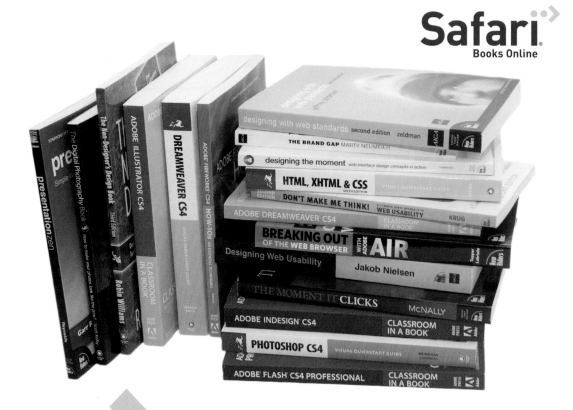

Safari
Books Online

Get free online access to this book for 45 days!

And get access to thousands more by signing up for a free trial to Safari Books Online!

With the purchase of this book you have instant online, searchable access to it for 45 days on Safari Books Online! And while you're there, be sure to check out Safari Books Online's on-demand digital library and their free trial offer (a separate sign-up process). Safari Books Online subscribers have access to thousands of technical, creative and business books, instructional videos, and articles from the world's leading publishers.

Simply visit www.peachpit.com/safarienabled and enter code XASBIWH to try it today.